Wonders of Nature in
South-East Asia

To Pam.

A small thank you for
giving me the opportunity
of sharing a wonderful
holiday with you.

Love,
Bren.

Wonders of Nature in South-East Asia

EARL OF CRANBROOK

With a Foreword by
VICTOR T. KING

KUALA LUMPUR
OXFORD UNIVERSITY PRESS
OXFORD SINGAPORE NEW YORK
1997

Oxford University Press

Oxford New York
Athens Auckland Bangkok Bombay
Calcutta Cape Town Dar es Salaam Delhi
Florence Hong Kong Istanbul Karachi
Madras Madrid Melbourne Mexico City
Nairobi Paris Shah Alam Singapore
Taipei Tokyo Toronto

and associated companies in
Berlin Ibadan

Oxford is a trade mark of Oxford University Press

Published in the United States
by Oxford University Press, New York

British Library Cataloguing in Publication Data
Data available

Library of Congress Cataloging-in-Publication Data
Cranbrook, Gathorne Gathorne-Hardy, Earl of, 1933–
Wonders of nature in South-East Asia / Earl of Cranbrook; with a
foreword by Victor T. King.
p. cm. — (Oxford in Asia paperbacks)
ISBN 967 65 3088 3 (paper)
1. Natural history—Asia, Southeastern. I. Title. II. Series.
QH193.S6C73 1997
508.59—dc20
96-25056
CIP

Typeset by Indah Photosetting Centre Sdn. Bhd., Malaysia
Printed by Kyodo Printing Co.(S) Pte. Ltd., Singapore
Published by Penerbit Fajar Bakti Sdn. Bhd. (008974-T),
under licence from Oxford University Press,
4 Jalan U1/15, Seksyen U1, 40000 Shah Alam,
Selangor Darul Ehsan, Malaysia

Foreword

VICTOR T. KING

As our compiler indicates in his Introduction to this volume, the passages were selected because they seemed to possess 'literary merit' and to provide lively and interesting descriptions of the significant aspects and elements of the South-East Asian environment. Even certain of the more academic extracts, originally intended for the instruction of students and teachers, do manage to give us a sense of what it is like to experience the wondrousness of tropical nature.

The Earl of Cranbrook has presented us with a remarkably varied range of records of the natural marvels of South-East Asia. Perhaps his task has been made a little easier in that we are fortunate in having an exceptional literature on the fauna, flora, landscapes, and seascapes of the region. The writers who described these wonders include a large number of distinguished scholars, scientists, and public figures—among them the eminent geographer Professor Charles Fisher, journalists of the calibre of J. R. Logan, famous explorers and travellers such as Henri Mouhot and Carl Bock, several major naturalists, including Alfred Russel Wallace, Odoardo Beccari, H. O. Forbes, Charles Hose, Captain F. Kingdon Ward, Tom Harrisson, and Gathorne Cranbrook himself, and renowned proconsuls like Sir Thomas Stamford Raffles and Sir J. G. Scott.

What is of special significance in this volume is that many of the contributions capture a now fast-changing world, but which at the time of writing had not yet experienced to any degree these dramatic human-induced transformations. During the last three decades, the natural environment of South-East Asia has been subjected to the needs of modernization and economic growth on an unprecedented scale. Of course, these processes had been set in motion during the European colonial period and even prior to that when early traders from India and the Middle East came to 'Chryse the Golden' in search of gold, diamonds, and other precious objects. But the momentum of change has since accelerated rapidly, particularly in regard to the exploitation of the region's natural products—its forests, minerals, and maritime resources. One can still enjoy the natural wonders celebrated in this volume, but increasingly they are artificially preserved and protected in national parks such as Kinabalu in Sabah and in forest reserves; ecotourists can now gaze upon them at a price.

What this anthology will undoubtedly impress upon the reader is the abundance and diversity of South-East Asian nature; and as Charles Fisher has said appositely, 'the exuberance of organic growth'.[1] The richness and proliferation of life are the result of an ample supply of light, warmth, and moisture. Yet, this very amplitude of sun and rain, and the intensity of energy also unleashes potentially destructive natural forces—typhoons, violent electrical storms, torrential downpours, and sudden floods. The rain forest with its incredible variety of fauna and flora is also, as Henri Mouhot, the famous French traveller, warned, 'the seat of malignant fevers'.[2] The climate can also be debilitating and uncomfortable. The geographer Charles Fisher, who has probably provided academe with one of the best general texts on the physical and human geography of South-East Asia, describes in measured and well-crafted prose the physical processes which give rise to the climatic patterns of monsoon Asia. However, in an otherwise sober technical account, he cannot resist giving us a few tips for coping with some of the

[1]Charles A. Fisher, *South-East Asia: A Social, Economic and Political Geography*, 2nd edn., Methuen and Co. Ltd., London, 1966, p. 43.
[2]Henri Mouhot, *Travels in the Central Parts of Indo-China (Siam), Cambodia, and Laos during the Years 1858, 1859, and 1860*, John Murray, London, 1864, p. 62.

problems of heat and moisture. This experienced resident and traveller in South-East Asia tells us that 'the effects of the dampness of the air both on bodily discomfort and in the form of the damage which it causes to almost every kind of fabric are the most unpleasant features of the climate during the rainy seasons of the year. Thus if clothing is to be preserved for more than a few weeks it will need frequent and systematic airing and elaborate care is required to prevent fungoid growths in footwear and the sticking together of postage stamps in one's wallet.'[3]

The natural environment of South-East Asia, embodying, as it does, these contrasts between abundance and destruction, beauty and danger, turbulence and tranquillity, has also evoked the whole range of emotions in our writers. The marvels of nature have excited all kinds of imaginings in European observers, particularly at the time when the first travellers and explorers were charting previously unknown and untouched regions. One cannot help but be captured by Sir Hugh Clifford's absorbing account of the French Mekong expedition of 1866–8 of Doudart de Lagrée and Frances Garnier; his powerful and evocative description of what confronted Garnier at the Sombor rapids above Kratie is for me one of the most arresting passages in Clifford's book. The bordering forest and the mighty Mekong River are depicted as both beautiful and savage, but Clifford brings us closer to their wildness and strangeness by describing them in human terms. 'On each bank of the great river rose marvellous tangles of untouched forest—giant trees with buttress-roots, treading on one another's toes, standing knee-deep in striving underwood, their branches interlocked, and bound each to each by vine and creeper, shaggy with ferns and mosses, draped with hanging parasitic growths, and set here and there with the delicate stars of orchids.... [T]he great river rolled, sullen and persistent, its brown waters sweeping downward with irresistible force their freight of wallowing

[3]Fisher, op. cit., p. 26.

tree-trunks, rushing with a fierce hissing sound through the brushwood on either bank, foaming and fighting around the islands which here bespatter the surface of the stream, and squabbling noisily with the rough-hewn outcrops which form at this point a broken bar at right-angles to the current.'[4] The tangled greenness and the 'whirling wilderness of troubled waters', we are told, 'filled' Garnier's eyes 'with seeing'.

So this anthology takes the reader from the majesty of the mountains of mainland South-East Asia and the broad sweep of the large inland lakes of the Toba Highlands and the Upper Kapuas basin to the spaciousness of the deltas and lowland plains of the Irrawaddy, Me Nam, and Mekong, from the 'placid loveliness' of the coasts, and the stillness of limestone caves, some of which were used as native burial places, to the potential turbulence of the volcanic belt of island South-East Asia, among which we find the famous Krakatau. We also have extracts on the more notable land mammals— the red ape (the orang-utan or 'man of the forest'), elephants, and bearded pigs; on many of the remarkable birds of the region—the hornbill, the megapode, the argus pheasant, birds of paradise, and cave swiftlets (the source of the important ingredient for the Chinese delicacy 'birds' nest soup'); descriptions of forest-dwelling flying lemurs and pythons, and of cave-dwelling bats and marine turtles. A number of these creatures, like the orang-utan, hornbill, and python, also have important positions in native folklore and custom, and traditionally the feathers and casque of the hornbill, for example, were used for decorative purposes in native costumes.

The anthology also gives us a picture of the teaming insect life of the rain forest—those unpleasant to humans—the malaria-carrying mosquitoes, blood-sucking leeches, and stinging ants—and those of beauty—the fireflies, moths, and butterflies, including Rajah Brooke's Birdwing. Only a few

[4]Clifford, Hugh, *Further India: Being the Story of Exploration from the Earliest Times in Burma, Malaya, Siam, and Indo-China*, Alston Rivers, London, 1905, pp. 168–9.

examples of the South-East Asian flora can be taken to illustrate its diversity—but we get to know something of the useful plants, such as the ubiquitous bamboos, rattans, and palms, as well as some of the extraordinary ones like the strangling figs and the Rafflesia. David Attenborough's brief description of the parasitic Rafflesia, the 'biggest flower in the world', perhaps illustrates its fantastic qualities. 'The bloom measures a metre across and sits directly on the ground, leafless and monstrous. Its maroon petals, thick, leathery and covered with warts, surround a vast cup, the floor of which bristles with large spikes. From this comes a powerful stench of putrescence. It revolts human nostrils but it attracts flies in swarms, as rotting meat would do. It is they that pollinate it.'[5]

Other tropical plants, such as the orchid, have a range of qualities—they are exotic, exquisitely beautiful, fragrant, and are now the object of a large floral export industry and a tourist attraction in the Botanic Gardens in Singapore. Yet, in terms of the unusual and extraordinary, it is still probably the durian which will continue to have a special place—it has a smell and taste like no other fruit and Alfred Russel Wallace provides us with a sense of its qualities. 'A rich butter-like custard highly flavoured with almonds gives the best general idea of it, but intermingled with it come wafts of flavour that call to mind cream-cheese, onion-sauce, brown sherry, and other incongruities.'[6]

For the opportunity to sample these and many other natural wonders, we are grateful to the Earl of Cranbrook. In this anthology he enables us to partake of some of these sensations of colour, taste, smell, and touch which nature provides, and like Garnier gazing on the mighty Mekong at Sombor, to fill our eyes with seeing.

[5]David Attenborough, *The Living Planet: A Portrait of the Earth*, William Collins and British Broadcasting Corporation, London, 1985, p. 103.

[6]Alfred Russel Wallace, *The Malay Archipelago: The Land of the Orang-Utan, and the Bird of Paradise. A Narrative of Travel, with Studies of Man and Nature*, 1st edn., Macmillan and Co., London, 1869, p. 57.

Acknowledgements

IN roving across this terrain, I have been much helped by the perceptive eye of Janet Probyn, who scoured London libraries for me, including those of the Royal Geographical Society, the Royal Asiatic Society, and the School of Oriental and African Studies, University of London. In these libraries and in others, notably the Linnean Society of London and the Library Services of the Natural History Museum, London, librarians have been unfailingly helpful. I am also grateful to those living authors who kindly consented to the inclusion in this anthology of the products of their pens, namely, Professor Emeritus Michael Audley Charles, Professor Emeritus John Corner, FRS, and Mr John Wyatt-Smith, CBE. Dr Gaden S. Robinson and Argus Gathorne-Hardy helped in the search for some key references. To all I record my warmest thanks.

Great Glemham, Saxmundham   EARL OF CRANBROOK
England
August 1996

Contents

CONTENTS

CONTENTS

Gold of the Chersonese

Introduction

EARL OF CRANBROOK

THIS anthology dips into writings on South-East Asia from ancient classical times to the present. The theme develops progressively to illustrate and explain the wonders of the earth, of mountains and volcanoes, rivers and estuaries, shore strands and island-studded seas, of rivers and the forests they traverse, and the plants and animal wildlife of this enthralling quarter of the globe.

Archaeology has shown that ancestral humans were present in this region three-quarters of a million years ago. The earliest South-East Asian remains of modern mankind were dated at 38,000 years BP (before present) by the excavators. Pollen grains in peat deposits give evidence of land clearance as long as 7,000 years ago, and the first signs of rice grown in the archipelago have been dated around 4500 BP. Over the millennia, there can be few places where people have not ventured and left some mark of their activity. Until recently, however, across much of the region the sum of these impacts was trivial and near pristine conditions persisted.

Yet, in the short period since many writers in this anthology were witnesses of the natural wonders, the countries of South-East Asia have been subject to unprecedented change. Half a century ago, world war enveloped the region. Subsequently, some nations have suffered further turmoil, in the struggle for independence, in revolution, or in continuing insurrection. At the same time, South-East Asia overall has experienced a huge population increase. Many governments have responded to the needs of their people by making massive investments in rapid industrialization and in rural development.

From these and other causes, vast tracts of landscape have been permanently altered. Natural vegetation has been swept aside and, with it, the wild creatures that once abounded. In their times, the earlier contributors to this anthology encountered lands and wildlife no longer to be found. Their collected jottings must be valued as postcards from that country of the past, to which no one can now return.

Through the centuries from the appearance of the first written accounts of South-East Asia, there has been progressive advance in human comprehension of the natural world. Perhaps the mystery has diminished but, as I hope this anthology displays, the marvel grows no less wondrous with understanding. My choice of passages was based on simple criteria. Each abstract, short or long, itemizes some detail of the natural environment and its wonders as directly experienced by the writer. The net has been cast wide. Many excerpts have been culled from the broad literature of travel. Authenticity is the most important standard. Some well-known writers have met this test but, in order to achieve full cover and dependable accounts of these marvels, other passages have been mined from professional or semi-technical sources that the general reader rarely encounters. These writers did not aim to produce gems of literature, but their descriptions gain from a measure of scientific insight.

The technology of printing—colour printing, in particular—has developed to such an extent that it is no longer difficult to find, nor costly to buy, an abundance of books that illustrate quite brilliantly the wonders of the natural world and surviving wildlife of South-East Asia. There has also been a matching surge of writing in books, scientific journals, magazines, and popular periodicals, informing and enlightening a world-wide readership. Thousands of people, local or foreign, nowadays enjoy environmental tourism in the region. A rich hoard of publications—the 'travelogues'—exists to serve this interest. Environmental issues are high on national and global agenda. Many universities and research

institutes are involved in the scientific investigation of ecological systems in South-East Asia.

The selection in these pages bridges the gap between the
restless plethora of modern publications and the more sedate
and considered writing of past generations. I have drawn on
authors who lived in the region, as well as others who stayed
only a short while or passed through on their travels. When
the light of modern research and understanding is needed to
appreciate the true wonder, I have included works of the late
twentieth century. Most selections reach back further into
history. In those times, the traveller progressed more slowly
but thought no less deeply and, by pen and ink rather than
digit and byte, recorded as carefully the powerful impact of
the wonders of the natural world in South-East Asia. The
introductory passages provide a commentary from the perspective of today and touch on wonders that the modern
visitor can still relish from the printed page, in the comfort of
an armchair or under the tropic sun.

Invocation

GEORGE MAXWELL

THE opening invocation was uttered by a rattan (cane) collector on entering the Malayan forest almost a century ago. The words were written down by George Maxwell, who was the third generation of his family to reside in the Malay States and to pursue a distinguished career in public service. Maxwell's book, *In Malay Forests*, was evidently based on his early life. It has become a classic of its kind, showing close intimacy with the land, the people, and the natural environment of what is now Peninsular Malaysia. His translation follows the original Malay language version.

As-salam aleikum.
Aku datang ini bersahabat sehaja.
Sehaja 'nak mencari hal kehidupan.
Janganlah engkau menggaru-garu ku,
Dan anak isteri ku,
Dan rumah tangga ku,
Dan segala kampung laman ku.
Aku 'nak tumpang bersahabat ini,
Mintalah selamat pulang balik.

Peace unto ye all!
I come as a friend, not as an enemy.
I come to seek my living, not to make war.
May no harm come to me, nor mine,
To my wife, my children, or my home.
Because I intend no harm, nor evil,
I ask that I may come, and go, in peace.

George, Maxwell, *In Malay Forests*, William Blackwood and Sons, Edinburgh and London, 1907, p. 9.

Marvels of the Ancients

∾

1
Golden Island

RUFUS FESTUS AVIENUS

'India Trans-gangetica', 'Nanyang', 'Suvarnabhumi'. To the ancient civilizations of Europe, China, or India, this corner of the Asian continent was a distant region of the strange and the precious, the 'Golden Chersonese'. Early writers—geographers, historians, or encyclopaedists—gleaned what they could from scant sources. The tales told by returning adventurers (some of the hardiest being pilgrims or missionaries of the world's great faiths) often relied much on hearsay and, down the years, repetition and faulty transcription embellished the sketchy accounts of these pioneering travellers. Thus, the earliest geographies told of island-strewn seas and wild shores, rich minerals, a terrain of mountains, rivers, and forests, lands populated by unknown peoples, strange creatures, and unusual plants. Merchants' stories, focusing on the chances of trade, listed precious ores and other natural products, some familiar, others weird and marvellous.

Typical is this short quotation from a versified *Description of the World*, written about AD 370 by Avienus, a Roman poet best known as translator and versifier of the works of others (including the early Greek author, Aratus, and the second-century geographer, Dionysius).

1

… *T*UM *cynaeis erepit ab undis*
Insula, quae prisci signatur nominis usu
Aurea, quod fulvo sol hic magis orbe rubescat

… Then there emerges from the azure waves an island which by ancient usage is known as 'the Golden', because there the yellow orb of the sun glows with a ruddier light.

Paul Wheatley, *The Golden Khersonese: Studies in Historical Geography of the Malay Peninsula before AD 1500*, University of Malaya Press, Kuala Lumpur, 1961, p. 133.

2
Vayu Purana

ROLAND BRADDELL

The compilers of this information in ancient times, often using scripts ill-suited for the purpose, strove to transcribe the names of strange provinces and settlements, peoples and products. Many accounts mixed geography, history, and opinion with a measure of licence. Most, inevitably, were coloured by the social and cultural perceptions of the writer. Apart from this overlay, a quotation from *Vayu Purana* (one of the eighteen Great Puranas of the historic Sanskrit corpus, dating back to the fifth century BC with additions up to the sixth century AD), purveys much the same information as would have been known to a contemporary classical Greek geo-grapher or Imperial Chinese court historian.

The translation is by Dato' Sir Roland Braddell, British-born but residing in Singapore or Malaysia for most of his long life, and honoured both by his adopted and his natal countries. He has been described as the scholar whose magisterial series of papers laid the foundation of our present knowledge of early Malaya.

S OUTH of Bharata Varsa, beyond a distance of 10,000 yojanas by sea, there is a dvipa—three thousand yojanas long and one third as broad. It is full of varieties of flowers and fruits. There is in that island a famous kulaparvata Vidyutvanta with many crests. There are thousands of rivers and tanks with clear and sweet waters. In the different parts of the mountain are towns where lived men and women in happiness. People there have long moustaches, are dark in hue, become aged 80 at the time of birth, live on roots and fruits like monkeys, and devoid of acaras (religious observances) like cattle. That island is full of such men and manikins.

Round about are other islands spreading over twenty, thirty, fifty, sixty, eighty, a hundred, and a thousand yojanas; these are small islands scattered in groups, and collectively known as Barhinadvipa.

There are six other provinces (pradesa) of Jambudvipa in different shapes. These are Anga dvipa, Yama dvipa, Malaya dvipa, Sankha dvipa, Kusa dvipa, and Varaha dvipa. Of these Anga dvipa is of a large size and is full of different clans and groups of *mlecchas*, and contains many rivers, trees, forests and hills, famous for its mines of gold and coral, being near the salt sea. There in the midst of Nagadesa is a mountain Cakragiri which contains a number of waterfalls and caves, and which touches the sea on either side with its extremities.

Yama dvipa again is full of mines. The hill here is known [as] Dyutiman, the source of rivers and of gold. In the same way Malaya dvipa has mines of precious stones and gold, besides sandalwood and ocean mines. It is full of groups of mlecchas and has many rivers and hills. The hill here is Malaya and contains silver mines. The noble mountain is reputed as the Mahamalaya. A second mountain (is there) Mandara by name, a beautiful hill with flowers and fruits resorted to by *devarsis* (Divine Sages). There is the venerable abode of Agastya revered by devas and Asuras. There is Kancapada other than the Malaya hill, and it is the holy hermitage rich in kusa grass and soma. It is a veritable

3

Paradise. In every parva it is said that Heaven descends here.

Roland Braddell, 'An Introduction to the Study of Ancient Times in the Malay Peninsula and the Straits of Malacca', *Journal of the Malayan Branch of the Royal Asiatic Society*, Vol. 15, Pt. 3, 1937, p. 115.

3
The Poison Tree from Macassar

GEORGIUS EVERHARDUS RUMPHIUS

As the centuries advanced, geographical knowledge of the region improved among the nations of Europe and Asia. In the East, reports of the sea routes, the lands, and the peoples encountered by Chinese merchants and trading fleets were compiled and repeated in general works as well as official dynastic histories. In West Asia, Arab authors drew mainly on sailors' yarns, producing renowned navigators' directories and fabulous compendia of wonders such as *Akhbar as-Sin wa'l-Hind* or the text we know as the *Thousand and One Nights*. From Europe, the first navigators reached South-East Asia in the sixteenth century. They and their early successors returned with novel merchandise, objects of curiosity, and tales of marvels enough to satisfy the credulity and eager pockets of their sponsors. Unduly obsessed with the bizarre and unusual, their stories unfortunately fail to provide us with reliable comment.

The earliest compendium of objective observations of the natural world, including true wonders, has come to us through the writings of Georg Everard Rumpf (1628–1702), published under the Latinized version of his name, Rumphius. Having enlisted as a volunteer soldier in the Dutch East Indies Company, Rumpf arrived in Batavia in 1653 and was posted to the island of Ambon. Here he spent the rest of his life as an administrator and collector and cataloguer of natural objects, although blind (possibly from glaucoma) from 1670. He became famous in his lifetime through his correspondence with notable naturalists in Europe and his meticulously annotated and illustrated manuscripts, the most important of which (*Thesaurus Amboinensis* and *Herbarium Amboinense*) were not published until long after his death.

Yet even this industrious and scholarly naturalist combined meticulous first-hand reports with fantastical hearsay, as in his strange account of *Arbor Toxicaria*, the Poison Tree from Macassar or *kayu upas*. This is nowadays known to systematic botanists as *Antiaris toxicaria*, an unremarkable large tree of the rain forest. Its sap does indeed provide a constituent of blowpipe dart poison, but it is not encircled by bare ground and its fruits are harmlessly ingested by frugivorous birds.

WHETHER it bears fruit or not no one can tell me, not even those who have been beneath it for gathering the poison. Under this tree and for a stone's throw around it, there grows neither grass nor leaves, nor any other trees, and the soil stays barren there, russet, and as if scorched. And under the most pernicious ones one will find the telltale sign of bird feathers, for the air around the tree is so tainted that if some birds want to rest themselves on the branches, they soon find themselves get dizzy and fall down dead. The branches that had been sent to me from Macassar, in a large Bamboo that was tightly shut, were still powerful enough that if one stuck a hand in there one felt a tingling as one does in frozen limbs after returning to where it is warm. Everything perishes that its wind touches, as so too do all animals shun it when they pass this tree, while the birds fly over it.

No Person dares approach it without having swaddled his head, arms, and legs with cloths, or he will become aware of a strong tingling in his limbs that will make them stiff and insensible. When drops from those leaves fall on someone's body it will make it swell up; nor should one stand under the tree with his head uncovered or his hairs will fall out. And so it seems that death has pitched his tents near this tree.

'The Upas, or Poison Tree of Java'. From *The Gallery of Nature and Art*, R. Wilkes, London, 1814.

The only thing that lives under it is a horned snake that cackles like a hen or, as others are wont to say, crows like a cock, and by night has fiery eyes.

E. M. Beekman (ed. and trans.), *The Poison Tree: Selected Writings of Rumphius on the Natural History of the Indies,* University of Massachusetts Press, Amherst, 1981, p. 129.

4
The Archipelago

J. R. LOGAN

It is mainly in publications of the nineteenth and twentieth centuries that we can look for reliable and authentic descriptions. Through the writings of this era—by travellers, residents, administrators (and their wives), journalists, collectors, scientists, and others—we can explore the wonders of the natural world—seas, islands, mountains, rivers, waterfalls, caves, forests, and beasts—tantalizingly hinted at in the ancient literature.

True to their profession, journalists have painted the most vivid pen portraits. In years past, at a period when the hand of man still lay lightly on the land, several saw a world little changed from its pristine state. They witnessed something of the magic that, at second hand, had inspired Avienus or the Sanskrit writers of the sixth century. J. R. Logan was editor of the *Penang Gazette*, a member of the Asiatic Society, a corresponding member of the Ethnological Society of London and of the Batavian Society of Arts and the Sciences, and obviously relished his widespread connections with the world of literature, science, and administration. Drawing on these sources, the two volumes of his *Journal of the Indian Archipelago* contain a wealth of remarkable descriptions of the natural world of a region he clearly loved.

WHEN we enter the seas of the Archipelago we are in a new world. Land and ocean are strangely intermingled. Great islands are disjoined by narrow straits, which, in the case of those of Sunda, lead at once into the smooth waters and green level shores of the interior from the rugged and turbulent outer coast, which would otherwise have opposed to us an unbroken wall more than two thousand miles in length. We pass from one mediterranean sea to another, now through groups of islets so small that we encounter many in an hour, and presently along the coast of those so large that we might be months in circumnavigating them. Even in crossing the widest of the eastern seas, when the last green speck has sunk beneath the horizon, the mariner knows that a circle drawn with a radius of two days sail would touch more land than water, and even that, if the eye were raised to a sufficient height, while the islands he had left would reappear on the one side, new shores would be seen on almost every other. But it is the wonderful freshness and greenness in which, go where he will, each new island is enveloped, that impresses itself on his senses as the great distinctive character of the region. The equinoctial warmth of the air, tempered and moistened by a constant evaporation, and purified by periodical winds, seems to be imbued with penetrating life-giving virtue, under the influence of which even the most barren rock becomes fertile. Hence those groups of small islands which sometimes environ the larger ones like clusters of satellites, or mark where their ranges pursue their course beneath the sea, often appear, in particular states of the atmosphere when a zone of white quivering light surrounds them and obliterates their coasts, to be dark umbrageous gardens floating on a wide lake, whose gleaming surface would be too dazzling were it not traversed by the shadows of the clouds, and covered by the breeze with an incessant play of light and shade.

J. R. Logan, 'The Present Condition of the Indian Archipelago', *Journal of the Indian Archipelago*, Vol. 1, 1847, pp. 4–5.

5
Placid Loveliness

JOHN CAMERON

John Cameron was a contemporary journalist, editor of the then youthful *Straits Times*, who intentionally promoted the delights and wonders of the British settlements on the west coast of the Malay Peninsula and in Singapore in 1865 on the eve of their incorporation into the Indian Empire of Queen Victoria. Of this romantic idyll, can some reminders still be found by the observant?

I have seen both Ceylon and Java, and admired in no grudging measure their many charms; but for calm placid loveliness, I should place Singapore high above them both. It is a loveliness, too, that at once strikes the eye, from whatever point we view the island, which combines all the advantages of an always beautiful and often imposing coastline with an endless succession of hill and dale stretching inland. The entire circumference of the island is one panorama, where the magnificent tropical forest, with its undergrowth of jungle, runs down at one place to the very water's edge, dipping its large leaves into the glassy sea, and at another is abruptly broken by a brown rocky cliff, or a late landslip over which the jungle has not yet had time to extend itself. Here and there, too, are scattered little green islands, set like gems on the bosom of the hushed water, between which the excursionist, the trader, or the pirate, is wont to steer his course. 'Eternal summer gilds these shores'; no sooner has the blossom of one tree passed away than that of another takes its place, and sheds fresh perfume all around; as for the foliage, that never seems to die. Perfumed isles are in many people's minds merely fabled dreams, but they are easy of realization here. There is scarcely a part of the island, except those few places where the original forest and jungle have been cleared away, from which at night time, on the first breathings of the land winds, may not be felt those lovely forest perfumes, even at the distance of more than a mile from shore. These land winds—or, more properly, land airs, for they can scarcely be said to blow, but only to breathe—usually commence at 10 o'clock at night and continue till within an hour or two of sunrise—they are welcomed by all; by the sailor because they speed him on either course, and by the wearied resident because of their delicious coolness.

The old Strait of Singhapura, that lies between Singapore and the mainland of Johore, at what we now term the back of the island, presents, probably, the most attractive scenery. There the hand of man has been but little at work, and nature has been left to paint her own picture. Besides this, the

9

narrowness and tortuous character of the straits at many places gives the appearance of lake scenery, and the invariable glassy stillness of the sea increases the similitude.

John Cameron, *Our Tropical Possessions in Malayan India*..., Smith, Elder and Co., London, 1865, pp. 27–9.

6
Tropical Scenery

RAMON REYES LALA

Ramon Reyes Lala, in 1898, viewed the tropical scenery of the Philippines at an equally historic juncture as the American intervention replaced the long colonial occupation of (in his words) 'the Spaniard [who] looks upon nature with a lazy eye, troubling himself little about anything that cannot be put to some immediate use. And he has jealously guarded the islands against alien footsteps, putting annoying obstacles in the way of all that sought to explore the interior'!

T ROPICAL scenery cannot be pictured in words. It must be seen to be comprehended. One need not, too, go beyond the environs of Manila—that Venice of the East, with its labyrinth of canals and estuaries,—through which the tides of the broad bay daily ebb and flow,—and with its wealth of brilliant flowers and tropic verdure—to imagine oneself in a new world. Its surroundings are a dream of beauty.

Take any of the roads that run outward from the city. Say, starting from the Malecon promenade: one passes through stretches of country verdant with groves of graceful bamboos, lofty cocoanut palms, flowing-leaved plantains, and all the wonderful variety and luxuriance of tropical vegetation. Upon it the eye gazes unsated, the leaves and flowers alike being rich and gorgeous in tint and form. Often have I wandered, entranced, up the eddying Pasig, enraptured by the beauty of its scenery and the charm of its coloring, viewing, also from its leafy banks the splendors of sunset skies, grand and glowing to a degree seldom seen in temperate zones.

Further inland the mountain scenery never fails to charm, with the varied pictures presented by its forest-growth. A grotesqueness of form is often assumed by the trunks and limbs of tropical trees, and this, with the glossy green foliage, the rich hues and attractive shapes of the blossoms, the novel forms and colors of the fruits, the dash and sparkle of mountain streams, here and there breaking into lovely cascades, all co-ordinated to the eye, compose a spectacle of beauty seldom excelled.

Of all those plants, the tall and graceful bamboo ranks among the most beautiful. Everywhere it is found, growing in groups and clusters, scattered with great profusion and variety over hill and plain, along the streams, and around the native huts and villages. At the slightest breeze its fleecy tops and supple branches wave gracefully in the air, giving to the foliage the charm of perpetual motion. In addition, too, to its almost endless variety of uses, it has a mission beyond that of utility,—the mission of beauty, and it may justly be viewed as one of the choicest decorations of the island scenery.

The bamboo never grows monotonous. It presents forms and colors of wonderful attractiveness and variety, and so fully dealt with has it been by the brush of the painter and the pen of the poet, that it might well be given a fine-art gallery and a library of its own.

Ramon Reyes Lala, *The Philippine Islands*, Continental Publishing Co., New York, 1898, pp. 153–5.

Continents Adrift

❧

7
Physical Review

J. R. LOGAN

It was reasonable, in the mid-nineteenth century, to assume (as did Logan) that the physical connections of this region with the main Asian continental structure were ancient and enduring.

T HE first and most general consideration in a physical review of the Archipelago is its relation to the Continent of Asia. In the platform, on which the largest and most important lands are distributed, we see a great root which the stupendous mass of Asia has sent forth from its south eastern side, and which, spreading far to the south beneath the waters of the India and Pacific Oceans, and there expanding and shooting up by its plutonic and volcanic energy, has covered them, and marked its tract, with innumerable islands. That there is a real and not merely a fanciful connection between the Archipelago and Asia is demonstrable, although, when we endeavour to trace its history, we are soon lost in the region of speculation.

J. R. Logan, 'The Present Condition of the Indian Archipelago, *Journal of the Indian Archipelago*, Vol. 1, 1847, p. 2.

8
Dispersal of Gondwanaland

M. G. AUDLEY-CHARLES

Only from the mid-1950s did speculation give way to theory as geologists began to elucidate the extraordinary processes by which the present continents have separated from a primordial single land mass, drifting apart over the global surface on deep magmatic convection currents. Not until 1985 was the complex and truly wondrous tectonic history of South-East Asia deciphered with some confidence.

In brief, the earth is about 5,000 million years old. There are, however, few places where exposures of rocks older than 600 million years can be found. Direct geological knowledge is therefore limited mainly to this time-span. At an early stage, it appears that the land formed one huge, single continent for which the name Pangea has been coined. In time, a huge rift developed across this continent, allowing it to be flooded by sea. Along the rift line, convection currents in the hot, underlying mantle of the globe emplaced new crustal material on either side, so that the sea floor spread progressively, forcing apart the two arms of Pangea. By about 300 million years ago, the two were fully separated as vast supercontinents, northern (called Laurasia) and southern (Gondwanaland), between which lay a newly formed ocean, the Tethys.

The southern supercontinent, Gondwanaland, comprised South America, Antarctica, Africa with Madagascar, Australia, and land that now forms a large part of southern Asia, from Turkey to Indo-China, including greater India. Subsequent rifting has divided Gondwanaland into these component parts. Over the past 300 million years, they have drifted apart infinitessimally slowly, by the same process of sea-floor spreading which has successively opened up new oceanic extensions, called Tethys II and Tethys III.

From the north-eastern shore of Gondwanaland, then lying roughly at latitude 30 °S, first to separate (some time after 300 million years ago) was an elongated coastal strip that now extends from Turkey through Iran and northern Tibet to Indo-China. About 200–160 million years ago, further rifting parallel to the coast opened up Tethys III and launched an element now forming connected land and islands from southern Tibet through Burma (Myanmar), western Thailand, and Peninsular Malaysia to western Celebes (Sulawesi). Eastern Celebes, with Timor and Seram, remained joined at that time to the New Guinea/Australian arm of Gondwanaland, although probably being submerged as continental shelf.

Around 140 million years ago, India began to rift apart from Gondwanaland. A spreading sea-floor ridge became part of the future Indian Ocean and carried India by increasing separation northwards. At the same time, subduction trenches developed at the northern shores of the Tethys, where the ocean crust descends back into the mantle (where it originally formed) and is remelted. As the Tethys ocean floor underwent this inevitable process of collapsing back into the mantle, successive Gondwanan continental fragments carried by the northward motion collided with Laurasia. These collisions have produced the huge Himalayan mountain chain and the tumbled highlands that adjoin it. The disposition of continental fragments assumed the present orientation only some 10 million years ago, so that the final stage of this astounding natural process is regarded as very recent on the geological time scale.

The tectonic history of South-East Asia has been re-interpreted by M. G. Audley-Charles, now retired Emeritus Professor of the Department of Geological Sciences, University College London. His text is highly technical, but the illustrations provide a brilliant graphic synopsis of the progressive separation, drift, and ultimate reassembly of the component elements. Note the lapse of up to 50 million years between successive frames! (See the figures on pp. 15–17.)

M. G. Audley-Charles, 'Dispersal of Gondwanaland: Relevance to Evolution of the Angiosperms', in T. C. Whitmore (ed.), *Biogeographical Evolution of the Malay Archipelago*, Clarendon Press, Oxford, 1987, pp. 5–25.

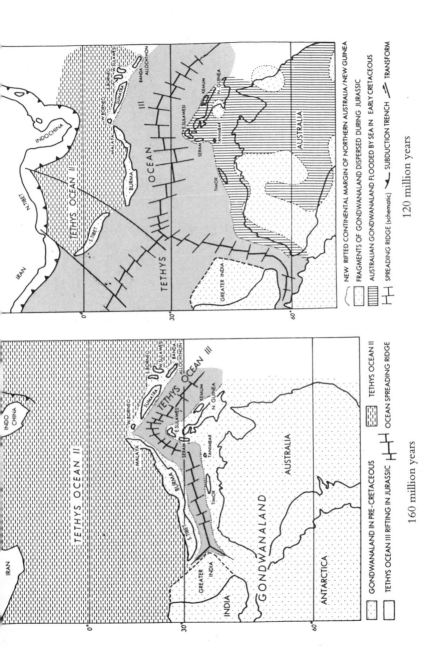

160 million years

☐ GONDWANALAND IN PRE-CRETACEOUS	☐ TETHYS OCEAN II
⫩⫩ TETHYS OCEAN III RIFTING IN JURASSIC	☐ OCEAN SPREADING RIDGE

120 million years

〰 NEW RIFTED CONTINENTAL MARGIN OF NORTHERN AUSTRALIA / NEW GUINEA	
☐ FRAGMENTS OF GONDWANALAND DISPERSED DURING JURASSIC	
⫩⫩ AUSTRALIAN GONDWANALAND FLOODED BY SEA IN EARLY CRETACEOUS	
☐ SPREADING RIDGE (schematic) ⟋ SUBDUCTION TRENCH ⟋ TRANSFORM	

15

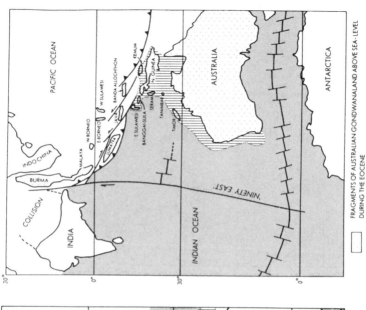

FRAGMENTS OF AUSTRALIAN GONDWANALAND ABOVE SEA-LEVEL DURING THE EOCENE

AUSTRALIAN CONTINENTAL MARGIN FLOODED BY SEA THROUGHOUT THE EOCENE

40 million years

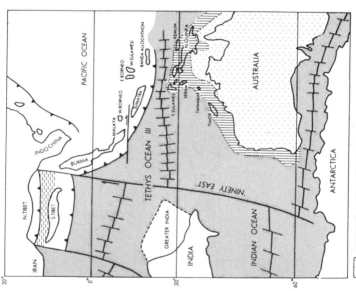

FRAGMENTS OF AUSTRALIAN GONDWANALAND DISPERSED IN THE JURASSIC

AUSTRALIAN GONDWANALAND FLOODED BY THE SEA IN LATE CRETACEOUS

REMNANT OF TETHYS OCEAN II

90 million years

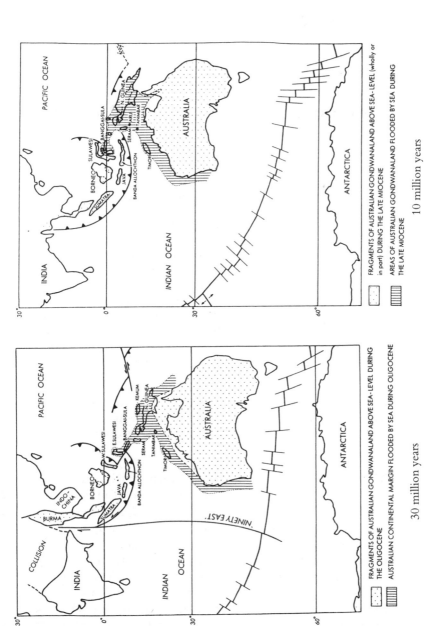

FRAGMENTS OF AUSTRALIAN GONDWANALAND ABOVE SEA-LEVEL DURING THE OLIGOCENE

AUSTRALIAN CONTINENTAL MARGIN FLOODED BY SEA DURING OLIGOCENE

30 million years

FRAGMENTS OF AUSTRALIAN GONDWANALAND ABOVE SEA-LEVEL (wholly or in part) DURING THE LATE MIOCENE

AREAS OF AUSTRALIAN GONDWANALAND FLOODED BY SEA DURING THE LATE MIOCENE

10 million years

17

Mountains and Mountain Ranges

❧

9
Earth Storm

CHARLES A. FISHER

The vast, earth-shaping tectonic processes described in the previous section have left their signature in the land-form of South-East Asia. One such mark is the dramatic change in orientation of the mountain ranges that delimit the region from the rest of Asia. The latitudinal axis of the Himalayas is prolonged eastwards as the Nanling range; connected escarpments extend to the South China Sea as the border watershed between the Red River of northern Vietnam and the Sikiang in China. South of this line, the mountain ranges are longitudinal in orientation, running predominantly north–south. The geographical scene is set in a textbook by Charles Fisher, former Head of the Department of Geography in the School of Oriental and African Studies and Professor of Geography with reference to Asia at the University of London.

T HUS the majestic east–west sweep of the Himalayas abruptly gives place on the borders of Burma to the north–south trend of the Arakan ranges and, although in the south the great arcs of Indonesia again show a more or less latitudinal alignment through Java and the Lesser Sundas, the islands which lie to the north and east of these present a more controversial pattern as they approach the Pacific. Moreover, while the most recent 'earth storm' has already passed its climax on the mainland, this stage has probably not yet been reached in the Malaysian archipelago and active orogenesis is still continuing, notably in the vicinity of the Banda sea.

Charles A. Fisher, *South-east Asia: A Social, Economic and Political Geography*, 2nd edn., Methuen and Co., London, 1966, pp. 11–12.

10
The Shan Plateau

F. KINGDON WARD

The irregular and deeply dissected topography of the land eastward of the Himalayas was familiar ground to a famous plant hunter. Captain Frank Kingdon Ward—explorer, dedicated plant collector, and prolific author—began his career as a schoolmaster in Shanghai (1907–9), but for most of his subsequent life travelled, collected plants, and wrote of his experiences in East and South-East Asia, from western China and Tibet to the hills of north-eastern India, through northern Burma, Thailand, and the Indo-Chinese region. In 1931–2, he was joined by my late father (4th Earl of Cranbrook), who was responsible for the zoological collections on their exploration of the upper Adung valley, leading to the Burma–Tibetan border.

In this passage, Kingdon Ward described the view from on high.

I was in the Shan country when the war spread to the Far East, travelling off the beaten track by mule-paths which led up and down over the steep hills from one fertile valley to another, from one village to another, while armies gathered from the east and from the west, to protect the frontier. But the Japanese did not strike from the east, from French Indo-China and from northern Siam as was expected, and the British, Indian and Chinese forces had to march south in a desperate attempt to save Lower Burma, leaving the Shans to their fate.

The Shan plateau forms the western edge of the great mountainous region of south-east Asia. Travelling north from Rangoon to Mandalay by the Burma railway, beyond Toungoo the escarpment comes into view, rising abruptly from the plain not many miles to the east. In the early morning mist it looks like a sea cliff blue, not white. There are few ways up the escarpment—the Thandaung road, from Toungoo, the Southern Shan States railway and road from Thazi, and the Burma Road and Lashio railway from Mandalay on a frontage of 500 miles; but once on the plateau, travel is easier than in most parts of Burma.

Although a plateau in the geographical sense, it must be remembered that it resembles the rest of Burma in being corrugated from north to south by parallel ranges of mountains which rise several thousand feet above the general level. Between the dark jungle-clad ranges, the open downs sweep in undulating curves, with tree-girt villages surrounded by rice fields hidden between the folds. Here and there a deep rift scores the country from north to south like a sword-cut, where a great river rolls southwards to the sea. But though the two largest rivers, the Salween and the Mekong, are much longer than the Irrawaddy, they flow, not through wide populous valleys, but through almost uninhabited gorges. Beyond the Mekong, which for nearly 200 miles forms the frontier between the Burmese Shan States and French Indo-China, there is no marked change. The country still consists of rolling plateaux, striped by parallel ranges of mountains and scored by deep valleys, whether it is called China, French Indo-China or Siam.

Captain F. Kingdon Ward, 'The Shans and Their Country', *Geographical Magazine*, Vol. 17, No. 8, 1944, p. 364.

11
The Blue-green Hill

R. RAVEN-HART

From the deeply cut river valleys of Upper Burma (Myanmar), the traveller catches only rare and tantalizing glimpses of the mountains. Boating down the Irrawaddy, Major Raven-Hart saw the high hills as blue.

T HIS freak direction gave us one of the best views of the day, some twenty miles of flat grey-green country, and then suddenly Mara Bum, the bold blue-green hill that lies opposite Myitkyina; and far beyond, so far that they looked bare although in reality covered with dense forests, the higher haze-blue hills that stretch towards Tibet. It was part of a rainbow, a magnification of the part of the spectrum from green to blue only: it was as difficult when looking at it to remember that reds and yellows existed as it is to imagine new colours when seeing the whole spectrum.

Major R. Raven-Hart, *Canoe to Mandalay*, The Book Club, London, 1941, pp. 40–1.

12
Wonderful Kinabalu

TOM HARRISSON

The summit of Kinabalu, at 13,455 feet (4100 metres), is the highest point in South-East Asia. Its soaring, jagged profile dominates the skyline throughout much of Sabah's west coast. The peak was formed 4–9 million years ago by a vast intrusion of underlying hot rock (a 'pluton') from the inner depths of the earth. Because it cooled slowly, large crystals formed in this rock, giving it a rough but startlingly beautiful, mottled appearance.

21

Born in 1911, Tom Harrisson was a co-founder of Mass Observation. He first visited South-East Asia in 1932 with the Oxford University expedition to Sarawak. In 1945, towards the end of the Second World War, he returned by parachute into the Kelabit uplands. He remained in Sarawak, holding the posts of Government Ethnologist and Curator of the Museum for twenty formative years during which he led research in ornithology, ethnology, and archaeology. He was killed in a traffic accident in Thailand in 1976.

K INABALU is one of the most wonderful mountains of the world. The outstanding mountains in the Andes and the Himalayas, in Europe and in Africa, have their separate, numerous splendours, but none exceed Kinabalu in what I can best term sheer strength and stark simplicity. The secret of this strength, this wonder, which stays with you from the very first sight through a lifetime, is the way the mountain is set; near the equator, rising darkly straight out of the tropical Forest, one continuous, clean, black, bare rock mass, to the summit. Because of its breathtaking isolation Kinabalu has its own climate, a constant flux of cloud and wind, rain and cold, and the warmth from the Forests below. So it is seldom in any sense a static mountain, one may be looking at it one moment, and the next it has disappeared. This feature is so unlike much of tropical, Bornean life, which is essentially continuous, even seasonless, that it plays a very important part in the excitement provided by Kinabalu.

Physically Kinabalu, at 13,455 ft, the highest mountain between the peaks of the Himalayas and Wilhemena in Irian (New Guinea), dominates most of Sabah. Spiritually, it dominates all of Sabah and much of Borneo. A coat of arms, a sentinel across so many horizons, it is a symbol in the lowland mind—how right the state government with unerring instinct, when it scrapped the tired name Jesselton for the State's capital and made it Kota Kinabalu. Much of

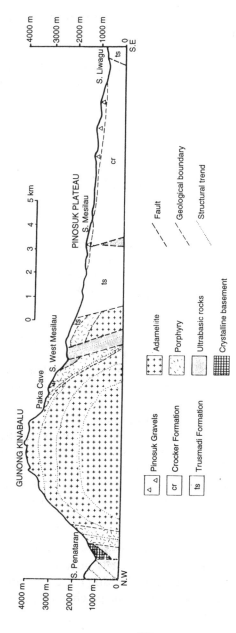

A diagrammatic geological section of Mount Kinabalu, from north-west (*left*) to south-east (*right*), showing the core of crystalline igneous rock known technically as Adamellite. From G. Jacobson, 'Geology', in E. R. Dingley (ed.), *Kinabalu Summit of Borneo*, Sabah Society Monograph, 1978.

23

what goes on in the capital is to some extent overshadowed from those great rock pinnacles.

T. Harrisson, 'Kinabalu the Wonderful Mountain of Change', in E. R. Dingley (ed.), *Kinabalu Summit of Borneo*, Sabah Society Monograph, 1978, p. 23.

13
A Virgin Peak

F. KINGDON WARD

The exultation of a professional botanist at gaining an unknown ridge-top summit in the steep, dissected terrain, and at the wondrous wildness found there, is evident in this short abstract of Kingdon Ward's story of his trip to the Ngawchang valley in the interior of Burma (Myanmar).

CLAMBERING up some cliffs in the crevices of which crouched half-frozen dwarf shrubs such as juniper, willow, rhododendron and gnarled cherry, we at last stood on the summit of the long ridge, where it joined the main range.

We had conquered our virgin peak.

The highest summit lay some distance away to the left, along the main ridge; fronting us was another deep valley at the bottom of which flowed a considerable stream, and beyond that again a jumble of ridges, spurs and valleys, but through the veil of swirling mist it was difficult to be sure of the topography. Sufficient was it for the moment that we had achieved our object.

The far side of the mountain sloped smoothly down to the stream just mentioned, and was embroidered with rhododendrons formed in the most enchanting patterns, within the web of which were included small patches of pure white quartz sand starred with the little bluish violet flowers of *Primula coryphæa*.

The rhododendrons were all dwarfs, not six inches high, bearing erect trusses each of two comparatively large flowers set horizontally, with widely gaping throats. They had white flowers, purple flowers, rose flowers, lemon-yellow flowers, port-wine flowers; but perhaps the most striking of all was one with pure white, waxen-looking flowers.

In this paradise we roamed for some time though shivering with cold as the raw wind beat through our drenched garments. Patches of snow still lay melting in the gullies; the mists gathered and dispersed whimsically. I would have given a lot to have seen these mountains bathed in sunshine.

Captain F. Kingdon Ward, *In Farthest Burma*, Seeley Service and Co. Ltd., London, 1921, pp. 90–1.

14
Dak Lac

NORMAN LEWIS

Since his first book, on Arabia, in 1938, and with twenty-five or more other major works (many of which have been revised and reissued) by the 1990s, the author and travel writer, Norman Lewis, has become recognized as one of the great observers of contemporary scenes and events. In the highlands of Vietnam in 1950, he witnessed the ever-repeated natural beauty of the daily cycle of morning mists, midday sunlight, and evening dusk, in a montane setting enhanced by the lakeside scene.

T HE whole district of the Dak Lac is seen as if through dark glasses. There is not a great deal of colour. It is a study in smoky blues, greens and white. The light has a cool Nordic quality and the lake itself is an Icelandic *vatyn* with the mountain reflections blurred in the dim sparkle of the frosted surface. The islands seemed edged with ice, but this edging is a packed fringe of egrets and when an eagle drops among them the ice dissolves as the egrets rise, to reform again as they settle. One's views of the lake seem always to be obtained through the spare branches of the frangipani or the *lilas de Japon*—negligent brush-strokes on silk, with a sparse adornment of white blossom.

In the morning the mountains float above a cauldron of mist in which islands slowly materialize, and along the near shore, below the administrator's bungalow, the topmost branches of the trees are elegantly supported upon layers of vapour. Later the scene solidifies and the lake is seen to be encircled by mountains, covered to their peaks by a tight webbing of jungle. The water's-edge is feathered by bamboos. As the sun drops in the sky, its light is no longer reflected from the moss-like sheath of vegetation on the distant highlands, which, instead of glowing with yellow light, as they would in Northern climes, turn to the darkest of smoky blue. Fishing eagles turning against this dark background show their white underparts and the end of their dive is marked by a fountain rising from the water. At this hour the butterflies appear and fly down to the lake. They are black, slashed with lemon and as big as bats. Egrets pass in drifts on their way to roost. The last movement is a curved line of cranes, with black, heraldic silhouettes against the darkening sky. All day and all through the night the cool sound of gongs comes over the water from unseen Moi villages.

Norman Lewis, *A Dragon Apparent*, Jonathan Cape, London, 1951, p. 101.

15
Bok-kor

ALAN HOUGHTON BRODRICK

The oldest land surface of this region occupies much of Cambodia and southern Vietnam. Here can be found exposures of the pre-Cambrian shield of ancient Gondwanaland, comparable to the Indian Deccan and the Australian interior, with which this land was once linked. The wonder of rocks more than 600 million years of age was lightly treated by the travel writer, A. H. Brodrick, describing the hills inland of Kompot which he visited in 1939.

B EHIND, and high up in the Elephant Ridge, is Bok-kor. It will take you two hours to drive through the Emerald Valley. The mountain road is bordered by thick forest whose trees shoot up, often, a hundred feet above you. The Emerald Valley shimmers in green mist. It is a world of leaves and lianas, of murderous thorns and monstrous trunks, it is a world quite uninhabited by man. This *Phnom Kamchhang*, as the Cambodians call it, is a compact mass of ancient (Triassic) sandstone riveted directly upon very antique rocks (pre-carboniferous strata). It has been dry land for countless ages and the ridge, so long and so often an island in the past has remained insular. It is an isolated outcrop rising abruptly from the plain. Cambodian legends shroud the place in mystery. It is the home of ghosts ... it is full of elephant, gaur, monkeys, panther, tiger, parrots, perhaps rhinoceros (but no one stalks them) and of deer.

A. H. Brodrick, *Little Vehicle, Cambodia and Laos*, Hutchinson and Co., London, *c*.1948, pp. 211–12.

Vulcanism

◌ↈ

16
Telluric Energy

J. R. LOGAN

Thrust up by the gargantuan forces of impact between tectonic plates, a striking array of parallel mountain ranges forms the northern continental boundary of South-East Asia, extending across the interior highlands of Burma (Myanmar) to Vietnam. Although a modern interpretation of the mechanisms of mountain-building was not known to him, Logan recognized the existence of the awesome forces that lie pent within the earth.

SERENE in their beauty and magnificence as these mountains generally appear, they hide in their bosoms elements of the highest terrestrial sublimity and awe, compared with whose appalling energy, not only the bursten lakes and the rushing avalanches of the Alps, but the most devastating explosions of Vesuvius or Etna, cease to terrify the imagination. When we look upon the ordinary aspects of these mountains, it is almost impossible to believe the geological story of their origin, and if our senses yield to science, they tacitly revenge themselves by placing in the remotest past, the era of such convulsions as it relates. But the nether powers though imprisoned are not subdued. The same telluric energy which piled the mountain from the ocean to the clouds, even while we gaze in silent worship on its glorious form, is silently gathering in its dark womb, and time speeds on to the day, whose coming science can neither foretell nor prevent, when the mountain is rent; the solid foundations of the whole region are shaken; the earth is opened to vomit forth destroying fires upon the living beings who dwell upon its surface, or closed to engulph them; the forests are deluged by lava, or withered by sulphureous vapours; the sun sets at noonday behind the black smoke which thickens over the sky, and spreads far and wide, raining ashes throughout a circuit hundreds of miles in diameter; till it seems to the superstitious native that the fiery abodes of the volcanic dewas are disembowelling themselves, possessing the earth, and blotting out the heavens. The living remnants of the generation whose doom it was to inhabit Sumbawa in 1815, could tell us that this picture is but a faint transcript of the reality, and that our imagination can never conceive the dreadful spectacle which still appals their memories. Fortunately these awful explosions of the earth, which to man convert nature into the supernatural, occur at rare intervals; and, though scarcely a year elapse without some volcano bursting into action, the greater portion of the Archipelago being more than once shaken, and even the ancient granitic floor of the Peninsula trembling beneath us, this terrestrial instability has ordinarily no worse effect than to dispel the illusion that we tread upon a solid globe, to convert the physical romance of geological history into the familiar associations of our own lives, and to unite the events of the passing hour with those which first fitted the world for the habitation of man.

J. R. Logan, 'The Present Condition of the Indian Archipelago', *Journal of the Indian Archipelago*, Vol. 1, 1847, pp. 6–7.

17
A Volcano and an Earthquake

ALFRED RUSSEL WALLACE

In the archipelago of South-East Asia, other mountains witness a different manifestation of continental drift. The sweeping curves of the subduction zones, shown on Audley-Charles's final map of 10 million years ago (Passage 8), mark the lines where the expanding sea floors of the Indian and Pacific Oceans thrust under the margins of the crustal plate and are reabsorbed into the underlying fiery magma. Along these lines there is constant seismic activity and long chains of volcanic mountains rear their fiery peaks. These curving volcanic belts were recognized and mapped (in 1868) by A. R. Wallace, in the most famous and enduringly readable of all books on the region.

Born in 1823, Wallace left school at thirteen and initially trained as a surveyor until the opportunity arose for him to turn his deep enthusiasm for natural history to good use, as a professional collector. His first experience of the tropical world was on expedition to the Amazon with his friend, Henry Walter Bates (1848–50). In 1853, he obtained a government passage to Singapore, and for the following eight years travelled widely through the Peninsula and islands that now comprise Malaysia, Singapore, and Indonesia. In 1858, from the Moluccas, he wrote to Charles Darwin who realized that they shared convergent ideas on natural selection. The two men are jointly credited with the origin of this fundamental theory on the origin of species and remained friends for life.

In the first passage quoted below, Wallace responded in a philosophical vein to his first sight of the volcano at Banda, in 1857. By 1859, he was familiar with the manifestations of the earth's internal energies and, in the second excerpt, was able to write light-heartedly about an earthquake he experienced at Rurukan village, Menado, Celebes (Sulawesi).

B ANDA is a lovely little spot, its three islands enclosing a secure harbour from whence no outlet is visible, and with water so transparent, that living corals and even the minutest objects are plainly seen on the volcanic sand at a depth of seven or eight fathoms. The ever smoking volcano rears its bare cone on one side, while the two larger islands are clothed with vegetation to the summit of the hills.

Going on shore, I walked up a pretty path which leads to the highest point of the island on which the town is situated, where there is a telegraph station and a magnificent view. Below lies the little town, with its neat red-tiled white houses and the thatched cottages of the natives, bounded on one side by the old Portuguese fort. Beyond, about half a mile distant, lies the larger island in the shape of a horseshoe, formed of a range of abrupt hills covered with fine forest and nutmeg gardens; while close opposite the town is the volcano, forming a nearly perfect cone, the lower part only covered with a light green bushy vegetation. On its north side the outline is more uneven, and there is a slight hollow or chasm about one-fifth of the way down, from which constantly issue two columns of smoke, as well as a good deal from the rugged surface around and from some spots nearer the summit. A white efflorescence, probably sulphur, is thickly spread over the upper part of the mountain, marked by the narrow black vertical lines of water gullies. The smoke unites as it rises, and forms a dense cloud, which in calm damp weather spreads out into a wide canopy hiding the top of the mountain. At night and early morning it often rises up straight and leaves the whole outline clear.

It is only when actually gazing on an active volcano that one can fully realize its awfulness and grandeur. Whence comes that inexhaustible fire whose dense and sulphureous smoke for ever issues from this bare and desolate peak? Whence the mighty forces that produced that peak, and still from time to time exhibit themselves in the earthquakes that always occur in the vicinity of volcanic vents? The knowledge from childhood, of the fact that volcanoes and earthquakes exist, has taken away somewhat of the strange and exceptional character that really belongs to them. The inhabitant of most parts of northern Europe, sees in the earth the emblem of stability and repose. His whole life-experience,

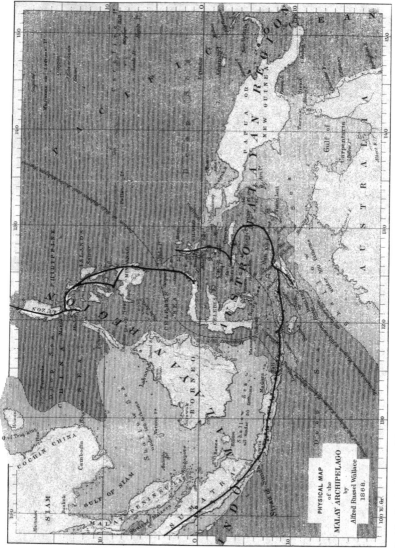

In his physical map of the Malay archipelago (1868), Wallace delineated the volcanic belts. (in bold line)

and that of all his age and generation, teaches him that the earth is solid and firm, that its massive rocks may contain water in abundance but never fire; and these essential characteristics of the earth are manifest in every mountain his country contains. A volcano is a fact opposed to all this mass of experience, a fact of so awful a character that, if it were the rule instead of the exception, it would make the earth uninhabitable, a fact so strange and unaccountable that we may be sure it would not be believed on any human testimony, if presented to us now for the first time, as a natural phenomenon happening in a distant country.

The summit of the small island is composed of a highly crystalline basalt; lower down I found a hard stratified slaty sandstone, while on the beach are huge blocks of lava, and scattered masses of white coralline limestone. The larger island has coral rock to a height of three or four hundred feet, while above is lava and basalt. It seems probable, therefore, that this little group of four islands is the fragment of a larger district which was perhaps once connected with Ceram, but which was separated and broken up by the same forces which formed the volcanic cone. When I visited the larger island on another occasion, I saw a considerable tract covered with large forest trees, dead, but still standing. This was a record of the last great earthquake only two years ago, when the sea broke in over this part of the island and so flooded it as to destroy the vegetation on all the low lands. Almost every year there is an earthquake here, and at intervals of a few years very severe ones, which throw down houses and carry ships out of the harbour bodily into the streets.

*   *   *

During my stay at Rurukan my curiosity was satisfied by experiencing a pretty sharp earthquake-shock. On the evening of June 29th, at a quarter after eight, as I was sitting reading, the house began shaking with a very gentle, but rapidly increasing motion. I sat still enjoying the novel sensation for some seconds; but in less than half a minute it became strong enough to shake me in my chair, and to make the house visibly rock about, and creak and crack as if it would fall to pieces. Then began a cry throughout the village of 'Tana goyang! tana goyang!' (Earthquake! earthquake!) Everybody rushed out of their houses—women screamed and children cried—and I thought it prudent to go out too. On getting up, I found my head giddy and my steps unsteady, and could hardly walk without falling. The shock continued about a minute, during which time I felt as if I had been turned round and round, and was almost sea-sick. Going into the house again. I found a lamp and a bottle of arrack upset. The tumbler which formed the lamp had been thrown out of the saucer in which it had stood. The shock appeared to be nearly vertical, rapid, vibratory, and jerking. It was sufficient, I have no doubt, to have thrown down brick chimneys and walls and church towers; but as the houses here are all low, and strongly framed of timber, it is impossible for them to be much injured, except by a shock that would utterly destroy a European city. The people told me it was ten years since they had had a stronger shock than this, at which time many houses were thrown down and some people killed.

At intervals of ten minutes to half an hour, slight shocks and tremors were felt, sometimes strong enough to send us all out again. There was a strange mixture of the terrible and the ludicrous in our situation. We might at any moment have a much stronger shock, which would bring down the house over us, or—what I feared more—cause a landslip, and send us down into the deep ravine on the very edge of which the village is built; yet I could not help laughing each time we ran out at a slight shock, and then in a few moments ran in again. The sublime and the ridiculous were here literally but a step apart. On the one hand, the most terrible and destructive of natural phenomena was in action around us—the rocks, the mountains, the solid earth were trembling and convulsed, and we were utterly impotent to guard against the danger that might at any moment overwhelm us. On the other hand was the spectacle of a number of men, women, and children running in and out of their houses, on what each time proved a very unnecessary alarm, as each shock ceased just as it became strong enough to frighten us. It seemed really very much like 'playing at earthquakes', and made many of the people join me in a hearty laugh, even while reminding each other that it really might be no laughing matter.

At length the evening got very cold, and I became very sleepy, and determined to turn in; leaving orders to my boys, who slept nearer the door, to wake me in case the house was in danger of falling. But I miscalculated my apathy, for I could not sleep much. The shocks continued at intervals of half an hour or an hour all night, just strong enough to wake me thoroughly each time and keep me on the alert ready to jump up in case of danger. I was therefore very glad when morning came. Most of the inhabitants had not been to bed at all, and some had stayed out of doors all night. For the next two days and nights shocks still continued at short intervals, and several times a day for a week, showing that there was some very extensive disturbance beneath our portion of the earth's crust. How vast the forces at work really are can only be properly appreciated when, after feeling their effects, we look abroad over the wide expanse of hill and valley, plain and mountain, and thus realize in a slight degree the immense mass of matter heaved and shaken. The sensation produced by an earthquake is never to be forgotten. We feel ourselves in the grasp of a power to which the wildest fury of the winds and waves are as nothing; yet the effect is more a thrill of awe than the terror which the more boisterous war of the elements produces. There is a mystery and an uncertainty as to the amount of danger we incur, which gives greater play to the imagination, and to the influences of hope and fear. These remarks apply only to a moderate earthquake. A severe one is the most destructive and the most horrible catastrophe to which human beings can be exposed.

Alfred Russel Wallace, *The Malay Archipelago: The Land of the Orang-Utan, and the Bird of Paradise*, 10th edn., Macmillan and Co., London, 1883, pp. 114–18, 249–51 and 286–7.

18
Mount Semiru

M. ZOLLINGER

The highest mountain in Java, Indonesia, is the exquisite Semeru (3676 metres), set spectacularly in the primordial volcanic land-scape of the Bromo–Tengger National Park. It was climbed in 1845 by M. Zollinger, a Swiss citizen nostalgic for his Helvetian homeland but, by his own evidence, by no means the first to do so. Semeru is still highly active, erupting every few minutes and over-hung by a smoky plume.

NO mountain in Java has so much reminded me of the mountains of my father-land as Semiru, not that it agrees more in its form than others with the granite moun-tains of the Alps. This resemblance on the contrary is less than in some of its brethren, but the circumstance that it is the highest of them calls back to my memory Mont Blanc, with which it agrees in another circumstance viz. the change of colour in its light according to the position of the sun. Above all its appearance is ravishing in early morning shortly before and at the up rising of the sun. The grey land that covers the top of the mountain then shews a rose-red glow, just as in the autumn at sunset the snow covered summits of the Alps, and above all those of Mont Blanc and Mont Rosa. If we have the fortune, shortly before the rising of the sun, to see one of the smoke clouds rising, which are expelled nearly every half hour or hour, we shall never forget the glorious

36

Mount Bromo in East Java is among the more spectacular of Java's live volcanoes, offering a view of Java's highest mountain, Semiru. From *Handbook of the Netherlands East Indies*, Department of Commerce, Buitenzorg, 1924.

sight. Slowly rises the cloud, slowly it spreads itself upwards by the development of the column turning spirally round the centre, until finally it appears to form a gigantic tree which depicts itself, rosy-red and indescribably beautiful, on the firmament, and is gradually lost in golden crowned flakes. So long as I remained in Lamajang it was particularly active. It expelled very frequently these smoke columns in such large volumes that in calms they in a short time wholly covered the mountain to a great depth beneath its top. With the fall of night, when all was become still, we could plainly hear a sound in the direction of the mountain like that of dull distant thunder, which sometimes lasted without interruption from 6 to 10 minutes. In the night of the 20th January, by clear moonlight I went in a small prahu from Pugor to Nusa Baron. About midnight I saw a large column of fire rise up out of the crater of Semiru (distant from me about 16 miles N.N.W.) which elevated itself for some time and finally sunk

37

into itself. This column must have consisted principally of glowing stones, for after it had fallen in, I saw, along the outermost slope of the mountain, sparks descending with lightning rapidity, and now disappearing and again appearing. This was certainly glowing stones rolling along the mountain, now concealed in the small isolated thickets and then again coming into view on the naked sand. How much more beautiful still would this sight have been without moonlight. It is remarkable that the Lamongan and the Bromo have for a long time remained unusually quiet. The crater of that mountain now evolves with difficulty some pillars of smoke. During an excursion to the south east foot of Semiru, I first saw that the eastern summit of this mountain, only possesses a crater, but in three deep clefts which open from its ruin, towards the south east, it has three solfataras, all of which emitted very much vapour and smoke.

M. Zollinger, 'Eruptions of Mount Semiru', *Journal of the Indian Archipelago*, Vol. 4, 1850, pp. 204–5.

19
Lombok Volcano

W. COOL

Wallace noted the volcanic peaks of Bali and Lombok as he sailed by, but did not attempt the climb. An early report was provided by Captain W. Cool of the Dutch Engineers (later to become Professor at the High School of War, The Hague), who observed the crater lake on Lombok in 1894.

T HE following day after climbing first one height and then another, we finally arrived at the top, towards three o'clock in the afternoon and then I discovered that this was not the real summit of the Peak at all, but a much more southern point.

Notwithstanding that this mountain top was enveloped by thick clouds, the sight I beheld was of the most imposing nature. The crest of the Peak is a vast lake, several pals long and wide; the different mountain tops within sight rise perpendicularly to from 2000 to 4000 feet above the ground which is covered by a small lake, lying about 2000 feet beneath me. The East border of the lake is skirted by a level tract, in the middle of which rises a cone-shaped carboniferous hill (rock) about 500 feet high, pouring forth smoke from every crevice and the ground is strewn with brimstone and other volcanic matter. The point which I had climbed was not the Rindjani but the G. Sankarean.

To proceed was out of the question; the descent from the point was almost vertical and I was separated from the nearest of the neighbouring summits by a ravine about 1500 feet deep. A furious East wind was chasing the clouds round the heights and creating such intense cold that the coolies were quite speechless and many of them had fever. They implored of me not to spend the night here and I myself felt but little inclination to unnecessarily prolong my stay in this inhospitable site.

Capt. W. Cool, *With the Dutch in the East*, Luzac and Co., London, 1897, p. 150.

20
The Lake of Taal

JOSEPH EARLE STEVENS

Lake Taal, Luzon, Philippines, is a huge flooded caldera marking the site of enormous past eruptions. The many visitors are reminded of the lake's origins by the growing active cone that rears from its exquisitely blue waters.

The prospect today can be compared with the scene viewed in the 1890s by J. E. Stevens, who was then the Manila representative of Henry W. Peabody & Co. of Boston and New York, in the interest of their hemp business.

OUR good friend at Taal went so far as to harness up a pair of ponies and drive us down to the river at four o'clock in the morning, and we found a large *banca*, previously ordered, waiting to take us up to the Lake of Taal and across to the volcano.

Our *banca* was of good size, was rowed by seven men and steered by one, and had a little thatched hen-coop arrangement over the stern, to keep the sun off our heads. We had brought one 'boy' with us from Manila, with enough 'chow' to last for two days, and soon all was stowed away in our floating tree-trunk. The river was shallow, and for most of the six miles of its length poles were the motive-power. It was slow work, and both wind and current were hostile. In due course, however, the lake came into view, and in its centre rose the volcano, smoking away like a true Filipino. The wind was now blowing strong and unfavorable, and we saw that it was not going to be an easy row across the six or seven miles of open water to the centre island. But the men worked with a will, and although the choppy waves slopped over into our roost once or twice so jocosely that it almost seemed as if we should have to turn back, we kept on. Benefitting by a lull or two, our progress was gradual, and at half after twelve, seven hours from Taal, we landed on the volcanic island and prepared for an ascent.

The lake of Taal is from fifteen to twenty miles across, is surrounded by high hills and mountains, for the most part, and has for its centre the volcanic island upon whose edges rise the sloping sides of an active cone a thousand feet high. The lake is certainly good to look at, reminding one forcibly of Loch Lomond, and the waters, shores, and mountains around all seem to bend their admiring gaze on the little volcano in its centre.

Filling our water-jug, we set off up the barren lava-slopes of this nature's safety-valve, sweltering under the stiff climb in the hot sun. Happily, the view bettered each moment, the smell of the sulphur became stronger, and we forgot present discomfort in anticipations of the revelation to come. After banging our shins on the particularly rough lava-beds of the ascent, near the top, we saw a great steaming crater yawning below us and sending up clouds of sulphurous steam. In the centre of this vast, dreary Circus Maximus rose a flat cone of red-hot squashy material, and out of it ascended the steam and smoke. All colors of the rainbow played with each other in the sun, and farther to the right was a boiling lake of fiery material that was variegated enough to suit an Italian organ-grinder.

It was all very weird, and if we had not been so lazy we should probably have descended farther into this laboratory of fire than we did. But is was too hot to make matches of ourselves and the air smelt like the river Styx at low tide. So we were contented with a good view of the wonders of the volcano from a distance, enjoyed the panorama from the narrow encircling apex-ridge, and cooled off in the smart breeze. Once more at the lake, and it was not long before we were in it, tickling our feet on the rough cinders of the bottom. The bath was most rejuvenating after a hot midday climb, and just to sit in the warmish water up to one's neck gave one a sort of mellow feeling like that presumably possessed by a ripe apple ready to fall on the grass.

J. E. Stevens, *Yesterdays in the Philippines*, Charles Scribners' Sons, New York, 1898, pp. 104–6.

21
Krakatoa

STANLEY COXON

The eruption of Krakatau was a stupendous event. The sounds were heard thousands of miles distant and the tremors felt even further. The tidal wave created had devastating effects on coastal settlements and there was huge loss of life. Following the initial cataclysmic explosion, continued activity at Krakatau has reconstructed new islands, which have been and are still progressively being recolonized by plants and animals.

One of the last to see Krakatau before it erupted was the mariner, Stanley Coxon, at that time serving as navigator on a coastal steamer around the Indonesian islands. His vivid first-hand account is a reminder of the gigantic forces unleashed.

B EFORE the Sumatra coast, we knew that next morning we should require to see the island of Krakatoa before shaping our course to enter the Straits. Krakatoa was in those days a large uninhabited mass of rock standing right in the middle of the entrance. Ever since we made Flat Cape, which is the southernmost point of Sumatra, we had experienced heavy torrential rain, and at 9 o'clock the captain sent for me and asked me to work out, as far as possible, the position of the ship. Knowing the danger of the situation, I was very particular as to the result, and, before taking it to the captain, got the first and third officers to make independent calculations. Taking the average of the three—and they were all within a mile or two of each other—I handed to my skipper the position of the ship at 9 a.m. as correctly as it was possible to ascertain it. But I am glad to be able to say that as a precautionary measure I wrote on my position slip that *no allowance had been made for any current one way or the other.* This made the ship to be at 9 o'clock that morning a clear twenty-six miles from the island of Krakatoa.

The captain, myself as navigator, and the third officer were all on the bridge. It was still raining heavily and nothing could be seen a hundred yards ahead of the ship. It was as if we were in a dense fog. At a quarter to ten, the captain, turning to me, said: 'I shan't risk it any longer; turn the ship round sixteen points.' 'Aye, aye, sir! Port the helm! Half speed. Steady. Stop her.' The ship was now facing exactly in the opposite direction, and the engines were only kept moving sufficiently to keep her head straight. About twenty minutes later the rain ceased, and on looking astern I saw what appeared to be a sheer precipice of rock directly over our flagstaff. 'Full speed ahead!' I yelled. Out came the sun, and the rock was the island of Krakatoa! We had on board at the time, all told, about 550 to 600 souls, and had the ship continued for another quarter of an hour on the course we were then steering, there would have been an accident almost as appalling as the loss of the *Titanic*.

It was fated to be the very last look we ever had of that island, for on the return journey it had practically disappeared off the face of the sea. We reached Batavia homeward bound just after the terrible eruption of Krakatoa—which it will be remembered occurred on the 26th August 1883—and were detained there pending the report of a Dutch man-of-war which had been sent to ascertain the extent of the disaster. As a matter of fact our ship was the first passenger ship allowed through, and we were warned that it would be necessary to exercise extreme caution. As navigating officer at the time, my place was on the bridge, and I would not have had it elsewhere for a great deal. More than two-thirds of the island had completely disappeared. Numerous other small islands and rocks had sprung up like mushrooms in the course of a night, and the channel through which we had passed on the outward journey was now completely blocked. Some idea of the appalling suddenness and magnitude of the disaster may be gathered from the fact that the air-waves of the great explosion are recorded as having been heard as far away as Diego Garcia and Rodriguez, which are respectively 2375 and 3080 English miles distant from the volcano. The eruption occurred at about 10 o'clock in the morning and by

11.20 there was complete darkness, which extended into the country for a distance of 150 miles. The damage to life and property throughout the Straits of Sunda was enormous, and the entire township of Anjer which existed on the southern or Java side of the Strait was washed off the face of the earth by the huge tidal waves which followed the eruption. By the inrush of these waves on to the land all vessels lying near the shore were stranded, and the various towns and villages devastated. Two of the lighthouses were also swept away, and the lives of 37,000 of the inhabitants, amongst whom were 37 Europeans, sacrificed. The height of the highest sea-wave which overswept Anjer is stated to have measured over 33 feet. Dead-slow was the order of the day, and groping our way through a sea of lava and pumice-stone, in which the wrecks of houses and other débris, floating corpses of men, women, children, and animals by the thousand, made our passage through the Straits on that occasion one of absorbing interest. I was on the bridge the entire time, and, from the numerous angles and cross-bearings we were able to take, compiled a chart of the New Channel, which together with my report appeared in one of the illustrated papers of the day. But for some reason or other it appeared under a name other than that of the author! Such is fame!

Stanley Coxon, *And That Reminds Me: Being Incidents of a Life Spent at Sea and in the Andaman Islands, Burma, Australia and India*, John Lane, London, 1914, pp. 26–8.

22
Submarine Volcano

HENRI MOUHOT

A submarine volcano, perhaps an incipient island, was witnessed
with wonder by Henri Mouhot in the Gulf of Siam, in 1859.

Born in France, at the age of thirty-two (apparently inspired by
Sir John Bowring's book, *The Kingdom and People of Siam*) Henri
Mouhot sailed for Bangkok in 1858. Over the next three years, his
journeys took him by boat along the eastern shore of the Gulf of
Siam, inland through Cambodia (including a visit to Angkor Wat),
and through eastern Thailand to Korat and Chaiyapoom and
ultimately to Luang Prabang, Laos, where he died in November
1861. His adventures are known through the posthumous publications of his notes and diary.

O N the morning of the 29th, at sunrise, the breeze less-
ened, and when we were about three miles from the
strait which separates the isle of Arec from that of the 'Cerfs',
it ceased altogether. For the last half-hour we were
indebted solely to our oars for the little progress made,
being exposed to all the glare of a burning sun; and the
atmosphere was heavy and suffocating. All of a sudden, to
my great astonishment, the water began to be agitated,
and our light boat was tossed about by the waves. I knew
not what to think, and was seriously alarmed, when our
pilot called out, 'Look how the sea boils!' Turning in the
direction indicated, I beheld the sea really in a state of
ebullition, and very shortly afterwards an immense jet of
water and steam, which lasted for several minutes, was
thrown into the air. I had never before witnessed such a
phenomenon, and was now no longer astonished at the
powerful smell of sulphur which had nearly overpowered
me in Ko-Man. It was really a submarine volcano, which

45

burst out more than a mile from the place where we had anchored three days before.

Henri Mouhot, *Travels in the Central Parts of Indo-China (Siam), Cambodia, and Loas during the Years 1858, 1859, and 1860,* John Murray, London, 1864, p. 151.

23
Hot Springs and Mud Volcanoes

ALFRED RUSSEL WALLACE

Finally, to close the litany of variation in volcanic activity, here is Wallace's account of two closely connected phenomena, hot springs and mud craters, which he saw near Menado, Celebes (Sulawesi).

THE next morning I went to see the hot-springs and mud volcanoes, for which this place is celebrated. A picturesque path among plantations and ravines, brought us to a beautiful circular basin about forty feet diameter, bordered by a calcareous ledge, so uniform and truly curved that it looked like a work of art. It was filled with clear water very near the boiling point, and emitting clouds of steam with a strong sulphureous odour. It overflows at one point and forms a little stream of hot water, which at a hundred yards' distance is still too hot to hold the hand in. A little further on, in a piece of rough wood, were two other springs not so regular in outline, but appearing to be much hotter, as they were in a continual state of active ebullition. At intervals of a few minutes a great escape of steam or gas took place, throwing up a column of water three or four feet high.

We then went to the mud-springs, which are about a mile off, and are still more curious. On a sloping tract of ground in a slight hollow is a small lake of liquid mud, in patches of blue, red, or white, and in many places boiling and bubbling most furiously. All around on the indurated clay, are small wells and craters full of boiling mud. These seem to be forming continually, a small hole appearing first, which emits jets of steam and boiling mud, which on hardening, forms a little cone with a crater in the middle. The ground for some distance is very unsafe, as it is evidently liquid at a small depth, and bends with pressure like thin ice. At one of the smaller marginal jets which I managed to approach, I held my hand to see if it was really as hot as it looked, when a little drop of mud that spurted on to my finger scalded like boiling water. A short distance off there was a flat bare surface of rock, as smooth and hot as an oven floor, which was evidently an old mud-pool dried up and hardened. For hundreds of yards round where there were banks of reddish and white clay used for whitewash, it was still so hot close to the surface that the hand could hardly bear to be held in cracks a few inches deep, and from which arose a strong sulphureous vapour. I was informed that some years back a French gentleman who visited these springs ventured too near the liquid mud, when the crust gave way and he was engulfed in the horrible caldron.

Alfred Russel Wallace, *The Malay Archipelago: The Land of the Orang-Utan, and the Bird of Paradise*, 10th edn., Macmillan and Co., London, 1883, pp. 258–9.

Wind and Weather

ॐ

24
Cochin-China: The Climate

DR GUTZLAFF

The awesome 'telluric' energy (to use Logan's term) that drives the drifting continents, builds the mountain ranges, and fires the volcanoes arises from the heat of decay of natural radioactive elements deep in the earth's core.

Most of the external energy impacting on the globe derives from the sun, in which nuclear fusion reactions raise stupendous surface temperatures (~ 6000 °C). Energy from the sun is distributed across space as short wave-length radiation, about half of which is within the visible range (i.e. perceived as light). Seasonal changes in climate arise because the globe is tilted (at 23° 30') to the perpendicular in its orbit round the sun. As a result, the latitude of the overhead sun (i.e. the zone of most intense insolation) progresses from the tropic of Cancer in June to the tropic of Capricorn in December, passing over the Equator twice each year at the equinoxes. Important effects in South-East Asia arise from the corresponding north–south progression of the zone of convergence of inflowing air, known as the Inter-tropical Front. In this zone, sailing ships encounter the doldrums, becalmed in still air or slight and uncertain breezes, helplessly drifting in the sea's currents.

Meteorology is a mass of statistics, inappropriate for this anthology. It is enough to remind ourselves that as latitude increases, on both sides of the Equator, seasonal changes are more pronounced. In our region, north of about latitude 10 °N the cycle is dominated by the monsoons. These are strong winds alternately drawn into central Asia by the heat of summer, or expelled from there by the prolonged, intense high pressure cell that develops in winter.

The vast weather system of the alternating monsoons affects local meteorology through much of South-East Asia in different ways. Thus, across central parts of the Indo-Chinese peninsula and into southern Philippines the south-westerlies carry summer rains whereas, on the eastern seaboard of the continental mainland and the islands, most rain falls with the north-easterlies in the other half of the year. North of about latitude 10 °N, other influences prevail. Here lies the typhoon belt where people, buildings, landscapes, and the entire natural world are at risk from the inexorable violence of these terrifying and destructive storms.

The scene is set by scholarly comment by Dr Gutzlaff, from whom the Royal Geographical Society received three detailed memoirs on the geography of China and the Indo-Chinese region in 1848–9.

K AMBODIA enjoys a delightful temperature, although the weather throughout the rainy season (May–September) is often very sultry: the dry monsoon during the remaining part of the year is clear and the heat very moderate, seldom exceeding 90°, and ordinarily being only about 80°. Cochin-China presents the very reverse of the seasons to Tunkin and Kambodia, on account of the ridge of mountains which breaks the clouds. From October up to January the weather is very boisterous, and typhoons are by no means uncommon—where in the former the wet season reigns, the latter is dry, and *vice versa*. The thermometer never rises there above 103°, nor sinks below 53°, and the climate throughout is healthy and agreeable. Tunkin in this respect resembles Bengal, but participates likewise in the oppressive heat and very disagreeable cold of China. Those who have never witnessed the *typhoons*, which sweep this country from one extremity to the other, will look upon a faithful description of this fearful visitation as overdrawn. Though earthquakes and the eruption of volcanoes may be far more terrific, still if one wishes to form an idea of the last moment when heaven and earth shall pass away, he may take the initiation of a *typhoon*. It is as if everything were devoted to destruction, and the world were again to return to a chaos. No words can convey an idea of such an awful moment, and the violence of the tempest in which man is scarcely an atom. Such is the scourge with which Tunkin is frequently visited, and in which northern Cochin-China occasionally participates.

Dr Gutzlaff, 'Geography of the Cochin-Chinese Empire', *Journal of the Royal Geographical Society*, Vol. 19, 1849, p. 101.

25
Climate of the Philippines

JOHN CRAWFURD

Typhoons are marked by dramatic falls in barometric pressure. Some 150 kilometres ahead of the advancing centre of this deep depression, dark nimbus clouds develop and torrential rain falls, accompanied by driving winds of enormous force that can attain speeds above 200 kilometres per hour. Each typhoon has a quiet 'eye', several kilometres in diameter, where the sky is relatively clear, winds are light or squally, and little or no rain falls. But behind this quiet centre, rain and howling winds resume with devastating violence, finally losing intensity as the storm passes.

The archipelago of those beautiful islands that form the Philippines lies athwart a zone subjected both to the seasonal cycles of the monsoons and to the intermittent rampages of typhoons. The consequences, in climatic terms, were succinctly summarized by John Crawfurd.

Born in Scotland in 1783, Crawfurd was a medical doctor employed in various capacities by the English East India Company. His service in South-East Asia began in Penang and continued in Java during the British occupation. In 1821, he was appointed leader of a mission to the Courts of Siam (Thailand) and Cochin-China (Vietnam). His *History of the Indian Archipelago*, from which this quotation is taken, was first published in 1820.

T HE climate of the Philippines varies with latitudes which range from 5° to near 20° from the equator. At Manilla, in latitude 14° 36', the difference between the longest summer and the shortest winter day is but one hour, 47 minutes, and 12 seconds. The monsoons are, the north-east and south-west, the first, as in all countries lying on the China Sea being the most violent, contrary to what is the case west of it. In the southern and western portions of the Archipelago the rainy season corresponds with the summer and autumn, but the case is reversed in the northern and eastern parts, occasioned by the ranges of mountains which run north and south, in the same manner as is the case on the eastern and western sides of Southern India. At the changes

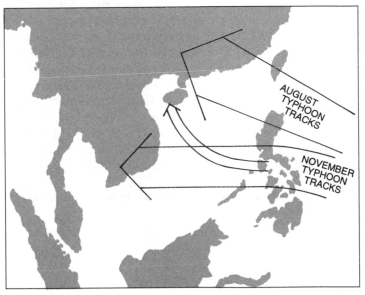

Typhoons of the South China Sea normally originate east of the Philippines. They occur at all times of the year, but are most frequent in July–November. During this period, the usual track trends progressively southwards. From E. H. G. Dobby, *Southeast Asia*, 11th edn., University of London Press, 1973.

from one monsoon to another take place those terrible hurricanes so well known to mariners as typhoons. These are most severe at the autumnal equinox, and the month of October is the most remarkable for them. From these scourges all parts of the Archipelago within ten degrees of the equator are exempt, which include the island of Mindano and the long chain of islands extending between it and Borneo. The rainy season commences in May, and lasts to September inclusive. At Manilla, which is not far from the centre of the Archipelago, reckoning from north to south, the lowest annual fall of rain is 84 inches, and the highest 114, giving an average of 98. A vast quantity of rain falls within a comparatively short space of time, and the consequence is that much of the low country is submerged,—the rivers overflow their banks and periodical lakes of many leagues in extent are formed. At Manilla Fahrenheit's thermometer never falls below 72°, nor rises above 95°, so that the range is but 23°. In the mountain valley of Banhao, 6400 feet above the level of the sea, and but 12 leagues from the city, the thermometer stands at from 45° to 47°. The greatest heats are experienced from April to August in the fair season, but Spanish writers declare that those of Manilla never equal those of Madrid in severity, although they last longer. A fall of hail is recorded to have taken place in the Philippines twice only since the Spanish occupation—once in May, 1749, and once February, 1803.

John Crawfurd, *A Descriptive Dictionary of the Indian Islands and Adjacent Countries*, London, 1856, p. 339.

26

Typhoon

JOSEPH EARLE STEVENS

The untamed power of typhoon winds can be felt ten or more times a year. The damage to trees and man-made structures can be extreme. Modern science has improved our ability to track typhoons, but not to avert them. The September typhoon in the Philippines, described below by an author we have already met, had many predecessors and many successors.

E ARLY in this eventful week, warnings came from our most excellent observatory, run by the Jesuit priests, that trouble was brewing down in the Pacific to the south and east, and by Friday signal No. 1 of the danger system was displayed on the flagstaff of the look-out tower. The news about the storm was indefinite, but the villain was supposed to be slowly moving northwest, headed directly for Manila. Saturday up went signal No. 2, and in the afternoon No. 3, and by evening No. 4. Still everything was calm and peaceful, and Sunday morning dawned pleasant but for the exception of a dull haze. Early in the afternoon up went signal No. 5, which means that things are getting pretty bad, and which is not far from No. 8, the worst that can be hoisted.

Everybody now began to get ready for the invisible monster. All the steamers and ships in the river put out extra cables, and the vessels in the Bay extra anchors. No small craft of any kind were permitted to pass out by the breakwater, and later navigation in the river itself was prohibited. Still everything was calm and quiet, but the haze thickened and low scud-clouds began to sail in from the China Sea. Shortly after tiffin at our residence by the seaside, our gaze was attracted by a native coming down the street, dressed in a black coat with shirt-tails hanging out beneath, and wearing white trousers and a tall hat. He carried a decorated cane, wore no shoes, and marched down the centre of the street, giving utterance to solemn sentences in a deep musical voice. In short, he was the official crier to herald the coming of the typhoon, and as he marched along the bells up in the old church beyond our house rang out what poets would call 'a wild, warning plea'.

The natives opposite began hastily to sling ropes over the thatch of their light shanties, and one of the Englishmen who lived not far back of us had already stretched good solid cables over the steep-sloping roof of his domicile. A sort of hush prevailed, and then sudden gusts began to blow in off the bay. The scud-clouds increased and appeared to be in a fearful hurry. The roar of the surf loudened, and one after the other of our sliding sea-shell windows had to be shut and bolstered up for precaution. The typhoon seemed to be advancing slowly, as they often do, but its course was sure. Our eight o'clock dinner-hour passed and the wind began to howl. Before turning in for the night, we moved out of our little parlor such valuable articles as might be most missed if they decided to journey off through the air in company with the roof, and later tried to sleep amidst a terrific din of rattlings. But slumber was impossible. Our house trembled like a blushing bride before the altar, and for the triumphal music of the 'Wedding March' the tin was suddenly stripped off our rain-shed roof like so much paper. And then the racket! Great pieces of tin were slapping around against the house like all possessed; the trees in the front garden were sawing against the cornices, as if they wanted to get in, and the rush of air outside seemed to generate a vacuum within.

At 3 a.m. things got so bad that it seemed as if something were going to burst, and my chum and I decided to take a last look into the parlor before seeking the safety of the cellar. No glass would have withstood the gusts that came pouncing in from the Bay, but our sea-shell windows did not seem to yield. The rain was sizzling in through the cracks like hot grease when a fresh doughnut is dropped into the spider, and the noise outside was deafening. As our house seemed to be holding together, however, we gave up going to the regions below, and turned in again, thankful that we were not off on the ships in the Bay. Now and then the wind lulled somewhat, and blew from another quarter, but by early morning came some of the most terrific blowings I have ever felt, resulting from the change of direction. Down came all the wires in the main street; over went half a dozen *nipa* houses to one side of us, and 'kerplunk' broke off some venerable trees that for many years had withstood the blast. The street was a mass of wreckage, as far down as the eye could see, and few signs of life were visible. During the rest of the day the wind blew most fiercely, but from the change of direction it was easy to see that the centre of the typhoon was passing off to the northwest.

I sallied out later in the afternoon, dressed in not much more than a squash-hat, a rubber coat, and a pair of boots, whose soles were holy enough to let the water out as fast as it came in. It was as much as one could do to stand against the blast, but I managed to keep along behind the houses, cross the streets, and reach the Luneta, where all the lamps bent their heads with broken glass, and where the huge waves were flying far up into the air in their efforts to dispose of the stone sea-wall. The clumps of fishing and bath houses which stood perched on posts out in the surf were being fast battered to pieces, and those which were not minus roof and sides were washed up into the road as driftwood. The natives were rushing gingerly hither and thither, grabbing such logs as they could find, while some of the fishermen's families were crouching behind a stone wall watching their wrecked barns, and sitting on their saucepans, furniture, and babies, to keep them from sailing skyward. The surf was tremendous, the vessels in the bay were shrouded in spray, and several of them seemed almost to be ashore in the breakers. A steamer appeared to have broken adrift and was locked in the embrace of a Nova Scotia bark. But everything comes to an end and as night drew on the winds and rain subsided and comparative quiet succeeded a season of exaggerated movement and din.

J. E. Stevens, *Yesterdays in the Philippines*, Charles Scribners' Sons, New York, 1898, pp. 128–34.

27
Seasonal Rainfall

E. BANKS

Close to the equator, at low latitudes north and south, lies a unique climatic zone where day-length varies by no more than a few minutes through the year and ambient temperatures, although warm, are uniformly equable and show no seasonal variation. At these equatorial latitudes, rainfall is generally local, irregular, and unpredictable. Total annual rainfall at any location is typically high (often exceeding 2000 mm), as is the number of rainy days (often more than 200 in the year). The wettest weather generally follows the passage of the inter-tropical front. When long-term records are analysed, monthly totals at most stations therefore show two broad annual peaks. Available weather data from stations in this zone up to 1933 were plotted and analysed by E. 'Bill' Banks.

Banks was appointed Curator of the Sarawak Museum in January 1925, and remained in this post until 1947, often acting for other State departments when their directors were absent. He suffered internment during the war, and subsequently retired to Minehead, Somerset, England. In the 1930s, he wrote prolifically on wildlife and the natural world for the *Sarawak Museum Journal*. Somewhat later, he privately published three books based on his experiences in Sarawak. In this short excerpt, he used the term 'Malaysia' to refer to the region now comprising Indonesia, with Brunei and Malaysia.

T HIS tropical rainbelt, extending a few degrees North and South of the Equator is naturally a region of calms, thunderstorms and rather heavy rainfall but is affected by the monsoons as well. Mountains sometimes place a station

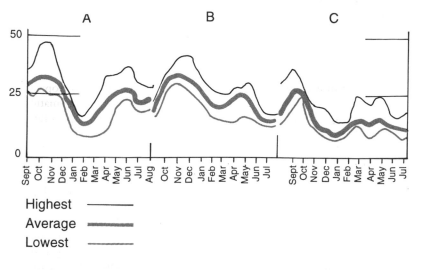

Plots of monthly rainfall records obtained at different periods between 1879 and 1933 at stations at (A) Miri, Sarawak, Labuan Island, and west coast of Sabah, (B) in Kalimantan Barat, Indonesia, and (C) in Perak, Penang, and Kedah, Malaysia, showing average values and extremes. After E. Banks, 'Seasonal Rainfall in Borneo', *Sarawak Museum Journal*, Vol. 4, 1935.

alternately to windward and leeward as the monsoon turns but the conditions are usually fairly local.

The Northern and Western portion of Malaysia come under the influence of the Asiatic monsoon type, a wet North-East monsoon from October to about the end of the year and a mild South-West monsoon from May to August. Southern and Eastern Malaysia fall under the Australian monsoon type, a dry East and a very wet West monsoon, with small rain about July to September. Apart from a few intermediate monsoon type stations all have seasons of calms and thunderstorms, with little air movement, in the periods between the monsoons.

E. Banks, 'Seasonal Rainfall in Borneo', *Sarawak Museum Journal*, Vol. 4, 1935, p. 363.

28

Storm

CHARLES HOSE

An enormous quantity of water vapour is carried in warm tropical air masses. Localized convectional rainstorms can be dramatic. Towering, anvil-topped cumulonimbus clouds develop, often 10 kilometres tall. Condensation in the cloud produces heavy rain which creates strong down-draughts as it falls. Opposing air movements in the clouds generate electrical charges, with repeated lightning flashes and resounding rolls of thunder. At ground level, these storms are typically heralded by violent, gusting winds; but, unlike the typhoon, the heaviest rain falls at the still centre.

Such a storm was experienced on the flank of Mt Dulit, Sarawak, in 1891 by Charles Hose. Born in England in 1863, Hose entered the administrative service of Sir Charles Brooke, second Rajah of Sarawak at the age of twenty. In 1888 he was appointed to the Baram district, in 1904 transferred to Sibu, and in 1907 took early retirement. He was an avid collector of animal specimens during his time in Sarawak and, after his retirement, published a series of books on the people and natural history of the State. He died in 1929.

T HE following morning we moved our camp higher up— to an altitude of 4000 feet, about that of the top of Ben Nevis—and while one party was doing so, the other brought down to the Store the specimens which we had collected. On the night of October 8, a terrible storm suddenly burst over the mountain. Gigantic trees and rocks, carrying all before them, came rolling down the sides. The roaring of the wind and the crash of falling timber and huge rocks with torrents of rain, such as the tropics alone can show, created a scene of wild portentous tumult that filled the mind with wonder and awe at the overwhelming power and grandeur of the forces of Nature. In the ghostly seclusion of this wooded mountain-side, perhaps never before trodden by the foot of man, we seemed to be in a world apart amid the spirits of the storm, while the voice of the tempest spoke to us in the language of overpowering might and sublimity....

We had fortunately taken the precaution to fell the trees near our encampment so that we escaped injury from the boulders and the uprooted trees that bore them along. When dawn came the storm had spent itself, but the mountain rivulet had become a small river with waterfalls of fifty to seventy feet in height. The noise of one of these new-born cascades near our hut made it impossible for us to make ourselves heard except by shouting. This streamlet the day before was so small that we had made spouts of bamboo to lead a few drops of water into a jar that we might procure enough to drink, while now the spray from the fall reached the hut, a distance of about twenty feet. Such are the latent forces that may break loose on the forest-clad slopes approaching the summit of Mt Dulit.

Charles Hose, *Fifty Years of Romance and Research or A Jungle-Wallah at Large*, Hutchinson and Co., London, 1927, pp. 166–7.

The Sea

❧

29
Typhoon in the South China Sea

EDWARD H. CREE

At sea, typhoons are as hazardous as on land. In his diary, Surgeon Edward Cree, RN, showed true Naval reticence but still could not disguise the risks.

Born in 1814, Edward Cree joined the Royal Navy in 1837 after studying medicine at Dublin and Edinburgh. From then, until the end of his last sea-going appointment in 1861, he kept a journal which ultimately amounted to twenty-one bound volumes, supplemented by some 1,700 water-colours and sketches. Cree spent a decade (1840–50) in eastern stations, and his combined record of words and pictures provides a fascinating contemporary observation of events in South-East Asia. In this abstract, he was sailing on HMS *Vixen* northwards past the scattered islets of the Paracels in the South China Sea in October 1844.

*T*UE. *1ST* Very hot weather—therm. 90°—no wind.

Fri. 4th Came on to blow from NE with a long heavy swell. Squally, with thunder and lightning. Sky very black and threatening. Making all secure for a typhoon.

Sat. 5th Wind and sea increasing and going round NW and W. 8 p.m. blowing a hurricane, a regular typhoon. Tremendous sea struck us on the quarter and stove in the deck lights, smashed the Captain's gig and the bulwarks, also the bulwarks forward, and part of the paddle-box. We shipped some heavy seas, and it was pitch-dark—deck leaking like a sieve, cabins swamped and altogether a miserable night. To add to the horrors we were somewhere near the Paracels shoals, but no observations having been made for a few days, all was uncertainty. If we had touched, no one would have lived to tell the tale. I tried to get a little sleep by spreading a mat under the table and getting an arm round one of the legs, but the rolling and pitching of the ship rendered rest impossible. Our three dogs huddled up to me for companionship, but we were all rolling about the deck with chairs and everything not made fast. The poor dogs were much distressed.

Sun. 6th The typhoon moderated somewhat, but no breakfast to be had except some cold meat and a bottle of beer. Cook's galley, as well as the cooks, nearly washed away and the crockery smashed, but the weather is clearing, wind veering to SW to S. and to SE. There was a magnificent sea, tumbling about from two or three different quarters. At sunset the waves looked like mountains tipped with gold as the slanting sunbeams came horizontally from under the heavy purple clouds, but the wind was falling and we were able to rattle along again towards the coast of China.

M. Levien (ed.), *The Cree Journals: The Voyages of Edward H. Cree, Surgeon R.N.*, Webb and Bower, Exeter, 1981, pp. 132–3.

30
Typhoon in the Visayas

MARY H. FEE

Captain B———, the pearl fisher, was unlucky in his encounter with the elemental ferocity of a typhoon at sea.

The story was told by Mary Fee, a teacher with the United States ATS, who was drafted to the Philippines at the time of the American intervention. Her journey started from San Francisco in the US Army Transport ship *Buford* and took thirty-eight days to reach Manila, via Honolulu and Guam. She was posted to Capiz,

Panay, where she had been living for six years at the time she wrote.

T HE storm had an aftermath in the rescue of an Englishman, Captain B——, a pearl fisher. He was anchored under the lee of a small island in the sea between Panay and Masbate. He was in a small lorcha, or sailing vessel, with no barometer, his glass having been left on a lorcha of larger tonnage, which was at another point. The heavy wind caught them without warning almost, and its impact soon pressed the lorcha over. Captain B—— found himself struggling in the water—able to swim, but drowning, as he expressed it, with the spindrift which was hurtling into his face. He kept one arm going, and partially protected his face with the other. Then in the inky dark he touched a human body. It was the leg of one of his crew, four of whom were clinging to one of the lorcha's boat's. It kept turning over and over, and they had to go with it each time. Captain B—— hung to the prow, so his circuit was not so wide as that of the others, but his body—arms, legs, and chest—was literally ploughed by the rough usage. Once he let go and lost the prow as it came up, and the fright of this was enough to strengthen his hold. They were in the water clinging to this all the rest of the night, the next day, and the next night. One man died of exhaustion, and one went mad and let go. On the second morning they succeeded in bailing it out by means of an undershirt, which Captain B—— had been wearing, and which, though torn to ribbons across the front, was whole in the back. They remained in the boat all day, beaten on by the tropical sun, having been thirty hours in the water without food or drink. Captain B—— said they were all a little mad. They saw the *Sam Shui*—the boat of the commanding officer of the Visayas—in the distance, but were too low to be sighted by her. They wore their finger ends down, tearing a plank off the side to use for an oar. Meanwhile the current carried them down closer to the Panay coast, and on the third day they were close enough to fall in with one of the big fishing *paraos*. This carried them into Panay, a town five or six miles east of Capiz. Captain B—— had just strength to write a line or two and sign his name. This was brought down to Capiz, and the constabulary officer on duty there went out immediately with a launch and brought him in. He was in the military hospital a long time. His attending physician said that between salt water and sun he had been literally flayed, and the flesh torn into ribbons and gouged by the impact of the boat.

The storm did frightful havoc all through the Visayas, and many lives were lost and vessels wrecked. The *Blanco* as usual made harbor all right, but another little Capiz boat, the *Josefina,* went ashore, and her captain and several others were lost. The adventurous *One Lung* was at Iloilo, and it was reported that she started out of the river without consulting her pilot, creating thereby general consternation among her sister craft.

M. H. Fee, *A Woman's Impressions of the Philippines*, A. C. McClurg and Co., Chicago, 1910, pp. 176–7.

31
The Straits of Bali

DANIEL BEECKMAN

The sea approaches in the South-East Asian archipelago confronted early European venturers with mysterious hazards. Although time was needed to comprehend the local vagaries of wind and tide, by trial and error a patient navigator such as Captain Daniel Beeckman could turn their properties to his ship's benefit.

Beeckman's voyage from London to Borneo and back, commanding the New East India Company's vessel *Eagle Galley*, took place during 1713–15. As was customary in that age, the route started westward across the Atlantic to the West Indies, thence south to latitude 20 °S where favourable winds were found to take the ship via the Cape of Good Hope, across the southern Indian Ocean to Java, gateway to the South-East Asian archipelago. In this excerpt, Beeckman described how he learnt to circumvent the peculiar local winds to gain a passage through the dangerous currents of the Straits of Bali.

T HAT Night we had a violent Tornado, that forc'd us to Sea, with the Loss of a new Anchor and Cable, and drove us over to the aforesaid Bay on the Island of *Madura*. From our first sailing from the said Bay, to get through the Streights of *Bally*, we were fifteen Days, though it be not above thirty Leagues, and in the westerly Monsoon; at which time a Person, who is a Stranger to the Coast, wou'd think it not above 24 Hours Work. At last we fell into the following Knowledge and Method, otherwise we cou'd not well have got through at all; for once in 24 Hours you have a southerly Wind from the Sea, blowing through the Streights, and is right against you, coming on like a Tornado, and blowing with such Force (being always attended with violent Rain) that at first coming on you'll be oblig'd to hand all your Sails, 'till the Strength of it be over. The Reason I take to be (for on the other side of the Streights, in the Road of *Palamboan*, or *Ballamboang*, you shall only see it, and never feel it) because the Streights, not being wider than the River *Thames*; and having steep Mountains on each side, whose Tops generally overlook the Clouds, the Wind coming out of the wide Sea, though in a gentle manner, gathers, hangs to, and is encreas'd by those Clouds; so that it is obstructed and contracted by the narrowness of the Passage, 'till it forces its way through at once, in a manner like Wind forc'd through a Tube, or through the Nozzel of a Pair of Bellows, but seldom lasts above an Hour or two; though not a quarter of an Hour in its greatest Violence.

You always have timely notice before it comes, so that when you wou'd pass to the Southward, it is adviseable to keep the Coast of *Java* on board, steering along Shore within a Mile or two with the northerly Sea-breeze, which lasts 'till

The north entrance to the Straits of Bali, from a sketch made in January 1714 for Captain Beeckman.

The North Entrance of the Streighll of BALLY

A. Cape Zandareen S.³⁄₄E.
and the Entrance
AB The N.E part of Java
DC The NW part of Bally
R. Several Rocks & Shoals

the other comes from the Southward, 'till you run four or five Leagues to the Southward of the N.E. end of *Java*. Then you will open a black Sandy Bay, which reaches to *Poolo Gilleboang*; and when you see the Tornado beating up in the Streights a-head of you, which may be discern'd for about an Hour before it reaches you, then get near enough into that Bay to anchor; for it will suddenly fall calm, and the Current will horse you out again: However, the Current runs not always to the Southward, but you will find many Eddies; so you must Night and Day attend the northerly Breezes, and anchor in that Bay, before the other comes on; otherwise you'll lose by the latter more than you gain by the former, and never get through. *Note*, That there is no safe anchoring before you reach that Bay.

On the 15th of *January* we were in the Streights; and it was but a very dismal Prospect to see those vast Mountains on each side, which by the narrowness of the Passage seem ready to fall upon your Head; and the Noise which the Sea makes in the Hollows of the Rocks is most frightful. Sometimes you have Gusts of Wind from the Hills flying round the Compass in three Minutes time, and then as suddenly it becomes calm; so that I would advise you to keep a Boat a-head, to prevent your being swung round by the circling Eddies, occasion'd by the Rapidity of the Current to the Southward; by which means, when once you are entered the narrowest part, you are soon through, and the Danger is not by half so great as may be imagin'd.

Captain Daniel Beeckman, *A Voyage to and from the Island of Borneo in the East-Indies*, T. Warner and J. Batley, London, 1718, pp. 164–7.

32
Ampanam Bay

ALFRED RUSSEL WALLACE

In these seas, violent currents and dangerous surf can surge along-side inspirational views. Wallace experienced both when landing in June 1856 on Lombok, the island east of Bali in the Lesser Sunda chain, Indonesia.

L EAVING Bileling, a pleasant sail of two days brought us to Ampanam in the island of Lombock, where I proposed to remain till I could obtain a passage to Macassar. We enjoyed superb views of the twin volcanoes of Bali and Lombock, each about eight thousand feet high, which form magnificent objects at sunrise and sunset, when they rise out of the mists and clouds that surround their bases, glowing with the rich and changing tints of these the most charming moments in a tropical day.

The bay or roadstead of Ampanam is extensive, and being at this season sheltered from the prevalent south-easterly winds, was as smooth as a lake. The beach of black volcanic sand is very steep, and there is at all times a heavy surf upon it, which during spring-tides increases to such an extent that it is often impossible for boats to land, and many serious accidents have occurred. Where we lay anchored, about a quarter of a mile from the shore, not the slightest swell was perceptible, but on approaching nearer undulations began, which rapidly increased, so as to form rollers which toppled over on to the beach at regular intervals with a noise like thunder. Sometimes this surf increases suddenly during perfect calms, to as great a force and fury as when a gale of wind is blowing, beating to pieces all boats that may not have been hauled sufficiently high upon the beach, and carrying away incautious natives. This violent surf is probably in some way dependent on the swell of the great southern ocean, and the violent currents that flow through the Straits of Lombock.

These are so uncertain that vessels preparing to anchor in the bay are sometimes suddenly swept away into the straits, and are not able to get back again for a fortnight! What seamen call the 'ripples' are also very violent in the straits, the sea appearing to boil and foam and dance like the rapids below a cataract; vessels are swept about helpless, and small ones are occasionally swamped in the finest weather and under the brightest skies.

I felt considerably relieved when all my boxes and myself had passed in safety through the devouring surf, which the natives look upon with some pride, saying, that 'their sea is always hungry, and eats up everything it can catch'.

Alfred Russel Wallace, *The Malay Archipelago: The Land of the Orang-Utan, and the Bird of Paradise*, 10th edn., Macmillan and Co., London, 1883, pp. 152–3.

33
Sarawak Approaches

JAMES BROOKE

How cautiously, in 1842, did the newly appointed Rajah explore the coastal approaches to Sarawak, the State of which he was now ruler under Brunei suzerainty. Once ashore, 'no place could surpass it'! Captain R. Mundy, RN, retold the tale by abstracting Brooke's journal in his *Narrative of Events in Borneo and Celebes*.

Born in 1803, James was the fifth child of Thomas Brooke, a judge of the High Court of Benares employed by the East India Company. At the age of twelve, James was sent to England to board at Norwich Grammar School, which he hated and from which he ran away. At sixteen, he was commissioned ensign in the 6th Madras Native Infantry, and returned to India. In 1825, seriously wounded in the war against Burma, he was taken back to England to recuperate. Still on the books of the East India Company, he tried to return in 1829, was shipwrecked, sailed again in 1830 but had by then overrun his leave, resigned, and returned once again to England. In 1835, on his father's death, he inherited a large fortune with which he bought an armed yacht of 142 tons, the *Royalist*. In this vessel, he sailed once again for the East in December 1838, reached Singapore in June, and on 11 August 1839, for the first time, came in sight of Santubong mountain, at the mouth of the Sarawak River. The rest is history.

*M*AY 1.—We dropped down the river last evening, and pulled in the morning to the Samarahan, but found no Dyaks, as reported. The entrance is incorrectly laid down by Mr Murray, by placing it as disemboguing to the northward, whereas it is to the westward, and some miles farther than he makes it. Hence, we retraced our course, and, passing Tanjong Po, coasted along the head-lands to Tullok Limow, where the Dyaks were encountered before. Here, however, we found no fresh traces. These head-lands are bold with rocks, and moderately elevated cliffs, and white sandy beaches, fringed with intervening trees. The crags have a weather-beaten aspect, the vegetation on them showing the effects of the high winds in the north-east monsoon.

To the westward of Tanjong Po, rocks lie off a mile and a half or more, but otherwise there is no visible danger. Tullok Limow is protected by an island, and an anchorage *might* be found for vessels in the north-east monsoon; but I had not time to examine. Between this island (which from seaward appears the westernmost head-land) and Tanjong Sipang, the land falls into a deep sandy bay, in which are the three rivers Sirai, Tabo, and Buntal, all of which are connected one with the other, and with the main stream of Sarawak. The river Sirai joining the Sarawak, too, reaches beyond Santong, the Buntal nearer the Batu Boyar entrance, and the connecting rivers branch into so many smaller streams, that they form, as I have before observed, a net-work of water wherein a boat may easily lose its way. No vessel should venture into this bay, as the sands extend a long way out to sea. The entrance of these rivers is very shallow, and at the Tabo and Buntal dries at half ebb, in consequence of which there is a remarkable irregularity of the tide. The first of the flood not finding its way in from the sea, the flood-tide of the Sarawak fills the river, which appears to run ebb until the sands at the mouth are covered, when the regular flood from the sea makes in. Thus half the flood was towards the sea, and half into the country: the same with the ebb tide, the first half of which runs out regularly; but when the sand dries, the last half appears to run flood, and escapes by the Sarawak mouth.

We brought up at sunset at the embouchure of the Buntal, and had a long walk with our guns over the sands. The scenery is striking, and the mountains of Santobong form a beautiful contrast with the sandy beach. No place could surpass it for the purposes of exercise and enjoyment. Fish is to be found in abundance, and deer and hogs are plentiful; the latter I might have shot, but could not come within reach of the former; those I saw were of a decided reddish colour. A huge lizard, or biawak, was likewise seen, but escaped: its length appeared full five feet. It is a land crocodile, but harmless. After dark we pulled away for Batu Boyar, and there passed the night, after a hard day's-work for the men.

Captain R. Mundy, RN, *Narrative of Events in Borneo and Celebes*, John Murray, London, 1848, Vol. 1, pp. 298–9.

34
Tide and Wind

TOM HARRISSON

In the 1950s, a century after the arrival of Rajah James Brooke, the tides and the breezes remained the most important elements controlling the pattern of existence of those Sarawak people who still drew their livelihood from sea and shore. The perfect integration of these natural cycles with human activities seemed marvellous to Tom Harrisson. Bako Bay is now included in one of Sarawak's treasury of National Parks. Its lively beauty has enthralled thousands of visitors. Tom Harrisson was commissioned by the UK Colonial Office to produce a report on the Malay people of Sarawak and, during my attachment to the museum (1956–8), I assisted in the field-work for this project.

I T is not the date nor the heat that determine the main doings of Malays outside the towns or government service. It is the cycle of the sun in the year and its seasons, of the moon in its monthly and daily cycle of tides and their breezes. These play an overwhelmingly important part in the day (and night) life of the coastal and riverine Malay. The stars are mere subsidiaries, since all navigation is by sight or experience. . . .

There are times (not clocked), of course, when you may find a whole village empty, its men out at work, in the middle of the night; all, naturally enough, asleep next noon. Such 'times' are decided, in these communities, by outside phenomena, and not by any contract, numbered code— sometimes not by any process consciously known and worked out at all.

In the sun cycle, the difference between the monsoon (*landas*) and the quieter summer (*tedoh*) dominates the long-term activities of Malays in the south-west. The monsoon falls varyingly, from the second half of October and goes on to mid-April, roughly. The 'summer' time of calm seas is the best. There are no other clear-cut seasonal differences; even these two are extremely variable, sometimes obscured.

The rainfall throughout the delta is over 150 inches a year, and you would need a rain gauge as a hat to distinguish in any precise way between the amount of rain that falls upon you, moving around from one month to another. The important consideration is not the rain (except in so far as this directly affects the important side-lines of rubber-tapping and rice) nor the temperature, humidity, visibility and other meteorological considerations. What matters here is wind and especially its effect on the surface disturbance of the waters.

Whatever the above-water surface-wind and below-water surface-movement, they can largely be offset by technical methods of boating, fishing or the fish themselves! But rough weather brings sea-fishing to a standstill and leaves, in a literal sense, everyone high, though not dry. And all wind (with tide) influences normal movement, in estuary river, to and fro.

*   *   *

A wonderful landfall on Borneo: one sails from Santubong round below the lovely moulded peaks of Tanjong Sipang, which according to some versions of the saga the Datu Merpati's son, Jepang, maybe knew and named—out at the eastern end of the range, the old 'island', and then one turns past the strange, jungle cliffs, suddenly into the wide-open box of Bako Bay. There, at the entrance to the bay, stretching from Tanjong Sipang away east to Tanjong Po, the South China Sea shelves suddenly from blue into shallow, silted-up water. Even in calm weather, as the tide turns, there are rollers, hurled gathering into the bay, running uninterrupted four or five miles along its wide quadrangle to break on the white beach sand, cockled mangrove mud and occasional sand patch of coconuts at the far end.

Tom Harrisson, *The Malays of South-West Sarawak before Malaysia*, Macmillan and Co., London, 1970, pp. 76–7 and 287.

Coasts and Islands

೧

35
Work of the Dragon

ANON.

From ancient times, as exploration extended the mariners' familiarity with these seas, few could fail to marvel at the natural wonders of the coasts and islands. The sea route from southern China leads first to the magical Bay of Along, on the approaches to Haiphong, Vietnam. Here, the scenic beauty and curiosity of the astonishing drowned karst landscape have been renowned for centuries. A popular French guidebook of the 1930s summarized past commentaries and abstracted a contemporary Gallic pen-portrait (in translation).

T HE bay has been classified by the native Sovereigns as among the natural marvels of the country of Annam, and all the travellers and tourists who have been here are at one in their enthusiastic descriptions of its magnificence....

'Imagine to yourself a mountain range suddenly engulphed by a cataclysm, with nothing emerging, above the now peaceful waters, but the highest summits torn by the thunderbolts, the gigantic peaks, sharp needles and topmost plateaux. It is in the midst of all these that you sail along between stupendous walls, here brightened and polished by time, there carved as by the chisel of some capricious sculptor. Here there are semi-circular vaults; there a pointed arch arises. A little farther on, there is a tunnel, the farther orifice of which is marked by a dazzling point of light. Then there are caves with menacing stalactites; of some, the floor is above water, with its covering of fine sand; under others of these vaults the sea intrudes its sheet of sleeping waters. Elsewhere, a lake lies in the depths of a crater; a tortuous passage leads to it, indiscernible when we have reached the middle of the circus. Under the burning rays of the tropical sun, the play of light and shade made on the surface of the water by this wilderness of rocks forms a changing spectacle that beggars description. At the setting of the sun, a perfect blaze lights up and invests this gigantic chaos at the moment of its apotheosis with a splendour as of fairyland. But the spectacle is even more impressive if you contemplate it in the moonlight, when the sea-birds, the only inhabitants of these rocks, are sleeping, and the great solemn silence reigns. Then you witness something phantomlike and utterly unreal; you glide between the most fantastically improbable pieces of architecture, castellated forts raised on dizzy peaks, such as Gustave Doré limned in his fantastic illustrations, giddy cathedrals, lofty obelisks, towers that lean over as it about to fall on you and crush you. These are sights such as can never be forgotten.

Guide Madrolle: Indo-China, Hachette, Paris, 1931, p. 168.

36
Baie d'Along

LORD MOYNE

The landscape of Along Bay has also been described by a prominent Anglo-Irish millionaire and politician, Walter Guinness, created the first Lord Moyne in 1932, and later assassinated in Cairo in 1944.

Lord Moyne toured the region on his yacht *Rosaura* in 1935–6, collecting ethnographic material for the British Museum and live animals for the London Zoo. Even the natural reticence of such a man succumbed to the inspirational beauty of the scene.

E ARLY next morning we took on a pilot at the entrance to the Baie d'Along. He told us that we had struck on the first clear day for six weeks. We were indeed lucky to see this wonderful scenery under perfect conditions, but in spite of the sunshine the weather was very cold. For about twenty miles from north to south and about thirty miles from east to west, countless islands of fantastic shape stud the deep blue water. Big ships go up to the town of Hongay on the north side of the Bay to load the coal which is there quarried from surface workings, but we preferred to anchor half-way up the Passe Henriette near the Ile de la Surprise. From there we threaded our way back by motor launch through islands great and small to the Ile de la Paix at the entrance to the Passe. The *trois cirques*, or lakes contained by this island, are the most unique feature of the Bay. At the foot of a sheer cliff of limestone an inconspicuous entrance admits to the first lake. It was impossible for a launch to pass under the low roof and we had to transfer to a sampan which was fishing near-by and even in this little boat we had, in places, to lie almost flat. After about fifty yards of tunnel we came out on a lake surrounded by steep walls of limestone, hundreds of feet high and in shape curiously like a volcanic crater. From this first lake passages admitted to two others, of which, owing to the state of the tide and the lowness of the roof, we were only able to visit one.

Lord Moyne, *Walkabout: A Journey in Lands between the Pacific and Indian Oceans*, William Heineman Ltd., London, 1936, pp. 215–16.

37
The Coast of Cochin-China

JOHN WHITE

South from Haiphong, the wonders and hazards of the sweeping coast of Vietnam and the wildlife treasures of its islands were described by John White, Lieutenant of the US Navy in command of the brig *Franklin*. The tragic conflict of our present century has marked this bountiful shore, but its natural resources hold the power of restoration.

Born in Massachusetts, USA, in 1782, White was commissioned to undertake a voyage through these seas in 1819–20, with the principal aim of establishing commercial contacts with Vietnam. He wrote his account of the voyage for deposit in the archives of the East India Marine Society of Salem, USA, but was persuaded by friends to publish the manuscript. He was promoted to Commander in 1837 and died in 1840.

T HE chain of mountains from Cape St. James to the gulf of Tonquin takes the direction of the coast, forming a natural barrier, or rampart, against the encroachments of the sea; receding from the shore a few leagues in several parts of the middle provinces, imparting to the features of the country, in those spaces, the most picturesque and fruitful appearances, and affording sites for several towns and villages; and the various small rivers and indentations on the coast afford a great number of secure, and several capacious harbours. In the interior, and forming the western frontier of the country, is a chain of mountains, clothed with large timber, and abounding with numerous wild beasts; the intermediate country is champaign, fruitful, and healthy, presenting some of the most beautiful scenery in nature. The coast is bold, abounding in great varieties of fish, and affords every facility to the navigator, having good anchorage in every part (though near Cape Avarella, the easternmost land of Cochin China, the soundings extend but a short distance from the shore); and there is no invisible danger on the coast, excepting

Holland's bank, which lies three or four leagues to the north-west of the island of Pulo Ciecer de Mer (between which two there is a safe channel), Britto's Bank, (situated near the main land, on the same parallel as Pulo Ciecer de Mer), and a shoal bank, situated between Pulo Ciecer de Terre and Cape Padaran, but the latter is not in the way of ships navigating along the coast.

On the 14th, at two o'clock a.m., we descried the island of Pulo Ciecer de Mer, and at daylight we had passed it. This island is of a moderate height, nearly two leagues in length from north-east to south-west, and has a hill at each extremity, which circumstance gives it the appearance of two islands when first discovered; but, on a nearer approach, the intermediate land is perceived. It is considered very valuable by the Cochin Chinese, being fruitful, and the cliffs and precipices affording large quantities of the edible birds' nests, and the surrounding sea producing *biches de mer* in abundance, and great varieties of fish.

John White, *A Voyage to Cochin China*, Longman, Hurst, Rees, Orme, Brown, and Green, London, 1824, pp. 72–3.

38
As Far as Champawn

H. WARINGTON SMYTH

Stretching towards the Equator, the coast of Thailand running south to Chumporn and beyond, to its narrowest point at the Isthmus of Kra, presented a scene of remote and untouched wonder in the late nineteenth century. Local folklore, as so often in South-East Asia, explained prominent features of the topography in legendary terms with tales of giants, love, and violence.

Warington Symth was employed by the Royal Thai government from 1891–6 as Director of the Department of Mines. He published an account of his experiences in his book (1898), which is exerpted later. A Fellow of the Royal Geographical Society, he gave several talks to members based on his life and times in the country. This abstract is from a paper describing an official journey he undertook from Bangkok in 1896, to visit the chief tin-producing states on the east coast of the peninsula.

T HE coast as far as Champawn is characterized by a number of wide bays stretching their spotless sand-beaches in scarcely perceptible curves to the horizon. Behind lies the sombre ever-piping jungle, relieved here and there by some jaggary or coconut palms, and an occasional cottage roof. Detached masses of limestone occur at intervals on steep-sided islands or high-peaked promontories, their serrated ridges, sometimes 2000 feet in height, forming conspicuous landmarks to the seafaring people using the gulf, and affording here and there good harbours for small craft. In the intense clearness of the early morning atmospheres, we used to see Sam Roi Yawt like a distant island 45 miles off. This headland is the noblest of all, and dominates the gulf like a huge cathedral—and aptly is it named the three hundred peaks.

The relations of these various rock-masses to one another have been long ago lucidly set forth by Siamese geologists, and, what in geological matters is more remarkable, all the authorities are unanimously agreed upon the subject. It appears that one Mong Lai and his wife once inhabited the neighbourhood (they were giants), and each promised their daughter in marriage, unknown to the other, to a different suitor. At last the day of the nuptials arrived, and Chao Lai and the Lord of Muang Chin both arrived to claim the bride. When the horrified father found how matters stood—having a regard for the value of a promise which is not too common in the East—he cut his daughter in half, that neither suitor should be disappointed. Chao Lai, in the mean time, on finding that he had a rival, committed suicide, and the peak of Chaolai is the remains of his body. The unfortunate bride is to be found in the islands off Sam Roi Yawt, the peaks of which are the remains of the gifts which were to be made to the holy man who was to solemnize the wedding; while Kaw Chang and Kaw Kong, on the east side of the gulf, are the elephant and buffalo cart in which the presents were brought.

Inland the densely wooded granites of the main ridge, forming the divide between Siam and Tenasserim, tower up into the monsoon clouds. At no point are they very distant from the coast-line, and the streams which drain their eastern slopes are but short and rapid mountain torrents.

The shoulders of the hills in places jostle the north and south trail out on to the beach, and the land wind comes off them laden with jungle fever. Except behind the bolder headlands, there is scarcely any flat land available for padi culture. Between the rich plain of Petchaburi and that of Champawn, there is not more than one acre of cultivation to every square mile of forest. The villages are few and the population small. A group of houses generally nestles under each of the great headlands, and the people are mostly fishermen, who do a little gardening, and take an occasional cargo of jungle produce (rattans, horns, buffalo-skins, etc.) to Champawn, Petchaburi, or Bangkok. In the four provinces of Pran, Kuwi, Bangtapan, and Patiyu there are about 6000 people.

From Champawn southwards, a new phase of scenery is entered on. The great axial range retreats further westward, and the country is more productive and more populous. The low hills of the coast-line are comparatively bare of heavy timber, thanks to the heavy gales and the ever-advancing jungle fires.

H. Warington Smyth, 'Journeys in the Siamese East Coast States', *Geographical Journal*, Vol. 11, 1898, pp. 466–7.

39
Junkceylon

G. E. GERINI

Cross to Thailand's west coast, and there on the shore a century ago lay a wonderful bounty of the traditional natural merchandise of the Chersonese. Who among today's tourist hordes expects to find such conchological richness still on the beaches of Phuket Island (Hujung Salang or 'Junkceylon' of the past)?

The author of this abstract, Colonel G. E. Gerini, became a senior official in the Royal Siamese government in the late nineteenth century and was fascinated by the land, the people, and the culture amongst which he found himself. He acquired a reputation locally as an amateur anthropologist and theologian, and was among the enthusiasts active in the early years of the Siam Society. He was also involved in the production of the Siamese section of the catalogue for the 1911 Paris Exhibition of Industry and Labour.

B Y the edge of the beach stretch smooth, flat banks of pure, cystalline sand; on the right hand side runs a fringe of Casuarina trees. Intermingled with the gravel and sand of the shore are shells of divers brilliant hues, blended in the most curious manner. One sees cowries of various sizes, white, yellow and of other tinges strewn about in hundreds of millions; many of them are quaint and lovely to behold in their kaleidoscopic wealth of colours. Some are of a bright red like sapan-wood dye; some black, and others speckled, or streaked with beautifully delineated veins; some are of a vivid yellow like sandal-wood; all charming and worthy of admiration. Nor are there wanting Sankha (chank) shells of the much prized variety whose whorls wind rightwise.* There is, in short, a superabundance of magnificent things, not least among which are brilliant-white oyster shells treasuring globular pearls. In these waters ambergris is also to be found.

---

*This is the sacred shell used in Brahmanical water-sprinkling ceremonies.

80

Tossed by the waves it is cast ashore up to the top of the broad beach, and while drying it exhales a foul carrion-like stench. But when dried and freed from all impurity it acquires an agreeable perfume, besides turning into a golden yellow resembling amber in appearance.

G. E. Gerini, 'Historical Retrospect of Junkceylon Island', *Journal of the Siam Society*, Vol. 2, Pt. 2, 1905, p. 101.

40
Northward from Dongalla

WALTER G. HARRIS

Even in the late 1920s, the timeless prospect of forested islands, mountain peaks, cliffs, and caves still lay to be revealed to the voyager on board his ship, sailing (in the manner of ancient times) up the west coast of Celebes (Sulawesi).

Walter Harris was such a voyager, a journalist with many years experience in the French areas of influence in North Africa and South-East Asia, and a Fellow of the Royal Geographical Society of London and the Society of Arts. In 1927–8, he spent eight months on a leisurely tour of the region, as he wrote, 'in a welcome atmosphere of peace, amongst surroundings often of surprising beauty and always of great interest'.

S TEAMING Northward from Dongalla we continued along the West coast of Celebes within a few miles of the shore. High hills rise directly from the sea, covered with dense jungle, though here and there, but rarely, there were clearings near the beach. A few native villages, recognizable by a glimpse of thatch roofs, or more often only by a column of pale blue smoke that rose from the groves of coco-nut palms that line the coast, tell that the region is inhabited. Away inland rose the crater of a volcano. As the steamer proceeded Northward the coast is more broken, and a succession of inlets studded with small wooded islands is passed. Once or twice we were only a few hundred yards from the shore. At one spot there was a narrow, sandy beach backed by high rocks full of sea-worn caves and crowned by jungle. Many of the trees had toppled over the cliff's edge, or been pushed over by their neighbours in the struggle for space and light. They lay with upturned roots, gaunt skeletons, upon the yellow sands below. The living wall of trees looked, and no doubt was, impenetrable. Tangled creepers interlaced the branches.

* * *

As we steamed Northward from Oena-Oena, nature exhibits various examples of her handiwork, careless and untidy excesses in the way of volcanic upheavals and more leisurely and successful efforts in the formation of coral islands; little, low white strands with surf breaking over the reefs and in the centre a dense mass of vegetation. At one moment half a dozen of these islands were in view at one time, none of them probably more than a third of a mile in length and one or two considerably smaller. The trees were full grown and towered above the rank undergrowth, and creepers had climbed their trunks and hung in long, trailing festoons from their branches. These are the islands that have reached completeness. In other parts of the Tomini Gulf we passed many still in a state of formation. In some cases the only sign of their existence was indicated by the breakers on reefs still below the surface. In others the line of coral was visible. Here and there a little sand and soil had collected and a stunted bush or two had taken root, the seed carried by bird or currents. In other cases, again, the vegetation, still young, took the form of low jungle, while near-by were islands on which the forest trees had reached their full dimensions. There cannot be many places where every period of the

formation of coral islands is exhibited at the same time as in
these waters of the Tomini Gulf.

W. G. Harris, *East for Pleasure: A Narrative of Eight Months Travel in Burma,
Siam, the Netherlands East Indies and French Indo-China*, 1929, pp. 200–1
and 231.

41
Cagayan Sulu

W. CHIMMO

The astonishing topography of Cagayan Sulu, lying in the Sulu Sea
about 95 kilometres north-east of the Borneo coast, was investigated
in 1871 by a visiting British naval Captain.

This abstract is from a paper published as an 'Additional Notice'
appended to Vol. 15 of the *Proceedings* of the Royal Geographical
Society. Apart from his rank and service (the Royal Navy), no
details of Chimmo were given. The reference to St John's views
reflects a contemporary controversy.

T HE whole island, as well as the group of small islets off
it, is evidently volcanic. On the two grassy-green hills
which face the south-west anchorage are the sites of two
extinct volcanoes, the craters of each being about 600 feet in
diameter, and about 80 feet deep, the circular lips inclining
to the south-east, as indeed they all do.

There are also several other craters, one on the north-east
side, one on the east extreme; but the most remarkable
and interesting one is on the south face of the island, which
is entered over a coral reef, through which a passage is formed
in the narrow neck of cliff, consisting of thin layers of trap,
sand, gravel, and stones, and communicates with the sea.

I visited this crater in the midst of a torrent of rain, thunder, and lightning, which seemed as if the heavens had

opened to swamp us while sounding its depths. This remarkable crater lake, which is nearly circular, having a basin of deep, dark-blue water of 320 feet in depth, the cliffs around clothed with trees reflecting their dark shadows on its surface, with 90 feet depth at the distance of a boat's oar (17 feet) from the rocky margin. The temperature of the bottom of the lake at that depth (53 fathoms) was 83°, its specific gravity 1·0220, while the surface water was 83°, and the air 78° only, after a heavy rain; while at the ship's anchorage the sea was 81°, and the density 1·0222.

The bottom in the centre consisted of soft yellow adhesive mud, with a strong sulphuric smell perceptible the moment the cup-lead, which brought up several pounds of it, came to the surface. This mud, when thoroughly washed and placed under the microscope, although impalpable and free from all grit to the touch, revealed the most marvellous field of minute and microscopic beauty, including many *Foraminifera* and *Diatomaceæ*.

Climbing a rugged and slippery network of roots, ferns, and stones to a height of about 100 feet through a solid and perpendicular stone gap, we saw to the eastward another lake of fresh water as large as this one, and into which a stone was let fall. The same perpendicular cliff was a wall for both lakes. It was impossible without great delay to get a boat on this lake to ascertain its depth. It was nearly circular, and its waters gushed through fissures in the rock, near some caves or grots, at an elevation of 40 feet above the salt lake, the temperature of which was 84°, quite warm to the feeling, and disagreeably warm to drink. In the sediment of this water were some minute *Algæ*, a snake-like form jointed and spined (microscopic), and a few small globular bodies darting about among the *Algæ*. The natives say that there are alligators in this lake, and of course there must be fish.

The gap of perpendicular massive walls formed between the cliffs, dividing the salt-water crater from the fresh, was very grand, and upwards of 200 feet high, the top bare, but the base clothed with creepers, ferns, areca palms and other trees, the ledges of some forming the resting-places for sea-fowl, and especially for the white and grey heron, and had a very curious effect from the sea, appearing at the distance of five or six miles like a huge building, with numerous people looking out from the tiers of balcomies.

Captain W. Chimmo, RN, 'Account of Cagayan Sulu, near Borneo', *Proceedings of the Geographical Society*, Vol. 15, 1871, pp. 384–6.

42
Banda Islands

ALBERT S. BICKMORE

The Banda Islands are volcanic in origin, as we have seen, and represent the remains of a vast, partially drowned caldera. The first full description of the group in English was written by Albert Bickmore, who had sailed in 1865 from Boston, USA, to Batavia (Jakarta) and then on to Ambon in order to collect specimens of the marine shells that had been figured in Rumphius's *Rariteit Kamer*. Having completed this task, he was invited to accompany the Dutch Governor (Arriens) on a visit to the Banda Islands. His note was communicated to the Royal Geographical Society of London, and printed in 1868 as an 'Additional Notice'.

E ARLY the next morning Banda, or more properly the Bandas, were in full view. They are ten in number; the largest, Lontar, or Great Banda, is a crescent-shaped island, about six miles long and a mile-and-a-half wide in its broadest parts. Its eastern horn curves towards the north, and the other points to the west. In a prolongation of the former lie Pulo Pisang, 'Banana Island', and Pulo Kapal, 'Ship Island'. The first is only about two-thirds of a mile long and half as wide, and the last is merely a high rock, resembling the poop of a ship, hence its name. Within the circle of which these islands form an arc, lie three other islands. The highest and most remarkable is the Gunong Api, or 'Burning Mountain', apparently attaining a very considerable elevation because its sides rise so abruptly up from the sea. Between the Gunong Api and the northern end of Lontar lies Banda Neira, about two miles long and less than a mile broad. North-east of the latter is a small rock called Pulo Krakka, or 'Women's Island'. The centre of the circle of which Lontar is an arc, falls in Sun Strait, a narrow passage separating Gunong Api from Banda Neira. The diameter of this circle is about six miles. Without this another concentric circle may be drawn, which will pass through Pulo Ai (Wai), 'Water Island', on the west, and Rosengain on the south-west; and outside of this a third concentric circle, which will pass through Pulo Swangi, 'Sorcery', or 'Spirit Island' on the north-west, Pulo Run (Rung), 'Chamber Island', on the west, and the reef of Rosengain on the south-west. The total area of the whole group is only 17·6 geographical square miles. . . .

Our fast yacht rapidly brought us nearer over the quiet, glassy sea. This is Pulo Ai on our right. It is only from 300 to 400 feet high, and, as we see from the low cliffs on its shores, is mostly composed of coral rock. This is also said to be the case with the other islands outside of the first circle, and we notice that they are all comparatiely low.

We now change our course to east, and steam up under the high, steep Gunong Api. On its N.N.W. side, about one-fourth of the distance from its summit down to the sea, there is a deep wide gulf, out of which rise thick, opaque clouds of white gas, that now, in the still clear air, are seen rolling grandly upward in one gigantic expanding column to the sky. On the top, also, thin clouds occasionally gather, and then slowly float away like cumuli, dissolving in the pure ether. These cloud masses are chiefly composed of steam and sulphurous acid gas, and, as they pour out, indicate what an active laboratory there is within the bowels of this volcano.

The western horn of crescent-shaped Lontar is before us. Its shore is composed of a series of nearly perpendicular crags, 200 or 300 feet high; but on the north side the luxurious vegetation of these tropical islands does not allow these rocks to remain naked, and from their horizontal crevices and upper edges hang down thick wide sheets of a bright green unfading verdure. The western entrance to the harbour, through which we are now passing, is between the abrupt magnificent coast of Lontar on the right, and the high, overhanging peak of Gunong Api on the left, and, as we advance, these separate and open to our view the steep lofty wall that forms Lontar's northern shore. This is completely covered with one dense matted mass of vegetation, out of which rise the erect columnar trunks of palms, from whose crests, as from sheaves, long feathery leaves hang over, and slowly and gracefully oscillate to and fro in the slight air which we can just perceive fanning our faces. Now Banda Neira is in full view. It is composed of hills, which gradually descend to the shore of this little bay. On the top of one near us is Fort Belgica, in form a regular pentagon. At the corners are bastions surmounted by small circular towers, so that the whole exactly resembles an old feudal castle. Its walls are white and almost dazzling in the bright sunlight, and beneath is a broad neatly clipped glacis, forming a beautiful, green, descending lawn. . . .

Our first excursion was to the western end of the opposite island, Lontar,—the Malay name of the Palmyra palm, *Borassus flabelliformis*, whose leaves were used to write upon over all the archipelago before the introduction of paper by the Arabs or Chinese; and in some places even at the present time. Lontar, as already noticed, has the form of a crescent. Its inner side is a steep wall, bordered at the base with a narrow band of low land.

On its outer side, from the crest of the wall many radiating ridges descend to the sea, its south-western shore is a series of little points separated by small bays. . . .

From Neira a large cutter took us swiftly over the bay to

Banda, showing the volcano Gunung Api on the left and Banda Neira on the right. From *Het Kamerlid van Berkenstein in Nederlandsch-Indie*, Leiden, 1888–9.

Selam,—a small village containing the ruins of the old capital occupied by the Portuguese during the sixteenth and early part of the seventeenth centuries, while their rights remained undisputed by the Dutch. This western end of Lontar is about 400 feet high, and is composed of coral rock of very recent date. Walking eastward we next came to a conglomerate containing angular fragments of lava. This was succeeded on the shore of the bay by a fine-grained, compact lava, somewhat stratified, and this again by trachytie and basaltic lavas. Indeed nearly this whole island is composed of such eruptive rocks, and Lontar may be regarded as merely a part of one immense crater about 6 miles in diameter, if it were circular, though it may have been more nearly elliptical. Pulo Pisang and Pulo Kapal, already noticed as falling in this circle, are two other fragments of the old crater walls—all the rest have disappeared beneath the sea. Here then, is another, enormous crater, greater even than that seen among the Zeugger Mountains on the eastern end of Java, whose minor and major axes severally measure *three miles and a half* and *four miles and a half*, and whose floor of naked sand is well named by the Malays 'the Sandy Sea'. Banda Neira represents the extinct craters rising in that Sandy Sea, and Gunong Api has a complete analogue in the still active Bromo. The enclosed bay, where vessels now anchor in 8 or 9 fathoms, is the bottom of this old crater, and, like that in the Zeugger Mountains, is composed of volcanic sand.

The radiating ridges on the outer side of Lontar represent the similar ridges on the sides of every volcano that is not building up its cone by frequent eruptions at its summit.

Lastly, the islands crossed by the second and third circles are so many cones on the flanks of this great volcano. True, those parts of some of them now above the sea are largely composed of coral rocks, like the west end of Lontar; but undoubtedly the polyps began to build their massive walls on the shores of islands of lava rock. They are doing this at the present moment. Every island in the group is now belted with a fringing reef, except at a few places where the shore is a perpendicular precipice, and the water of great depth. The western entrance through which we came to the roads is already quite closed up by a broad reef of living, growing coral....

A. S. Bickmore, 'A Description of the Banda Islands', *Proceedings of the Geographical Society*, Vol. 12, 1868, pp. 324–8.

43
Arru Islands

ALFRED RUSSEL WALLACE

Wallace reached the easternmost extreme of the Indonesian archipelago in 1857. He was fascinated by the extraordinary topography of the karstic islands of the Aru group, where he remained from January until June. Since these islands lie within the 100 fathom contour on the Sahul continental shelf, Wallace was undoubtedly correct to assume that, formerly (i.e. during the Pleistocene Ice Ages, when sea levels were greatly lowered world-wide) there must have existed closer terrestrial connections between these islands and New Guinea.

This abstract is taken from a paper read to a meeting of the Royal Geographical Society, London, on 22 February 1858. Wallace himself, of course, was not present but the audience included John Crawfurd, who was able to comment from his own observations.

T HE Arru group may be said to consist of one very large central island with a number of smaller ones scattered around it. The great island is called by the natives and traders 'Tanna busar' (great or main land), to distinguish it as a whole from any of the detached islands. It is of an irregular, oblong form, about 80 miles from north to south, and 50 from east to west, in which direction it is traversed by three channels or rivers dividing it into four portions. The northernmost of these, the river Watelai, I passed through, and found the entrance about 25 miles S.S.E. from Dobbo, in the southern angle of an extensive bay. The entrance is about a quarter of a mile wide, with low undulating land on each side. It gradually narrows to about the eighth of a mile, which width it retains, with very little variation, till on approaching its eastern mouth it again spreads out to about one-third of a mile. Its course is winding moderately, with a general direction of E.N.E., the extreme range of the bearings in passing through it being 105°. The banks (except near the eastern extremity, where there is much tidal swamp) are dry and moderately elevated. In many parts there are cliffs of hard rock, more or less worn away by the action of the water. A few smaller streams enter it right and left, at the mouths of which are some small rocky islands, and on the whole it has every feature of a true river. It is, in fact, difficult to believe you are in a small island, and not on a fine river watering some extensive country. But that the clear, cool water around you is briny as the ocean there is nothing to undeceive you. The depth of this stream is pretty regular, being from 10 to 15 fathoms. Its length is, according to the best estimate I could make, about 44 miles. The other two rivers, whose names are Vorkai and Maykor, are stated to be very similar in general character. Between these two, however, which are near together, the country is flat and swampy, and there are innumerable cross channels cutting the land up in every direction. On the south side of Maykor the banks are very rocky, and from thence to the extreme southern end of Arru, near the small island of Kri, is an uninterrupted extent of rather elevated and very rocky country, penetrated by numerous small streams in the high limestone cliffs, bordering which the larger portion of the edible birds' nests are obtained. The two southern rivers are universally declared to be longer than Watelai.

The whole country of Arru is very low, but by no means

so flat and swampy as has been represented, or as it appears from the sea. By far the greater part of it is dry rocky ground more or less undulating, now rising in abrupt hillocks, now cut into steep and narrow ravines. Except the actual tidal swamps, which extend on one side or the other at the mouths of most of the small rivers which everywhere penetrate it, there is no level ground, although the greatest elevation is probably not more than 200 feet. The rock, which everywhere appears in the ravines and brooks, is a coralline limestone, in some places soft and friable, in others so hard and crystalline, as to resemble the mountain limestone of England. The small islands which surround the central mass are very numerous, several hundreds in number. On the west are very few, Wamna and Pulo Babi being the chief. On the north-west extremity of the main land of Wokan is Ougia, and a little beyond it, Wassia, the north-westernmost of the group. To the east of these, and all along the east coast, are an immense number, extending to the extreme south, but nowhere reaching more than 15 or 20 miles from the central island. All are contained in a very shallow sea full of coral, and producing the pearl shells, which form the principal article of commerce in the islands. The whole of the islands are covered with a dense and very lofty forest.

The physical features here described are of the greatest interest, and probably altogether unique, for I have been unable to call to mind any other islands in the world which are completely divided by salt-water channels, having the dimensions and every other character of true rivers. What is the real nature of these, and how they have originated, are questions which have occupied much of my attention.

Alfred Russel Wallace, 'On the Arru Islands', *Proceedings of the Geographical Society*, Vol. 2, 1858, pp. 163–5.

Estuaries

࿖

44
The Bight

H. WARINGTON SMYTH

On the sheltered coasts of South-East Asia where great rivers discharge their silt-laden flow, unimaginably vast tracts of gleaming dark mud or dun-coloured sand-flats are exposed at low water. For the early voyager, lacking accurate charts and ignorant of the changing courses of tidal channels, reaching the land could be a slow and risky process. On such a shelving shore on the east coast of southern (peninsular) Thailand, Smyth witnessed the turbulence of the tides as his boat inched through the waters of the bight.

I T took us a whole day to get in, as we had to sound and survey the channel first of all, which involved many hours' work in the skiff, and the sea on the flats when it is blowing hard is not in favour of taking bearings from a small boat.

The scenery of the bight is quite peculiar. At low water immense tracts of mud and sand are laid bare, for the edification of flocks of pelican, cormorants, and herons. As the tide comes in, the whole becomes a boiling mass of foam, and an uneasy little sea gets up, with a short, uncomfortable motion. The birds betake themselves to the far-off shores, and a few boats come out and cut across from creek to creek. As the water falls again it becomes smoother, and long fishing-canoes come out, their Malay crews wading with their seine nets along the sands. Far to the southward dense masses of vapour condense about the summits of the Lakawn range, at a height of from 5000 to 6000 feet above the sea.

H. Warington Smyth, 'Journeys in the Siamese East Coast States', *Geographical Journal*, Vol. 11, 1898, p. 473.

45
Influenced by the Tide

ODOARDO BECCARI

On the sheltered muddy coasts and huge river deltas of South-East Asia, a shining green forest advances over dark mud-flats through the intertidal zone. This is the mangal or mangrove forest, a uniquely tropical vegetation type of extraordinary interest, yet rarely attracting the attention of any but the most dedicated naturalist.

Let the intrepid Italian botanist and palm specialist, Odoardo Beccari, explain why, despite its enormous botanical interest, he found this vegetation 'monotonous, weird and desolate'. A native of Florence, Italy, Beccari (1843–1920) was a passionate plant collector from the age of thirteen. He made three important expeditions to South-East Asia and New Guinea. Of these his first, to Sarawak in 1865–8, is best known to the English reader through the publication of his book of 1904, translated by F. H. H. Guillemard and illustrated by photographs provided by the Ranee Margaret of Sarawak.

ACCORDINGLY, in the beginning of January, I started up this trusan with my men, and entered the Mattang channels. We stayed here for about ten days, at a place called Salak, where nipa palms grew in abundance, so that my men had every facility for making the ataps I required. During the excursions I made all round I had ample opportunities of investigating the peculiar vegetation along the streams and estuaries which are influenced by the tide.

Descending the Sarawak river, just below Kuching, the 'kayu p'dada'. or 'peddada' of the Malays (*Sonneratia lanceolata*, Bl.), abounds, a mere variety of *S. acida*, which is not, however, strictly an estuarine plant, for it thrives also in places where sea and fresh water do not mix. Together with the *Sonneratia*, but usually farther away from the water, the predominant trees on the lower Sarawak are *Heritiera litoralis* and three species of *Brownlowia*. On the banks of the river *Acanthus ilicifolius*, with glossy and spinose leaves, is about the only herbaceous plant which grows. The true ligneous salt-water plants on the Sarawak river are about ten species; amongst these are *Skyphiphora hydrophyllacea*, *Lumnitzera coccinea*, *Excæcaria agallocha*, *Ægiceras major*, and *Sonneratia alba*; all shrubs, which grow in the foremost ranks. True mangroves, or *Rhizophoræ*, are represented by three species: *Brughiera gymnorhiza*, *B. cylindrica*, and *Randelia Rheedei*, and mixed with these, two trees are always found—*Carapa moluccensis* and *Avicennia officinalis*.

Two of the most characteristic plants on the banks of the Sarawak river, near the sea, are the nibong, already mentioned, and the nipa. The first is an invaluable palm to the natives, who generally use its straight and tough stems in house building, especially as piles. Splitting the stems longitudinally, they obtain long, slender slips, which, tied neatly together side by side with rotang, form 'lanté', a light, strong flooring which is excellent for houses and boats.

The nipa palm (*Nipa fruticans*) forms usually a dense hedge in front of the masses of arboreal vegetation as far as salt water extends. It evidently requires a swampy ground, on which it spreads its big stems, which resemble both in aspect and dimensions those of a coconut palm lying on the ground, while like the latter they show the big cicatrices left by detached leaves. But the nipa stems are flattened, and from their lower side, in contact with the ground, a number of rootlets grow. The head of the palm, too, is never raised any height from the soil. The fronds of the nipa, which may exceed thirty feet or more in length, resemble those of the coco.

The uses of the nipa are innumerable, and from it are produced sugar, wine, vinegar, and salt. The fruits grow close
together, forming a great ball a foot across, and each fruit,
when immature, contains, like the coconut, a watery liquid
and the soft edible albumen of the seed. Of the young white
leaves bags are made, and mats called 'kajang', very serviceable for covering boats or making partitions in houses. From
the same leaves, taking away the harder part and leaving the
epidermis, cigarette papers are obtained, and the 'rokos', or
cigarettes, which Malays continually smoke with great zest,
are all thus rolled. The nipa serves many other purposes, and
the natives, practised in the art and craft of backwoodsman-
ship, know how to avail themselves of it under a variety of
circumstances.

Boating along the Sarawak river at low tide below
Kuching, an infinite number of living creatures can be observed on the exposed mud-banks. Small amphibious fish
with prominent eyes, which look as if they were being forced
out of their orbits (*Periophthalmus Kolreuteri*), flop about with
extraordinary agility; whilst quaint blue crabs move backwards and sideways in all directions. Here and there singular
straight elongated bodies resembling horns, conical in shape,
and from one to two feet in length, may be seen rising vertically out of the slush. At first they might be taken for young
plants shooting up, but they show no trace of leaves. They
are really organs produced mostly by the roots of the *Sonneratia*,
and are always to be found where this tree grows. It appears,
moreover, that all plants growing in estuaries influenced
by the tide produced analogous root-appendages. *Avicennia*
and *Carapa* have root-horns which are shorter, broader,
and less pointed than those of *Sonneratia*, but are otherwise
identical.

Odoardo Beccari, *Wanderings in the Great Forests of Borneo: Travels and
Researches of a Naturalist in Sarawak*, Archibald Constable and Co., London,
1904, pp. 80–4.

46
Mangrove Forests of the Malay Peninsula

J. G. WATSON

Along the estuaries and sheltered, muddy shores of equatorial South-East Asia, mangroves reach their greatest natural richness, without parallel elsewhere in the world. The economic potential of these coastal forests prompted early research into their growth and management. Peculiar adaptations include 'stilts', 'knees', and other kinds of aerial extensions to the roots. The strange habit of viviparity (i.e. germination of the seed before it has left the parent tree) is well developed. Most intriguing is the narrow tolerance of each kind of mangrove tree to tidal amplitude and salinity.

It was staff of the Federated Malay States Forest Department who, overcoming the deterrent aspects of this extraordinary environment, succeeded in interpreting the salient features of mangrove ecology. Although rather technical for the non-botanist, passages are abstracted below from the seminal research report for which J. G. Watson, as Deputy Director of Forests, was technically responsible. In the introduction, he acknowledged its origins in 'a bundle of manuscript handed to the writer by Mr J. P. Mead on the eve of his departure to France in 1916, containing a mass of valuable first-hand observations', and its subsequent evolution through the joint efforts of forest officers and rangers, and others who provided specialist help.

T HE mangrove forests (or swamps) of the Malay Peninsula cover an area of about four hundred and thirty square miles, almost all on the west coast. Over four hundred square miles have been constituted reserved forests....

On the west coast the mangrove belt is almost continuous from Kedah to Singapore. It varies in width from a few chains to a maximum of about twelve miles at the mouth of the Larut river in the Matang district of Perak; but the mangroves follow the rivers much further inland, extending along the banks of the Perak river up to Teluk Anson, a distance of about thirty miles from the sea. The belt is intersected

97

by numerous deep anastomising tidal creeks, which some-times exceed a mile in width, and which cut off from the mainland islands varying in size from a few acres to more than thirty square miles. On the Perak coast there is a con-tinuous inland waterway through the belt from Gula in the Krian district to Panchor on the boundary of the Dindings, a distance of over forty miles, while the main approaches to Port Swettenham (which lies at the back of a large mangrove swamp) are navigable by large ocean-going vessels at all states of the tide. Some of the islands, such as Pulau Trong and Pulau Klang, are entirely covered by mangrove....

Silt brought down by the rivers, and sand from the bed of the sea, are banked up by the combined action of waves, tides, and currents. When the banks have developed suf-ficiently they become covered with water-borne species, Avicennia (*api-api*) being usually the fist to appear. The seeds of this genus, being semi-viviparous, are able to start growing at once and, with the help of their hairy radicles, successfully to withstand the scour of tide and current. Not so easy to understand is the ability of Sonneratia (*perepat*) to establish itself; for the seed is neither viviparous nor armed with any special anchoring device. Yet this species is certainly one of the pioneers in the formation of mangrove forests, particularly where there is a high percentage of humus mixed with the silt. Moodie suggests that the small seeds, which do not float for any length of time, are carried along with the silt and deposited on the newly formed banks. Tree growth thus quickly covers the shoals, whose level is then more rapidly raised by mud and organic matter held up by the spreading network of roots, and by the peculiar development of the roots themselves. These banks are often entirely isolated, and may be some miles out to sea, the young trees being at first completely submerged twice daily, except during neap tides.

It is doubtful whether even *api-api* can withstand complete submergence twice every day for any length of time. The large expanse of unclothed mud exposed at low water suggests that it is necessary for the banks to remain uncovered for several days together before any form of land vegetation can establish itself. It is considered that the limit of tree growth is to be found round about the neap high-water mark, above which the ground remains unsubmerged for at least two days in every month. In rivers and sheltered situations the Rhizophoras may occupy flats that are covered by even the lowest neap tides, but here the superior length of the radicles enables even the seedlings to keep their heads above water....

J. G. Watson, 'Mangrove Forests of the Malay Peninsula', *Malayan Forest Records*, No. 6, 1928, pp. 1, 2, 9, 131–2.

47
The Lupar Bore

WILLIAM M. CROCKER

Under a regime of heavy rainfall, all the larger rivers of South-East Asia have built up extensive deltas. Their lower reaches show minimal fall, and the influence of the tide can extend far inland. At certain tides, the configuration of some estuaries creates a 'bore', a terrifying surge of water that advances up the river as one, or a short succession of steep and swiftly moving waves. In the estuary of the Lupar River, Sarawak, at certain tides, a spectacular bore is formed. In 1995, proposals were made locally to base a tourist attraction on its regular occurrence.

In 1881, when this description was read to the Royal Geographical Society of London, William Crocker had already been employed in Sarawak for sixteen years, for much of the time as Resident with authority (as President of the Administrative Committee) to take charge of affairs in the absence of the Rajah Brooke. He travelled widely in the State, and also crossed its borders to visit adjoining parts of (then) Dutch Borneo.

T HE first river in the Second Division is the Batang Lupar. Reference to the map will show this to be a river of considerable size. There is a bar at the mouth, giving 3½ fathoms at high water and 10 feet at low water, and the river is navigable for large vessels as far as Lingga, about 30 miles from the mouth. Just above this point the bore begins. A single wave rises to the height of about six feet above the level surface of the river, and rolls up for some 60 miles, with a roaring noise and foaming head, at a rate of several miles an hour, oversetting all it meets. This bore begins about three days before full and change, and lasts about three days after. The rise and fall of the tide is so great, and the river so full of shallows, that navigation beyond Lingga is always more or less dangerous.

W. M. Crocker, 'Notes on Sarawak and North Borneo', *Proceedings of the Royal Geographical Society*, Vol. 3, 1881, p. 196.

Rivers

∾

48
Rivers of Burma

J. ANNAN BRYCE

Along the northern boundary of South-East Asia, the collision of Gondwanan tectonic plates with Laurasia had a dramatic impact on the drainage pattern of central Asia. Squeezed by the rising mountain ranges, the courses of five huge rivers now run south, close together, in deep gorges around the eastern end of the Himalayas: the Tsangpo-Brahmaputra, Irrawaddy, Salween, Mekong, and Yangtse.

In this setting, the extravagances of the tropical climate have forged rivers of spectacular character. As we have seen, the volume of rain falling in any drainage basin fluctuates from zero to enormous—seasonally where the monsoons prevail, and as violent interludes in the typhoon belt or as intermittent localized rainstorms in the humid equatorial zone. The alternation of trickle and flood in the streams and river headwaters creates a very erosive regime. In the warm climate, soil-forming processes are rapid. Valleys are deeply incised and hillslopes often unstable. Landslips are frequent. Heavy loads of stone and soil falling into the rivers can be carried long distances in turbulent water. When they finally emerge on to the plains, the large rivers have deposited great depths of alluvium and many have built extensive deltas.

Early explorers and travellers marvelled at the great Irrawaddy, the principal river of Burma (Myanmar), which shows all these features. By 1886, when this scholarly review was delivered to the Royal Geographical Society of London, exploration had covered much of Burma. Mr Bryce himself was among the first to visit the Chindwin (Khyenwin) area.

101

T HE character of a country is most easily understood by beginning with a consideration of its mountain structure. If you look at the map, you will see that the great peninsula between the Bay of Bengal and the China Sea, known by the general name of Indo-China, differs in its conformation from India proper in this remarkable respect, that its mountain ranges all run north and south, while those of India run east and west. The map will show you further that these ranges, which have a very considerable, though not great, average elevation, say from 3000 to 5000 feet, are separated by valleys of no great width, and that the principal chains have their roots at the south-eastern extremity of the great Tibetan plateau. Now these physical features have important results. The north and south strike of the ranges, opening out a little towards the south, permits the mouths of the valleys where the rich delta land lies to receive the full force of the rain-bearing south-west monsoon, which passes obliquely up to the north-east. The elevation of the mountain ranges, while sufficient to secure the condensation of the monsoon clouds, is not great enough, as is the case with the Himalayas, to impede the passage of those clouds. The highlands, therefore, all over this region have an abundant supply of rain, which gives birth to a number of great rivers, the Irawadi, the Sittang, the Salween, the Mehkong, and the Mehnam. The direction and length of the mountain chains have determined the course and size of these rivers, of which all except the Salween, which flows during the whole of its long course in a very narrow valley, and has therefore a comparatively small drainage, bring down annually vast supplies of fertile alluvium, forming rich plains during their course, and great deltas at their mouths.

I have said that the deltas at the mouths of these valleys receive the full force of the south-west monsoon, and enjoy therefore an abundant rainfall. Their upper parts, however, have to depend for their water-supply mostly upon the inundations of the rivers, which are fed by the abundant rainfall of the mountains. You will see from the map that the

102

south-west clouds, before they reach the upper valleys, have to pass over one or more of the ranges. Now when clouds laden with rain pass over a range of hills which is able to condense them, they are in the habit of depositing the bulk of the moisture with which they part at that particular time on the side nearest the direction from which they come. Furthermore, if there be any considerable space at a much lower level between the ranges, the clouds will often pass over from one to the other without depositing any rain to speak of on the intermediate plain, and again condense on the range to leeward. Over all this region, therefore, you find that the plains of the upper valleys have much less rain than the mountains which bound them, and that the eastern sides of the ranges and the adjoining part of the plain have less rain than the western sides, and consequently that the streams fed from the eastern side are smaller. . . .

The river *par excellence* of Burma is the Irawadi. This great stream, which is navigable by steamers drawing five feet of water as far as Bhamo, 900 miles from its mouth, and its largest tributary the Kyendwin, form in Upper Burma several fertile plains, producing rice, cotton, wheat, and other valuable crops, while in the lower part of its course, in conjunction with the river Sittang, it forms a splendid delta, which is the main source of the world's supply of rice. The vast expanse of delta, nearly 100 miles each way, appears, indeed, one immense rice-field, stretching away illimitably, level as the sea. The aspect of this plain is changeful. In midsummer, after the first heavy rains, an unbroken sheet of water, it becomes carpeted, as the rice plant grows, with brightest green, which turns, ere December arrives, to waving gold, and then, after harvest, to a dreary grey flat of sun-baked mud, over which the smoke of the burning stubble hangs like a pall. Out of it rise, visible to great distances, the mighty masses of the great pagodas of Rangoon and Pegu, as changeful in their golden sheen of light, and yet as unchanging, as the wide plain over which they have looked for so many centuries. . . .

103

All this delta country, exposed to the full force of the south-west monsoon, has in the summer an abundant rainfall, as much as 100 inches in the southern part, but as one journeys north the country becomes drier till at the apex of it, about 170 miles from the sea, the rainfall is about one-half. About this point the ranges bounding the valley send out spurs, which again retire, leaving rich plain country on both sides, though on the left bank a low arid ridge intercepts the view of it, while to the west the eye ranges as far as the Arakan chain. In the plain country of the Upper Irawadi, as I have already said, there is but a small rainfall. This region, therefore, depends very largely for its water supply on the rises of the Irawadi and its tributaries, which are as much as 40 or 50 feet in height, and spread widely over the country, so that the course of the Irawadi and the Kyendwin present in places during the rains, the appearance of a great lake nine or ten miles in width. When the river falls, vast expanses of sand and mud are left exposed, and the stream narrows to a comparatively small volume, winding in devious channels among the sandbanks. In the spring months, when the strong southerly wind, the precursor of the monsoon, sets in, it raises clouds of sand, which, under the bright sunlight, overspread the horizon with a yellow glare. All around, the thorny vegetation of this dry region looks at this season bare and arid. Even the forest-covered hills, the leaves having now fallen, are grey and dreary, showing the parched ground between the leafless stems, and the only relief to the eye under the cloudless sky of brass are the clumps of evergreen mango trees and palms which mark the site of some village. The time to see this upper region in its beauty is at the end of the rains. The sandbanks then have sunk under the brimming river, into which dip feathery bamboos. Everything is clothed in green, while above, in a sky of deepest, softest blue, hang masses of white cumuli. The air, though hot, is exquisitely clear, while the mountains, clothed to their tops with verdure, are visible to immense distances. There is some good scenery in Burma. The Salween, just above Maulmain, flows among fantastic limestone mountains, which rise in great precipices out of deep tropical forests. The Irawadi, too, furnishes some fine bits. In Lower Burma the defile at Prome is highly picturesque. There are few finer approaches to a capital than the narrow passage where the river rushes between Ava and the pagoda-crowned ridge of Sagain—both of them once capitals—while the line of lofty and serrated crags forms a noble background to the rich plain where the battlements of Mandalay and the golden spire of its palace rise beneath its sacred hill. The long defile above the capital, called the third defile, is pretty, while the first and second defiles, one just above and one just below Bhamo, are, especially the latter, extremely grand. The river, contracted to a width of 250 yards, has forced through a ridge of hills about 1000 feet high a tortuous channel, down which it rushes in whirling eddies between vertical cliffs 700 feet high, from whose crest and face trees and shrubs, wherever they can find lodgment, wave pendulous towards the stream.

J. A. Bryce, 'Burma: The Country and People', *Proceedings of the Royal Geographical Society*, Vol. 8, 1886, pp. 481–4.

49
The Upper Defile

BEATRIX METFORD

The course of the Irrawaddy is marked by three great gorges, or defiles. These are navigable, but at a risk, as travellers have recounted. The spectacular features of the upper defile were described by Beatrix Metford, born in 1890, daughter of a Gloucester miller, who accompanied her first husband, V. Clart, on official tours and on other trips through north-eastern Burma and into China in the late 1920s and early 1930s. By her second marriage, in 1933, she became stepmother to another author in this anthology, John Wyatt-Smith.

T EN miles above Bhamo the Irrawaddy flows for forty miles through a narrow gorge, with mountains, 3000 or 4000 feet high, rising on either side. This gorge, or Upper Defile, as it is called, is famous for its wild and rugged scenery. During the rains the river at Bhamo is nearly two miles wide, and often rises as much as six feet in twenty-four hours, but in the Upper Defile its waters are confined to a narrow channel in places only fifty yards wide. Navigation through this gorge is only possible for six months of the year, and but few people get the chance to view the grandeur of its scenery, for the Irrawaddy Flotilla Company's vessels do not ply beyond Bhamo. Each time I went through the defile I gazed with wonder at the high-water mark, plainly visible on the rocks far, far above. On the rocky islets now towering out of the water could be seen uprooted tree trunks which had been torn from the banks and stranded on the rocks during the last high water. Well could I believe that those inky depths had never been plumbed, and that in years gone by one out of every three boats had been wrecked in the swirling waters, and their precious cargoes of jade from the mines in the north lost for ever.

Beatrix Metford, *Where China Meets Burma*, Blackie and Son Ltd., London and Glasgow, 1935, pp. 116–17.

50
The Second Defile

E. B. SLADEN

The second defile of the Irrawaddy is shorter than the first, but not inferior in its scenic impact.

In 1868, Major E. B. Sladen, at that time Her (Britannic) Majesty's Political Resident in Burma, spent nine months travelling some 1,000 miles through the 'hitherto forbidden tract' between what was then the Burmese frontier at Bhamo and south-western

China. His steamer ('the draught of which did not exceed 3 feet') was the first to prove that this sector of the Irrawaddy between Mandalay and Bhamo was navigable by such craft.

T HE second defile, which occurs only a few miles below Bhamo, is so graphically described by a traveller who passed through it in November last that I cannot help quoting a few extracts from his narrative. He says:—'About 11 o'clock we entered the second defile, which is about 15 miles in length. The scenery of this defile or gorge surpasses anything

'A vast perpendicular mass, rising apparently at least 800 feet above the glass-like river.' From R. Talbot Kelly, *Burma*, A. and C. Black Ltd., London, 1905.

I have ever beheld. The river narrows in, whilst the banks on either side rise to a height of from 500 to 800 feet, and are covered with thick woods. The most striking part of the defile is a huge rock, which is called Monkey Castle, from the number of monkeys which hang about it. This is a vast perpendicular mass, rising apparently at least 800 feet above the glass-like river. It is impossible to describe our impressions of the grandeur of this wonderful defile. During the couple of hours we were passing through, there was a continual change: sometimes the stream took a winding course between the elevated and precipitous banks, with their towering forests; at other places we came upon a long vista of wood and stream. Here and there was a pagoda, or a village, or a few fishermen in a boat. On the whole, I do not remember any scene so calculated to please and astonish the eye—not by rude, wild precipices, but by glorious heights crowned with forests, and throwing their dark shade upon the smooth water.'

Major E. B. Sladen, 'Expedition from Burma via the Irrawaddy and Bhamo to South-West China', *Journal of the Royal Geographical Society*, Vol. 41, 1871, pp. 258–9.

51
The Third Defile

G. T. GASCOIGNE

The third defile of the Irrawaddy, by contrast with the upper and the second, is almost bucolic in its charm as described in this brief abstract of the late nineteenth century.

AFTER leaving Kyaukmyaung, we passed into the third and lowest defile of the river, and the scenery became most captivating. Glorious wooded banks rose upon both sides of the stream, and many fascinating little native villages were dotted here and there. These picturesque little bamboo structures peeped forth from among thick groves of palms and bananas, while close beside them stood small groups of pagodas which are always the necessary attendants of every Burman village.

The bamboos grew in marvellous profusion, weaving themselves, in parts, into a dense, green wall, while the tamarind, mango, Ficus Religiosa, interspersed with the gorgeous crimson of the Butea Frondosa (or Dak), with occasional Bombax Malabaricum or silk tree, produced an amazing study of colour.

We spent the whole afternoon of the 25th in that delightful third defile. Each fresh reach of the river that was disclosed seemed more fascinating than the preceding one. Long stretches of blue, limpid water wandered away, and the brilliant foliage on the banks strayed down to the water's edge and peeped over, as if to gaze at their delicate, wistful reflections in the clear, glittering depths.

G. T. Gascoigne, *Among Pagodas and Fair Ladies: An Account of a Tour through Burma*, A. D. Innes and Co., London, 1896, pp. 176–7.

52
The Lower Irrawaddy

HENRY YULE

The great river Irrawaddy completes its journey placidly, traversing a fertile flood plain and debouching through a complex delta into the Bay of Bengal.

This abstract is from a paper presented to the Royal Geographical Society of London in 1857, when the British had already occupied Pegu and Martaban and were intensely interested in the lands of Burma and its tributary States to the north. Yule (later Sir Henry), a noted sinologist and scholar of Marco Polo, was then a Captain in the Bengal Engineers and secretary to Major Phayre, British envoy to the kingdom of Burma at Ava.

T HE Irawadi continues to flow between bold and wooded banks to Prome; and the whole breadth of the land thus far is more or less rugged. Below Prome the valley expands into an alluvial plain, intersected on both sides by low ridges, covered in the rains with the densest foliage, but in the dry season exhibiting a brick-dust soil beset with leafless stems. Twenty-five miles below Prome, where the cliffs of Akouk-toung protrude into the Irawadi, this level is on the western bank interrupted for a brief space. On the other side it unites with the fertile plain of Poungde, which stretches from the isolated Prome hills to the foot of the Peguan-Yoma; and passing southward continues to widen till lost in the vast plains of the delta.

The delta may be considered to commence at the bifurcation of the Bassein branch from the main stream, a little above Henzada. That branch, though affording the best and deepest access for ships into the heart of the delta, is now entirely cut off from the main stream during the dry season by a bank of sand which fills the head of the channel to a height of many feet above the surface of the river. In the rains, steamers drawing 10 feet water pass without difficulty. The harbour of Rangoon is connected with the Irawadi, by the channel called Panlang. This is not navigable by the steam flotilla in the dry weather, and at that season the vessels are obliged to make a detour, analogous to that forced on steamers bound from Calcutta for the upper Ganges, though of much less extent. They then ascend by the channel called by seamen China Bukeer, which is the shortest outlet of the Irawadi, though another, which keeps more the direction of the unbroken stream, retains the name. There is, however, no one of the ramifications which can claim to be the primary mouth.

A vast labyrinth of creeks and channels cuts up the lower part of the delta into an infinity of islands. Within the full tidal influence, these are lined with mangrove thicket; further up with forest of a nobler kind, or more commonly with a fringe of gigantic grasses.

Captain Henry Yule, 'On the Geography of Burma and Its Tributary States in Illustration of a New Map of Those Regions', *Journal of the Royal Geographical Society*, Vol. 27, 1857, pp. 79–80.

53
Shooting the Rapids

CARL A. BOCK

The courses of the Salween and Mekong diverge around the uplands of northern Thailand, which are drained by rivers that make up in scenic wonder for their relatively short lengths. The landscape of cliffs and rapids in the navigable river gorges may be insurpassable, but travellers were often preoccupied with other priorities!

Born in Oslo, Norway, in 1849, Bock was a naturalist and explorer who, through his writings, holds a recognized place among the cohort of Europeans—officials, merchants, collectors, and missionaries—who visited South-East Asia in the nineteenth century. His trips were all accomplished within a few years: the first, sponsored by the Marquess of Tweeddale, was to Sumatra (1878); his second, for which he is best known, a journey through Borneo from Kutai to Banjermasin, and his third, from which this abstract is taken, into northern Thailand and Laos.

A NOTHER day's journey brought us to Muang Hawt, a village famous for its six-toed fowls, and a halting-station on the road to Moulmein. The banks of the river are here hemmed in with limestone mountains, which stand out like silhouettes against the bright blue sky, studded to the top with trees and vegetation growing in bewildering but enchanting confusion. The whole face of the cliffs was alive with bats and swallows, flitting about their nests, scooped out in the soft stone. But we had not time to examine the beauties of the course of the river through this gorge. Already the current was becoming more and more rapid, necessitating the greatest care in steering our boats between the treacherous rocks, as we were impelled irresistibly towards a series of rapids, thirty-two in all, which would make the strongest claim upon our undivided attention. We arrived at Mutka about three in the afternoon, and I at once sought out the Phya, to present my 'passport', and get arrangements made for shooting the rapids on the morrow. The boats had to be specially prepared for the purpose, a double bulwark being placed round the bows, to prevent the ingress of water while plunging through the seething surf. The Phya was very attentive, and was very grateful for the small 'tip' of five rupees which I offered him, for, as he said, 'money was very scarce'.

Early the next morning we continued the journey down stream, having taken on board a steersman and two pilots for each boat. In the river were several dead buffaloes, on some of which vultures were feeding as they floated rapidly down towards the sea. The natives said a plague had carried off many hundreds of cattle, entailing heavy loss on some of the villages. Monkeys were numerous in the trees on the banks, and we passed adjutants and other wading birds in abundance. About three miles below Mutka broken water was reached—the first 'kong' or rapid—immediately below which is a small native village called Ban Kau, the inhabitants of which get their living by collecting bats' dung in the numerous caves in the neighbourhood, which they use in the manufacture of gunpowder.

Two or three hours' 'drifting' below this, the river runs between perpendicular walls of limestone rocks, the strata of which are distorted in a remarkable manner, sometimes lying almost at right angles with each other. Where the strata are horizontal, near the water's edge, the action of the stream has eaten out deep, narrow fissures, giving the rock the appearance of a huge series of neatly-wrought shelves. We put up for the night at Keng Soi, named after, or giving its name to, one of the rapids. Near here, on the top of a high hill on the right bank of the river, are a Wat and a phrachedee, both of them visible for many miles above and below. So long as the hill was in sight, I noticed my steersman, everytime a rapid was passed, bow reverently in its direction, with hands pressed tightly together and held close to the forehead.

Below Keng Soi the scenery on the banks became more rugged, an indication of our approach to still rougher water. The view was very impressive; at every bend of the river, which takes sharp curves just here, the landscape seems to change, not only in effect, but in character, according as the softness of the distance, or the rugged grandeur of the foreground, predominates. The edges of the stream are dotted with huge boulders, borne down with irresistible force in times of flood from the distant hills, and we are swiftly nearing Doi Omlo, the heaviest and most dangerous of the rapids. It needs strength as well as skill to avoid the sunken rocks, for the river takes so sharp a bend that it requires the united force of several men to keep the rudder in place. In sweeping round the curve my boat swerved broadside on, being twisted round by the constant eddies, and narrowly escaped collision with a rock, but, by dint of great shouting and exertion on the part of the crew, some of whom stood in the bow with their long poles, ready for such an emergency—though, had we struck, the force of the collision would have made matchwood of the stoutest bamboo—the boat was made obedient to the enormous rudder, and the danger was avoided. The second boat, however, was carried too near the shore, and the over-arching branches caught the attap roofing of the cabin, and stripped it off, while, more disastrous still, one of the pilots fell into the roaring current. How he escaped drowning is a miracle; but fortunately he was near the shore, and was able to reach *terra firma*, and, following us along the shore for some two miles, was subsequently taken on board with a sound, if a wet, skin. When we were safely

through the danger, the steersmen offered a short thanks-
giving to the mountain-spirit.

Carl Bock, *Temples and Elephants: The Narrative of a Journey of Exploration
through Upper Siam and Lao*, Sampson Low, Marston, Searle, and
Rivington, London, 1884, pp. 368–71.

54
Keng Karm

NOEL WYNYARD

The turbulence of the rivers of Thailand presented constant hazards
to travellers reliant on water transport for their business—and to
those daring ladies who accompanied their husbands.

Noel Wynyard sailed from Southampton port, England, to
Penang, Malaysia, in order to marry her fiancé. He was employed
in the teak forests of Thailand, and her book graphically describes
her experiences accompanying him on tour in the 1930s. Despite a
certain naïvety, her lively pen imparts the wonder of the untamed
river.

ON the third morning we set out again by boat for the
next camp, which was a day's journey downstream.
Passing through several minor rapids we shipped a considerable amount of water, but no harm was done. After about an
hour we arrived at a very big rapid down which the river
roared with such ferocity that it seemed impossible that any
boat could make the passage of it unscathed. We all got out,
having stopped at the edge of a quiet backwater, and most of
the heavy gear and all valuables were portaged over rocks
and boulders to the calmer water zoo yards below, where the
main body of turbulent water swept by a deep quieter pool.
Then the fun began. For the first 100 yards the boat was
lowered slowly downstream at the end of a long check-
rope which, hauled on by a dozen men and belayed round

114

projecting rocks, allowed the boat to arrive at the point below which any checked boat would instantly have been swamped. The rope was unhitched and away shot the boat. It really was a magnificent sight: three men standing poling and working as though their very lives depended on their strenuous efforts and perfect co-operation—and indeed this most certainly was the case, for no human swept into those turgid waters could have hoped to survive. The boat, looking absurdly small, must have been moving at twenty-five miles an hour. At one moment it would be riding high on a crest and at the next plunging almost completely under before being staggered by the broadside backwash from a huge rock, rolling so that it was a marvel that the bare-footed boatmen could keep any effective balance on the submerged bows and stern, washed as they were by wave after wave. When in the very middle of the worst part, his oar, jamming between two rocks, was whipped from the hands of the foremost boatman, he was thrown back on the man behind. The latter, thrown off his balance, missed his stroke and, to our dismay, we saw the boat hurtling down straight for a sunken rock over which the water splashed and swirled to the height of 2 ft. Nothing could avert disaster. The man at the stern, the only one of the three in commission, was powerless to turn the bows 50 ft. away from him. Within a second of losing his oar the bow man had grabbed another from the roof, but in so doing had blocked all sight from the second man owing to the extreme narrowness, and an instant later, with only one man effective, he at the stern, they hit the rock. They hit it head-on with a noise we could hear above the roar of the foaming, tossing waves, but Fate had postponed her obviously-intended calamity, and they were swept over intact, to reach the bank water-logged but floating. After bailing, we loaded up again, and it was midday before Fate acted.

Ahead, a rocky island divided the river, the water roaring past it on either side in a thundering rapid. To the right it took a right- and then a left-hand turn before hurling itself upon a welter of rocks with such foaming fury that no boat could have found a passage. To the left a bend finished in a long gradual right-handed sweep of turbulent water that, in a sense, resembled a gigantic snake-skin parted along the dorso-mesal line, and spread belly upward; the quieter water near the banks approximating to the dorso-lateral, and the rushing, central water, cross-scarred by 3-ft. and 4-ft. waves, to the ventral scales. This being a fairly dangerous rapid, we stopped to land the cook and three coolies, none of whom, it later transpired, could swim. The preliminary rapid was successfully negotiated, and on the left bank was a quiet narrow strip of water down which we started. Unluckily, a swirl from an unseen rock swept us into the main stream, into waves 4 ft. high, of which it took but the first under which we dived to sink us. Everything happened so quickly that I hardly realized we were sinking before my husband had driven the roof into the waters with a sudden heave of his shoulders and had flung me as far as he could towards the bank, shouting into my ear, 'Swim like the devil!' I am not a strong swimmer, but after what seemed like half an hour's struggle and fight which called upon reserves of strength that I had no idea I possessed, but which in reality only lasted about half a minute, I managed to clutch frantically on to some withies growing near the bank, from which I was swept by the fierce current, my knees and elbows scraping over the tops of rocks. I was again unlucky in my second effort to reach dry land. This time I clutched more branches with a firmer grip, only to be dragged completely under and to be forced to let go. Down I was swept again, this time to be brought up with a sickening thud that drove nearly all the wind from my body against a rock. I was nearly done for. With my wind went the remains of my strength. My salvation lay in the fact that I had been swept into the hollow of two rocks, where for a few seconds I remained, gasping and dazed, before clambering to safety.

Noel Wynward, *Durian: A Siamese Interlude*, Oxford University Press, London, 1939, pp. 127–30.

55
The Mekong

J. S. BLACK

In eastern Thailand, the rivers drain towards the Mekong which forms the national frontier for much of its length. The great Mekong is another enormously long river, changing character as it flows from the highlands to the sea. Its course is broken by three remarkable rapids which were even more hazardous for boat-farers than the Irrawaddy defiles.

J. S. Black assessed the prospects. In 1895, when he made this tour under the auspices of HRH Prince Damrong, Minister of the Interior, Black had already served seven years as the First Assistant of the British Consular Service in Siam (Thailand). He was a fluent Thai speaker, and familiar with Thai life and manners.

I T was at Nongkhai that I first gazed upon the great river of Indo-China, the Mekong. Even at this point, more than 1000 miles from its mouth, the Mekong is a magnificent stream, and the sight of this vast volume of water nearly half a mile wide, issuing from the unknown regions of Tibet and sweeping on grandly towards the distant ocean, gives rise to feelings of the deepest admiration and awe. My feelings of admiration and awe were, however, quickly changed to those of dismay and abhorrence when I reached the Chiengkhan rapids, and spent eight long and anxious days battling against the surging and boiling waters, creeping cautiously round jagged rocks, pulling strenuously with ropes, shoving with boat-hooks, struggling and shouting, or simply sitting helplessly in the bottom of the rude dug-out with secret terror in my heart, as I gazed at the wildly hissing water, and speculated how far a body would be carried before it reached the surface of these boiling whirlpools. Twice we had to unload the boats and transport all baggage across the rocks and sand, but this was the most difficult season of the year, on account of the lowness of the water. The river, of which the average width above the rapids is about half a mile, with say an

Passage of a rapid on the Mekong. From F. Garnier, *Voyage d'exploration en Indo-Chine*, Hachette, Paris, 1885.

average depth of 4 or 5 feet, here gets contracted into a narrow rocky channel not more than 60 or 100 yards wide in places, shut in by black and sharply jutting rocks from 10 to 30 feet high. In the rainy season the water rises and spreads hundreds of yards beyond this little channel, and then small boats creep along the banks in a somewhat easier fashion. The different rapids or shoots of water, which are each distinguished by a local name, number fourteen in all, and are spread over a distance of 50 miles. The intervening spaces are, of course, not so difficult as the rapids, but during the whole of these eight days the ropes were hardly ever cast off the boats.

As the river here literally forces its way through a range of hills, the scenery is wildly picturesque. Rugged forest-clad hills rear their lofty heads at every turn, and, after surmounting a fierce and impetuous rapid, it was a great pleasure to paddle along smoothly for a space and quietly enjoy the ever-changing aspects of this delightful mountain and river scenery. Inhabitants were almost entirely wanting, and every morning I was awakened by the crowing of jungle fowl, the calling of wild peacock, or the loud prolonged and intensely mournful howling of monkeys....

J. S. Black, 'Journey round Siam', *Geographical Journal*, Vol. 8, 1896, pp. 442–4.

56
Mother of Rivers

H. W. PONDER

The Mekong, like so many rivers in South-East Asia, has for long been a strategic navigation, especially in its lower reaches in Cambodia.

H. W. Ponder, a Fellow of the Royal Geographical Society of London, was a traveller and travel writer of the relatively calm decade preceding the Second World War. She was chiefly interested in places, the people, and their lives in what were then the Netherlands East Indies and French Indo-China. Some short descriptive passages in her writings have captured the wonder of the natural environment.

T HE Me-kong (Mekhong or Mekong), whose name means 'the Mother of Rivers'—is immense, melancholy, and mysterious. When day breaks the banks are so far distant on either side that there is nothing to tell you that you are not afloat upon some still grey ocean. There is little sign of life. Now and then a small island appears, looking in the distance like a great ship moored in a deserted harbour. The water is so smooth that even the occasional leap of a fish is startling; and the noiseless approach of one of the dugout canoes that the riverside natives handle so skilfully, seems a visitant from another world—as indeed it is. A world of which we know nothing and can never enter; and which doubtless has not changed at all since the days of those puzzling people whose secrets we try in vain to probe.

H. W. Ponder, *Cambodian Glory*, Thornton Butterworth Ltd., London, 1936, p. 18.

Floodplains

ॐ

57
Raheng Flood

HOLT S. HALLETT

In their lower reaches, the huge rivers of South-East Asia meander through the vast levels of their alluvial plains. Every year, somewhere in the region, a swollen torrent overspills its banks and calamity ensues.

Thailand suffered twice in the 1870s, as told in this traveller's tale. The author, Holt Hallet, was employed from 1868 until 1879 by the Public Works Department in Burma, mainly engaged in engineering works for the control of the lower Irrawaddy River. A passionate railway enthusiast, in 1883 he returned to the region to investigate a potential rail route from Burma, through the Shan territories of Thailand, towards the Mekong River and southern China. He described the journey at a meeting of the Royal Geographical Society of London (of which he was a Fellow for thirty years) in 1885 and in the pages of his book of 1890, from which this abstract is taken.

W HILE conversing about the country, Mr Stevens told me that in making railways in the plains of Siam, the occasional extraordinary rise of the rivers, and the consequent inundation of the country, would necessitate high embankments. At Raheng, in November 1878, he had the opportunity of observing the highest flood that had happened during the lifetime of the inhabitants. . . .

Rain being an unusual occurrence in Siam in November, Mr Stevens noted in his diary that on the 6th inst. it rained

120

heavily throughout the day, many logs of timber were drifting down the river, and that the water, topping the banks, inundated the city. During the night the river rose three feet, and rain continuing throughout the next day, the inundation increased, and the elephants were removed to the high ground. On Friday the 7th, the heavy rain continued, and there was a great rush of water from the hills at the back of his house, carrying everything before it; fruit-trees and the slab palisade, besides 40 of his teak-logs, being washed away, and the floating grass drifted off the lake at the back of his house; and the house, although built on posts well rooted in the ground, was in great danger. In the evening he removed what he could into boats, and left for the night. Several of the villages in the neighbourhood were swept away, the houses floating down the river with the people in them. There had never been such a rise since Raheng was founded.

Some of the governor's buildings were destroyed; rafts of timber were drifting past from Lakon; and the inhabitants of Raheng and the neighbouring villages all took refuge in their boats. The river rose two feet above the floor of his house, or 8½ feet above the river-bank. Several rafts broke up below the city, and 140 houses were washed away.

The next morning was fine, and the people returned to their houses, as the water was falling rapidly. The flood rose seven feet in twenty hours, and on its fall left a creek three feet deep on each side of his house. There was a great loss of property. Rice was not to be had, and many of the people found themselves starving on the Monday. The flood continued right down to Bangkok, and rose 10½ feet on the fields a gunshot distance to the west of the river at Kamphang Pet, 4½ feet on the fields to the east, and the same height under the governor's house at that place.

In the 'Siam Repository' for July 1873, there is a description of the great inundation which occurred in 1831, which, like the flood described by Mr Stevens, was due to heavy rainfall in the north. The flood lay from three-quarters of a fathom to one and a half fathom on the rice-fields of the northern provinces, varying with the height of the land. Flowing southwards, it swamped the low lands in the neighbourhood of Ayuthia, the former capital of Siam, to the varying depths of one and three fathoms, and the rice-fields and orchards of Bangkok to from three-quarters to one and a quarter fathom.

Within Bangkok the surface of the ground was covered to the depths of half and three-quarters of a fathom; and noblemen, great and small, whose duties required them to visit the king, paddled their boats to the doors of the inner palace buildings. Between Bangkok and Ayuthia, as the flood rose above the floors, which are raised several feet from the ground, the people elevated a temporary floor, and made egress and ingress through the windows. Some were obliged to erect the floor upon the roof-beams of their houses, and to enter and leave by the gable-ends. The great plains looked like a sea; and one night during a storm the drifting masses of floating plants, gathering against some houses, swept them away, many of the sleeping occupants perishing.

Holt S. Hallett, *A Thousand Miles on an Elephant in the Shan States*, William Blackwood and Sons, London, 1890, pp. 411–13.

58
Mattabong Plain

D. O. KING

The remarkable seasonal lakes of South-East Asia are formed where the annual flood is impounded by the natural topography of the plain. The largest, now usually known by its Cambodian name of Tonle Sap, was already famous in the mid-nineteenth century for its huge expanse at high levels and the abundance of fish harvested from its waters.

When D. O. King spent a year in 1857–8 travelling from Bangkok through what were then (to him and other foreigners) the 'unknown lands of Eastern Siam and Cambodia', the western part of the lake lay within Thai borders and was naturally seen as an extension of the Mattabong plain. King's paper to the Royal Geographical Society of London was posted from Newport, Rhode Island, and read to the Society in June 1859.

T HE provincial town of Mattabong is situated on both sides of a river of that name, in the centre of a large plain. The country, for nearly 100 miles around it, is flooded with water soon after the commencement of the rains; travelling becomes impossible, except in boats, and wild animals are driven off to the mountains. The existence of a large lake to the eastward has been reported to foreigners ever since their residence in Siam; and in the map accompanying M. de Pallegoix's work it is incorrectly inserted. The native accounts of its size were found to be not far from the truth; and I passed completely round the shores, everywhere being pleasantly diversified with forest and open prairie. The natives hold the lake in a sort of superstitious fear, its rough waves causing many accidents to their small canoes; and squalls and waterspouts are of frequent occurrence. During the months of January, February, and March, when the water has drained off the surrounding country, the lake appears alive with fish, and the inhabitants collect large quantities of them. From September to December the banks are overflowed from 10 to 20 feet deep. In the lake we failed to get bottom at 10 fathoms. At the close of the dry season, in May, frequent shoals occur in its bed, and a boat drawing 2 feet of water is all its shallowness will allow.

D. O. King, 'Travels in Siam and Cambodia', *Journal of the Royal Geographical Society*, Vol. 30, 1860, p. 179.

59
The Great Lake of Cambodia

HENRI MOUHOT

A second traveller of the 1850s, Henri Mouhot, passed through Cambodia to what was then a lacustrine frontier in the centre of Tonle Sap.

T HE entrance to the great lake of Cambodia is grand and beautiful. The river becomes wider and wider, until at last it is four or five miles in breadth; and then you enter the immense sheet of water called Tonli-Sap, as large and full of motion as a sea. It is more than 120 miles long, and must be at least 400 in circumference.

The shore is low, and thickly covered with treses, which are half submerged; and in the distance is visible an extensive range of mountains whose highest peaks seem lost in the clouds. The waves glitter in the broad sunshine with a brilliancy which the eye can scarcely support, and, in many parts of the lake, nothing is visible all around but water. In the centre is planted a tall mast, indicating the boundary between the kingdoms of Siam and Cambodia.

Henri Mouhot, *Travels in the Central Parts of Indo-China (Siam), Cambodia and Laos during the Years 1858, 1859, and 1860*, John Murray, London, 1864, Vol. 1, p. 272.

60
Tonle-sap

ANON.

In the 1930s, tourists could enjoy the sights of the great lake Tonle Sap from the deck of a steamer.

T HE steamer bears northwards, in the direction of the landing-stages on the opp. bank, across the *Tonle-sap*, or 'Great sheet of sweet water', by that part called *Great Lake*.

In summer, the Tonle-sap is a regular inland sea, subject to storms, whereas, after the winter, it is but one vast swamp, choked with reeds and traversed by shallow channels. This low-lying stretch extends, from N.-W. to S.-E., for a distance of 130 k. and serves a very special purpose, such as nature assigned to Lake Moeris, in Egypt, viz to act as a reservoir for the floods.

The Me-kong is swollen, in its upper reaches, by the heavy rains which drench the Yun-nan and the Laos from the end of May to Sept. Very soon the river swells inordinately, when its lower part, which in the dry season flowed down towards the sea, has a certain proportion of its yellow waters forced back into the arm of the lake, swamps the grassy stretches and reaches the trees on the fringe of the forest, while the mingled waters of the other rivers, one and all in spate, are lost in it. When the highest level is reached, the water is from 8 to 9 m. deep.

The area covered by the Lake, which at low-water-mark was but 2,000 sq. kil., is 9,000 sq. kil., when high-water is reached, storing up about 50,000 millions of cub. m. of water.

For a time, we keep fairly close to the banks, among the green tufts formed by the emerging tops of the trees, then the steamer stands off somewhat. The Lake, swollen and with its area increased to more than three times what it was, has all the appearance of a sea; to the r. and to the l. of us nothing but sky and water, the latter having put on an emerald hue under the sparkling rays of the tropical sun.

In December, when the river subsides, the direction of the current is reversed, the Tonle-sap is gradually emptied, but the waters, as they sink to a lower leave behind a portion of the wealth they contain: slime to ensure a rich crop of rice, fish caught in such quantities that they are the staple food of the natives, with a surplus for export to the Far East.

After February, the level of the water sinks rapidly, thousands of small boats engage in the business of fishing. Presently the lakes dry up to such a degree that the sampans have considerable difficulty in crossing them, and even have to be dragged sometimes, over the mud.

Beyond the fields fit for cultivation, there extends round the lake a belt of poor lands, fairly level in character, covered with light woods, which soon give way to the fine forest in which the more precious kinds of trees are to be found, and which is peopled by a plentiful fauna (tigers, panthers, leopards, wild boar, gaurs, buffaloes, wild oxen, stags, deer, etc.).

In the vicinity of the Lakes are to be encountered the cayman, the otter, the water-tortoise, the water-hen, the sultana hen, the water-rail, the teal, the small duck, the snipe, the diver, the cormoran, etc....

Guide Madrolle: Indo-China, Hachette, Paris, 1931, pp. 22–3.

61
Floods

E. J. H. CORNER

The periodic cycle of Tonle Sap is repeated on a smaller scale in many other places in South-East Asia where seasonal flood levels are controlled by the flow in connected river systems. The extraordinary experience of boating through the flooded forest at Danau (the name means 'seasonal lake'), near Mawai, in eastern Johor, Malaysia, in the late 1930s was described by John Corner.

As Assistant Director of the Gardens Department, Straits Settlements, from 1929 to 1945, John Corner was based in Singapore. During the pre-war years, he travelled widely in Peninsular Malaysia collecting and observing plants and fungi, at times with a trained monkey on his shoulder. He later taught botany at Cambridge University, England, and through the Royal Society of London (of which he is a Fellow) promoted tropical forest research and expeditions, several of which he himself led. Now Emeritus Professor of Tropical Botany, his eminence has been recognized by numerous awards. He has written many scientific papers and several books with an inimitable, lively style that has inspired a generation of younger readers.

I T happened, nevertheless, that I had planned to spend Easter week-end, 25–29 March 1932, on the Sedili Besar. It began to rain when I arrived at Mawai at 8 a.m. on Good Friday, but we took Sultan's motor-boat up to the floating house at Danau where we lodged for the next four nights. It poured incessantly until 3 p.m. when the skies cleared. Such bad luck for collecting had happened before and I gave little thought to it, but Hasan with long experience tied the motor-boat with two ropes to the upper part of the trunk of a little tree some fifty feet high, which stood on the bank beside the floating house. There were two or three of these rafts up river from Mawai, though none below. Big trunks were nailed and lashed together with poles to make a platform on which an attap hut was built, and the trunks were moored by stout rotans to two large trees on the bank. A Malay family lived in each on river-fish, fowls that ran about the platform, forest-produce, and such rice and other commodities that barter could obtain from Mawai. Each house had a dog to warn against the tiger, a *kerah* monkey whose screeching warned against the snake that might swim aboard, and a quantity of fish-traps, coiled rotans, fire-wood, and spare oars piled on the narrow platform. What with the unending gossip of adults on this occasion, the scrambling of the children, the snarling of the dog, the chattering of the *kerah*, the smoke, and the smell of dried fish, I decided to sleep in the motor-boat. It bumped all night against the raft. The rain recommenced, beat upon the awning, and splashed into the straining and jolting boat. At length, near dawn, I snatched some sleep of exhaustion, to be awoken by a strange and loud hissing that filled the ears and all around; the rain had stopped. I looked out on an unfamiliar expanse of water. Logs were swirling past half-submerged trees; their branches were swaying, tugging, and bobbing all around, and their leaves were jerking and swishing in the turmoil and eddies. The opposite bank with its small clearing was not there. I thought we had broken loose and were travelling down river, when a trunk rolled into view. I looked for the ropes, and they were not there. I could not recognise the scene of yesterday. Then I saw that the prow of the motor-boat was almost submerged and that the ends of the ropes passed vertically into the water. In fact the river had risen over twenty feet in the night and I was level with the crown of the little tree to which the ropes had been attached. We were *in situ* and, thankfully, just in time to avoid a sinking. A coil of rotan was produced; the boat was lashed to the raft, and the ropes untied from the prow; Sultan recovered them on his next journey up the river. The water stayed at this height during Saturday and Sunday but fell about two feet on Monday. It rained that night and was still raining when we left on Tuesday, but the river was falling. We reached Mawai after dodging many floating trunks and found the jetty still awash; it had been completely submerged and the ground-floors of the shops had been flooded, but my car had been parked, luckily, on high ground behind the village.

During the three days at Danau we paddled in a canoe through the flooded forest. The force of the flood was lost among the trees, though impossible to stem on the main river. I could stand up at a height of twenty feet above the floor of the forest and collect from the tops of the undergrowth trees, though the collections could only be bundled up in the hope that they would last until I returned to Singapore and could have them dried. Wherever we touched leaf, twig, trunk, or floating logs, showers of insects tumbled into the canoe. Everything that could had climbed above the water. Ants ran over everything. I bailed insects and spiders instead of water, even scorpions, centipedes, and frogs. All around there was the incessant swishing of the half-submerged leaves, the oblong lanceolate form of which was eminently successful for the occasion, and the incessant honking of frogs and toads. Lizards clung to the trunks; earthworms wriggled in the water, with snapping fish. I found in those short trees many birds' nests, one of which was a *reductio ad absurdum* for it consisted of two pairs of twigs crossed and entwined at right angles with one small egg perched over the central gap. As the water receded, there was the tell-tale smear of mud, and stranded trunks and branches were jammed into the small crowns suspended with débris of everything that could float. The subsiding waters revealed the tops of stilt-roots and I came, thus, to understand that the maximum height of these roots, which I had measured near Mawai as c. 30 ft. on trees of *Calophyllum* and *Palaquium*, was that of the rain-floods to which the trees were subjected. I realised the importance of the hillocks in and around the swamp-forest to animal life, for anything that could escape the flood must have fled there. We met no corpses. Pig, deer, tapir, rat, porcupine, leopard, tiger, monitor lizard, and snakes must have congregated on those hillocks in disquieting proximity. I saw, later, the trampling of elephants round the foot of Bt Kuing and Bt Tinjau Laut. The commotion of flood and feet must have churned up the statistical regularity of sediment beloved of numerical ecologists. Fallen trunks were shifted long distances by the floods;

On their way to Kinabalu, Burbidge and Veitch (see Passage 84) forded the swollen Tampusak River on buffalo-back. From F. W. Burbidge, *The Gardens of the Sun: Or a Naturalist's Journal on the Mountains and in the Forests and Swamps of Borneo and the Sulu Archipelago*, John Murray, London, 1880.

old trunks, buried in humus, were floated out and stranded upright in the crowns of small trees; all the upper soil-strata had been deranged. Bracket-fungi that had withstood the rush had a layer of debris deposited on them into which their hyphae would then grow as knobs, spikes and clavarioid branches among seedlings of epiphytes. Loose pioneer vegetation along the river was washed away; new debris accumulated in creeks to supply new niches for fortuitous seedlings. As for the trees themselves, none that could not survive the drowning of roots and bole for several days would survive; perhaps the pneumatophores had a store of oxygen that supplied the roots. How often big floods occurred I could not find out but, certainly, two or three times a year. They are the great test of fitness which rules the life of the swamp-forest; they are ecological experiments of a surpassing magnitude that need to be witnessed.

E. J. H. Corner, 'The Freshwater Swamp-forest of South Johore and Singapore', *Gardens' Bulletin*, Supplement No. 1, 1978, pp. 9–11.

62
Danau Lamadjan

ODOARDO BECCARI

The extensive lake complex in the Upper Kapuas River, West Kalimantan, forms by direct drainage of the surrounding land. It was visited by Beccari in May 1866.

O N the 13th, as soon as the welcome call of the 'Wa-wa' told us that dawn was nigh, I awoke my men, and for a wonder we actually managed to get off before sunrise.

It was one of those cool delicious mornings which are not infrequent in Borneo after violent rain. Many birds which had kept hidden during the bad weather were now flying from branch to branch. The river was still very full and the current strong, and our descent would have been rapid enough were we not often obliged to stop to remove the tree-trunks with which the flood had barred our way. By and by we came to the boat we had lost, caught in the fork of a tree above our heads and quite undamaged. The white and rosy flowers of a fine tree (*Dipterocarpus oblongifolius*, Bl.) perfumed the air strongly. Plants in blossom of many kinds which I had never seen beyond the hills increased in number as we progressed, taking the place of those which I had been wont to see on the Sarawak river. Often, within reach, we came across tree-trunks of overhanging branches loaded with epiphytes, amongst which the magnificent *Vanda suavis*, one of the most charming orchids of our hothouses, with its splendid racemes of big milky-white odorous flowers, was most conspicuous. Several species of *Ficus*, too, threw a cool shade over the water, attracting many birds who feed on their fruits.

The course of the river was very tortuous and its bed narrow, but the water spread widely in the forest on both sides. The space free of vegetation alone marked out its course, the banks being lost to view beneath the water. We paddled thus for six hours and my men slackened their work somewhat, being both hungry and tired. We landed at the first place where landing was possible, and cooked our rice. The river hereabouts had lost the aspect of a torrent, the flood of water having found its way through the forest. It was still very deep, however, but the current was less rapid. The trees along the banks no longer met overhead, but formed two high green vertical walls on either side. The light attracts the creepers towards the river, and among them a species of Connaracea (*P.B.* No. 3,384) was especially noticeable, having magnificent bunches of rosy flowers. Bauhinias and several Anonaceæ hung their festoons from tree to tree, giving an aspect of perfect impenetrability to the forest. Even the rotangs spread their great pinnated fronds towards the river, pushing through the dense surrounding foliage. To avoid several big bends and shorten the distance, we left the proper course of the stream from time to time, and cut through the flooded

131

forest. That navigation in the deep shade of the primeval trees is a thing never to be forgotten! We float amidst gigantic trunks as regular and straight as the columns of some immense basilica. It is high noon, and the powerful sun rays fall vertically on the dense cupola of foliage which, hungry for the light and heat, has fought its way upwards from the shade below. If here and there a straggling ray manages to penetrate the thick mass of leaves, it a reflected back by the black waters beneath.

At three p.m. we reached the Segrat hill, round whose base the river winds. This place is called Ujong Kayu Rattei, and has a Dyak village. The river assumes here the name of Umpanang....

As we approached the lakes the Umpanang increased in width; but, strange to say, the trees diminished in height, getting so low as to be not more than from ten to twenty feet above the water. But what surprises one most on entering the lake from the river is the very unusual colour of the great sheet of water before us. Looking straight down into its depths it appears so intensely black as to cause a certain sensation of fear. At times I felt as if the boat must sink in that unfathomable dark abyss! Our ideas on the specific gravity of water are naturally associated with the coloration which is familiar to us. They might be termed innate ideas; and even a child shows no surprise that a boat floats. But when waters show a coloration so different from the ordinary, even the notion one possesses instinctively of its specific gravity is shaken. These inky waters certainly do not tempt one to a plunge; whilst, as all know, the opposite feeling is elicited by limpid and transparent water, the mere sight alone of which is always pleasant and attractive.

The surface of the lake, clear and free from arboreal vegetation, extends only a few miles, but nowhere could we see a trace of dry land. As soon as we issued from the Umpanang, we sighted Lamadan, a village inhabited by Malays, towards which we proceeded. My people called the lake Danau Lamadjan, but I believe that it is better known to the Kapuas people as Danau Seriang....

The lacustrine region, as a whole, must be of wide extent, but the water surface free from trees is, perhaps, never more than five or six miles in length. The natives of Lamadjan asserted that in very dry seasons some of these lakes dry up, leaving a prodigious quantity of fish exposed or densely packed in small pools, where they can be caught by hand. They also assured me that there is no mud on the bottom.

Odoardo Beccari, *Wanderings in the Great Forests of Borneo: Travels and Researches of a Naturalist in Sarawak*, Archibald Constable and Co., London, 1904, pp. 180–4.

63
Lake Seriang

W. M. CROCKER

The Kapuas lakes of West Kalimantan, Indonesia, were later visited by W. M. Crocker in 1880.

I have very recently visited Lake Seriang, in Dutch territory. After a four days' journey up the Batang Lupar, in a canoe manned by fifty men, Mr Maxwell, the Resident of the district, myself, and party reached Lobok Antu Fort, walked to Nanga Badow, where the Dutch are building a small military station, and on the following day started at 6 a.m., and after a three hours' walk reached a small stream named the Pesaya, down which we pulled for about four hours before we reached the lake. During the last hour of our pull we found the whole neighbourhood under water, and passed through a desolate-looking country, there being nothing but a little brushwood above high-water mark, and the blackened and charred remains of what were once fine jungle trees.

This lake has been described as 25 miles long and 9 miles wide, and we found it a fine sheet of water, with four gunboats anchored off an island. Nevertheless, I was told that in

1877, after a drought, it quite dried up; in fact, the remains of a settlement, since abandoned, were pointed out to us on Majang Island, which was attacked by Dyaks, who took advantage of the drought to approach by land. The Dyaks were driven off, but they fired the jungle in their retreat, destroying the forest for miles around.

The following extract is taken from my Diary, written on Lake Seriang, Friday, February 27th, 1880:—

'A heavy squall during the night had cleared the air. I came on deck to find it delightfully cool, and the view over the lake very pretty. To the westward lie the nearest mountains, the highest being about 2000 feet. The lake in the wet season stretches away to the foot of the nearest of these hills, although there is now about two miles of jungle intervening. On all sides, at a considerable distance, mountains can be seen on a clear day, the several streams from which empty themselves into the lake. The only high land is a small island on which once stood a settlement. It is of no great extent, being at present only a few feet above high-water mark. A Malay told me yesterday that the last time he visited the lake the whole country was inundated. On that occasion he saw a Malay boy eating sugar-cane, and on asking where he got it, as he saw nothing but water, the boy told him he had dived down to their garden, which was on the island, and at that time several feet under water. Our boys amuse themselves fishing, and seem delighted at their success; the lake is literally swarming with fish, and in the dry season, when the waters abate, they are caught by the Malays in immense quantities, their roes only being preserved for the Pontianak market.'

W. M. Crocker, 'Notes on Sarawak and North Borneo', *Proceedings of the Royal Geographical Society*, Vol. 3, 1881, p. 203.

64

Peatswamp

J. WYATT-SMITH

The dark, acidic waters so daringly declared drinkable by Beccari are also characteristic of the peatswamp forests that lie behind the coastal mangrove belt at equatorial latitudes. The waterlogged peat is rain-fed, and overlies ancient estuarine mud. As observed in the extract that follows, the base of the 15-metre thick accumulation of peat near Marudi, Sarawak, now about 45 kilometres from the seashore, proved to be only some 4,250 years old. The huge tracts of peatswamp now extending behind sheltered coasts on Sumatra, Peninsular Malaysia, and Borneo apparently developed within the past 4,000 years advancing at a rate that, at times, must have averaged more than 1 kilometre per century.

A technical account of this strange, trackless terrain was compiled for the 1963 *Manual of Malayan Silviculture*, from which this abstract is taken. The information derived from the combined experience of many officers of the then Malayan Forest Service (MFS) and others. The principal author, John Wyatt-Smith, joined the MFS in 1939, retiring in 1963 as Silvicultural Research Officer. He was also President of the Malayan Nature Society and a founder member of the Malayan Scientific Association. He subsequently became Professor of Forestry, University of Ibadan, Nigeria, then forestry/natural resources adviser to the UK Overseas Development Administration and, finally, a well-respected international forestry consultant.

D ECAY of vegetation is prevented and peat formed where there is permanent water-logging and anaerobic conditions prevail, caused by the decrease of inflowing mineral water and a resulting acidity increase to a pH value of between 3 and 4. The water is almost black in appearance, but is clear when held up against the light and has been likened to tea or weak coffee.

The peat in the west is of varying thickness due to it overlying clay and sandy strips of higher land—the old banks of rivers and flood deposits—and which often still occur as islands and bars of dry land within the peat swamps. Some of these areas in the west certainly carried mangrove forest prior to the development of peat swamp forest; diatoms taken from mud beneath four feet of peat in Telok Forest Reserve south of Klang, Selangor, were almost all of marine origin, and a number of the species were common to those from surface mud of Port Swettenham mangroves about ten miles away, and plant remains of typical mangrove species such as *Carapa* and *Bruguiera* have been found in the 'peat' layer immediately above the clay in the same reserve. This has been confirmed in Sarawak where a pollen analysis of a core about forty feet in depth indicated that the peat developed over mangrove; the age of the peat at the base of the core was 4,270 (± 70) years. The depth of peat varies from a few to many feet; depths of over eighteen feet have been recorded in the Kuala Selangor area and of ten feet in a detailed survey carried out at the Federal Experimental Station, Chenderong, Perak. In the deep-peat areas there is usually several feet of peaty water between the true fibrous peat and the alluvial clay beneath. Levels have shown that the area covered by Kuala Langat North Forest Reserve is dome-shaped and that the clay layer is itself ten feet or more above sea level, the dome-shaped nature of the swamp is similar to that found in extensive peat swamps in other countries, and it probably occurs in other large peat swamps in Malaya. On the other hand it is probable that the level of some of the Malayan peat areas, and in particular the tongues up valleys, rises steadily the further the peat occurs inland.

Along the east coast the peat is less well developed and in general shallower than found in the west, though in south Pahang a depth of sixteen feet was recorded along a road trace to the west of Menchali Forest Reserve and of thirteen feet in the eastern part of Lesong Forest Reserve.

J. Wyatt-Smith, 'Swamp Forest', *Malayan Forest Records*, No. 23, 1963, pp. 111–15/3–4.

Trees and Forests

ॐ

65
Trees of Java

H. W. PONDER

Man and nature together, as partners, can do wonderful things. On tour in Indonesia in the 1930s, Ponder was amazed at the richness of the natural tree flora and entranced by the choice roadside specimens in Java, where an enlightened planting programme had created 'hundreds upon hundreds of miles' of avenues throughout the island.

T HE trees of Java have earned a whole literature to themselves. Forestry experts estimate the numbers of distinct sorts at anything between five and ten thousand. But without presuming to attempt to approach them on so devastatingly grand a scale, the few that the ordinary layman succeeds in identifying are quite interesting enough. Heading the list for sheer breathtaking magnificence is the *Poinciana*, well named by the French, in its native land of Madagascar, the 'Flamboyant', and by the English 'Flame of the Forest', for this tree in full flower must surely be nature's supreme achievement in the realm of colour. Bare in the dry East Monsoon, the branches break suddenly at the change of season into a dazzling blaze of scarlet blossom which spreads day by day until it is a mass of flaming glory almost too blinding for human eyes to bear. Then, as quickly, the foliage appears in feathery sprays, supplying a perfect setting to the flaming masses of bloom. For a month or six weeks the show

displays itself daily in all its glory in an ever increasing luxuriance of foliage, until at last there begin the gentle showers
of falling blossoms that cover the ground under the trees with
a brilliant carpet, swept up with meticulous care daily;
for these trees are mostly planted to form avenues along
important roads in the large towns. And then, slowly and
imperceptibly, for the process takes some weeks, the scarlet
seems to melt away as the green foliage thickens, as though it
had been submerged and drowned by the rising green tide.
And at last, 'flamboyant' no longer, the *Poinciana* enters upon
another phase as a gracious and lovely shade tree.

Only second to it in brilliance is the *cassia*, which bears
masses of yellow blossoms like those of our laburnum, and is
called *hoedjan mas* (golden rain) by the natives. Another
beautiful tree is one they call *daoen koepoe-koepoe* (butterfly
leaf) bearing dainty clusters of frail pink and white blooms
like flights of butterflies; and the *tamarind*, a native of tropical
Africa, with red streaked yellow flowers is also a familiar
roadside tree. It has a practical as well as an æsthetic value, its
pods making a delicious jam and a popular syrup known as
stroop asem.

Two another red blossomed trees which visitors sometimes confuse with the *Poinciana* are the *sepatoe dea*, or Forest
Tulip, and the *dadap*. The former is a native tree planted along
the roadsides at high altitudes too cool for the heat loving
Flamboyant. It bears flowers which grow singly, high among
the topmost branches, and are only visible as splashes of
brilliant colour against the sky. It is only when they fall that
the beauty of these strange blossoms can be seen. They are
not unlike immense sealing-wax red sweetpeas, and are as big
as a native woman's hand. The *dadap* has an equally bright
red flower of similar shape but quite small. It also is a native
tree, and is much planted for shade in coffee plantations, as it
grows quickly and does not exhaust the soil. Its seeds contain
a valuable alkaloid, and the bark of one variety, known as
dadap bong, yields the poison *erythrinine*. Several sorts of
Albizzia are also planted as shade trees with coffee or tea; and

so is *koveel toro*, from whose light, flexible wood walking-sticks are made.

Hundreds upon hundreds of miles of country roads, as well as those in the towns, have been converted into avenues in Java by the planting of shade trees. The favourite, and most familiar, is the stately *Kenari*, which grows to a great size, and whose nuts are much sought after by the Javanese, who eat them with their rice and also extract oil from them. The *Sana* is another the sight of which soon grows familiar, for it is easily recognised in its so called 'wintering' period when, like the teak, it sheds its leaves and stands looking strangely naked and forlorn against the background of rich tropic foliage. The timber from this tree is a beautiful reddish hardwood known as *lenggoa*, and trees sometimes attain such a size that table tops five or six feet in diameter have been cut from a single cross section of its trunk.

H. W. Ponder, *Javanese Panorama*, Seeley Service and Co. Ltd., London, 1942, pp. 185–6.

66
Amherstia

G. T. GASCOIGNE

Several of the most ornamental roadside trees that flourish in South-East Asia have been naturalized from other tropical regions. As Gascoigne noted, this is not so in the case of the exquisite Amherstia, which is truly native in Burma (Myanmar) and, in origin, exclusive to that country.

A MONG the most beautiful of the ornamental trees is the Amherstia nobilis, which is entirely peculiar to Burma. It has the most graceful of forms, with brilliant green foliage and glowing scarlet flowers, which fall droopingly from exquisite pendulous branches. The flowers partake a little of the Dielytria, and seem to drape themselves and hang like great crimson tassels. One of the most beautiful specimens of this tree that I saw grew in Mr Smeaton's garden at Rangoon; and many is the hour I have spent peering admiringly into its cool emerald depths, and letting my eyes feast on its glorious flowers. A very interesting and charming little account of it is given by Lieutenant-General Albert Fytche in his work on Burma, and I have ventured to quote his account of the tree in his own words: 'The Amherstia was first discovered near Trocla, on the Salween river, by Dr Wallich, and named by him after Lady Amherst, the wife of the then Governor-General of India. Dr Wallich says that there can be no doubt that this tree, when in foliage and blossom, is the most strikingly superb object which can possibly be imagined. It is unequalled in the flora of the East. Its precise habitat was unknown until 1865, when it was discovered by the Rev. C. Parish growing wild on the banks of the Yoondzaleen river. From the fact of old trees of this species being found only in the vicinity of sacred places, it was for a long time supposed not to be indigenous to Burma, but to have been introduced by Buddhist pilgrims from the Shan States or China. It is often planted in company with the Jonesia, which is called by the Burmese the wife of the Amherstia. The tree first discovered by Dr Wallich was growing beside a Jonesia; and the symmetry and numerous graceful raceme of crimson and orange blossoms of the latter well fit it for such companionship.

G. T. Gascoigne, *Among Pagodas and Fair Ladies: An Account of a Tour through Burma*, A. D. Innes and Co., London, 1896, pp. 213–14.

67
The Carmine Cherry

F. KINGDON WARD

Travelling in northern Burma in 1931 (on this occasion, with my father as his companion), Kingdon Ward was almost overwhelmed by the glory of the Carmine Cherry breaking into bloom.

T HIS, the most magnificent hardy flowering tree I have ever seen, is intimately related to *Prunus puddum*— perhaps only a form of that species. On March 20th, close to our camp, I noticed a big cherry tree about to flower. Two days later it was in full bloom. It was quite leafless and just a mass of blossom, stark crimson. For a minute I stood before it, unable to speak a word, drunk with the glory of it. It was not to be believed. When the everyday world came back to me, I was in doubt for a moment whether I wept, shouted, or said a prayer. And then I turned to Cranbrook and said 'Golly!' in a sort of awed whisper.

Prunus puddum, as it grows in the Adung valley, is one of the largest of the deciduous trees, only the elm outstripping it. It grows eighty to a hundred feet high, and its branches have a very wide spread. The ruby-red flower-buds appear about the middle of March, in compact clusters towards the ends of the branches, and the tree is swiftly transformed into a frozen fountain of precious stones. As the buds open the stalks lengthen till the flowers are hanging down. Then the whole tree bursts suddenly into carmine flame. To see the setting sun through its branches when the tree is in full bloom is a thing not easily put out of one's mind.

There were only scattered trees along the river bank, and all of them on the far, sheltered side, difficult to reach. But in the forest, up to the 7000-feet ridge, the carmine cherry stood out like beacon fires.

F. Kingdon Ward, *Plant Hunter's Paradise*, Jonathan Cape, London, 1937, pp. 149–50.

68
Along the Rawas

HENRY O. FORBES

The natural climax vegetation of the equatorial zone of South-East Asia is evergreen tropical rain forest. This marvellous forest is unrivalled in its stupendous grandeur and incalculable biological richness. These marvels were closely observed by Henry Forbes who travelled and collected in the region for five years as a bachelor (1879–84) and two (1885–6) accompanied by his young wife, Annabella. Henry's book, *A Naturalist's Wanderings in the Eastern Archipelago* (1885), turned an energetic and scholarly eye on the natural world; Annabella's, *Insulinde: The Experiences of a Naturalist's Wife in the Eastern Archepelago*, touched graphically on some of the tougher aspects of their early married life. Forbes later spent three years at the Canterbury Museum, New Zealand, until, in 1894, he took up the post of Director of the Liverpool Museums, UK, where he passed the remainder of his career.

In this short passage from his book, Forbes rhapsodized on the riparian forest of Sumatra and its wildlife.

T HE display of flower and fruit along the Rawas river … could scarcely have been richer. While Oak-trees in full blossom characterised the Rupit, *Dipterocarpeæ*, the family which gives us the Camphor-tree and supplies a great deal of the dammar of commerce, and some of which are among the tallest of trees, were along the Rawas the distinguishing feature—though clumps of oak were plentiful enough too—the brilliant pink and rose coloured 'wings' that adorn their ripening fruits having the appearance of tassels hanging from the tips of the branches all over their immense crowns. Over some of the highest trees, and spread continuously across the forest for hundreds of yards at a stretch, was a Leguminose climber (*Bauhinia*) with rich orange and scarlet flowers. Blue fishing-hawks (*Poliætus humilis*) sat in motionless watch on the projecting limbs of trees; Rhinoceros birds (*Anthracocerus convexus* and *Rhytidoceros subruficollis*) clambered on the fruit-laden fig-trees, conspicuous by the rich colour of their beaks—derived from the oilgland at the tail in *B. rhinoceros*. Herons and Bitterns hunted in the sandy bends, kingfishers flew out from every corner, and flocks of sand-plovers zig-zagged away with a frightened scream as we passed along; while on the projecting stones on the river, black cormorants (*Phalocracorax*) eagerly watched for their finny prey, and flocks of pure white egrets displayed to advantage their spotless plumage against the dark foliage of the tops of the trees.

Henry O. Forbes, *A Naturalist's Wanderings in the Eastern Archipelago: A Narrative of Travel and Exploration from 1878 to 1883*, Harper and Brothers, New York, 1885, p. 252.

69
The Forests

J. R. LOGAN

Logan, the pioneer journalist of the mid-1800s, painted a graphic picture of the tropical rain forests that spread from shore to shore across the lowlands of the South-East Asian archipelago in his time.

T REES of gigantic forms and exuberant foliage rise on every side: each species shooting up its trunk to its utmost measure of development, and striving, as it seems, to escape from the dense crowd. Others, as if no room were left for them to grow in the ordinary way, emulate the shapes and motions of serpents, enwrap their less pliant neighbours in their folds, twine their branches into one connected canopy, or hang down, here, loose and swaying in the air, or in festoons from tree to tree, and there, stiff and rooted like the shrouds which support the mast of a ship. No sooner has decay diminished the green array of a branch, than its places is supplied by epiphites, chiefly fragrant orchidaceæ, of singular and beautiful forms. While the eye in vain seeks to familiarize itself with the exuberance and diversity of the forest vegetation, the ear drinks in the sounds of life which break the silence and deepen the solitude. Of these, while the interrupted notes of birds, loud or low, rapid or long-drawn, cheerful or plaintive, and ranging over a greater or less musical compass are the most pleasing; the most constant are those of insects, which sometimes rise into a shrill and deafening clangour; and the most impressive, and those which bring out all the wildness and loneliness of the scene, are the prolonged complaining cries of the unkas, which rise, loud and more loud, till the twilight air is filled with the clear, powerful, and melancholy sounds. As we penetrate deeper into the forest, its animals, few at any one place, are soon seen to be, in reality, numerous and varied. Green and harmless snakes hang like tender branches. Others of deeper and mingled colours, but less innocuous, lie coiled up, or, dis-turbed by the human intruder, assume an angry and danger-ous look, but glide out of sight. Insects in their shapes and hues imitate leaves, twigs and flowers. Monkeys, of many sizes and colours, spring from branch to branch, or, in long trains, rapidly steal up the trunks. Deer, and amongst them the graceful palandoh, no bigger than a hare, and celebrated in Malayan poetry, on our approach fly startled from the pools which they and the wild hog most frequent. Lively squirrels, of different species, are everywhere met with. Amongst a great variety of other remarkable animals which range the forest, we may, according to our locality, en-counter herds of elephants, the rhinoceros, tigers of several sorts, the tapir, the babirusa, the orangutan, the sloth; and, of the winged tribes, the gorgeously beautiful birds of paradise, the loris, the peacock, and the argus pheasant.

J. R. Logan, 'The Present Condition of the Indian Archipelago', *Journal of the Indian Archipelago*, Vol. 1, 1847, pp. 7–8.

70
Tropical Dendrons

E. J. H. CORNER

John Corner, from the perspective of Emeritus Professor of
Tropical Botany at Cambridge University and a Fellow of the
Royal Society of London, has set the marvels of the South-East
Asian rain forests in their global and scientific context, and adopted
terms originally introduced to describe the South American
equivalent to this vegetation.

T HE lofty dipterocarp tree represents the culmination of
tropical rain-forest in Malaysia, where many species
of the family Dipterocarpaceae construct the most luxuriant
forest on earth. The immense trunk, superbly engineered
and, consequently for its destruction, in high demand for
timber, branches at a height of 100 ft. into the large canopy
of small leaves, many twigs, and spreading limbs along which
animals may travel from tree to tree, and eat, sleep, and give
birth without returning to the ground. That is tree life. The
small leaves glitter, reflecting light and transmitting sun flecks
into the depths beneath, where the slanting rays of the
ascending and descending sun penetrate.

Where tropical forest has been cleared by hand, for the
bulldozer smashes everything, a few big trees are left in the
open because they are the ironwood trees from which the axe
rebounds. In picturesque grandeur they relieve the sad
monotony of human endeavour until by decay, against which
their hard timber is no guarantee, they too succumb. We
used to call them tropical dendrons, so gracefully pruned in
forest shade of the lower limbs, and saw in them glimpses
that the older artists caught of the passing primeval forest of
Europe. Bereft of the close surround, exposed to wind, and
serving for the roosts of the birds that bring the seeds of
destructive mistletoe and strangling fig, they die back,

hollow, and decay. To catch these dendrons in their prime is a duty of the botanist; they may not be seen much longer.

* * *

High rainfall, sunshine, and temperature make the tropical forest the prime of plant life. Plants have never been able to work dry methods. By origin aquatic, they have inherited this need for water and, even on land, grow best where its supply is unlimited. But stagnant water is not enough. Roots prefer daily rain oxygenated by the atmosphere as the tidal substitute. Then, through photosynthesis and making of cellulose, the more the sunshine the bigger is the frame that the plant builds. Warmth increases the rate of all plant activities, but warmth with high rainfall is always tempered from excess: even on cloudless days the shade temperature in the rain-forest climate seldom reaches 38 °C. So, under the optimum set of conditions, the flowering plant has entrained fungus and animal to build in those fortunate parts of the world the finest forest; and to the whole extent of this primeval tropical forest the traveller Humboldt gave the name hylea, taken from the Greek word for aboriginal woodland.

As soon as plants go beyond the hylea, circumstances for their growth become difficult. Conditions become exacting; the plants need to be specialized; the vegetation that they compose begins to become characteristic. Rainfall lessens and the end is desert. Trees become deciduous; twigs are thin and dry, or thick and fleshy; desert plants tend to be leafless, spinous, or succulent. Seasons enter and lead to winter. Days lengthen, nights shorten; then days shorten and nights lengthen. Periods of prolonged activity are followed by periods of inactivity, imposed upon the plant in its vegetative state and while it is a seed. Temperate lands have the spring flush of leaves, the early summer flowering, the autumn fruiting, and, between times, the miscellaneous flowering, which is determined by the succession of lengthening or shortening days. Prairie, misty mountain-top, and tundra have their character as water, light, and temperature approach the minimum for plant growth.

The one thing that cannot be said about the hylean forest is that it has character. Its plants have, of course, specifically or generically, but as a whole it is far too manifold to be singular. Trees differ side by side, as do the epiphytes and climbers on them. One may be leafing, another flowering, and another fruiting. On the ground are palms, bananas, burrowing gingers, ferns, and dicotyledonous herbs of perennial or short-lived habit as different as they represent so many families. The ground flora has no uniformity whatsoever; nor have the trees. There are big trees and little trees. There are big-leafed trees with small flowers, and small-leafed trees with big flowers, as there are leafy parasites with small flowers (the mistletoe family), and leafless parasites with enormous flowers, as *Rafflesia*. Some leaf continually, others intermittently; yet others are deciduous. There are all kinds of flowers and fruits. There are big seeds and small, which sprout at once, and others that are dormant for various periods from a matter of days to a sleep of years. In the hylea the flowering plants have produced almost every variation that seems possible on every part of the original theme, and these variations fit into the growing complexity as a forest.

E. J. H. Corner, *The Life of Plants*, Weidenfeld and Nicolson, London, 1964, pp. 151–2 and 261–2.

71
Figs

HENRY O. FORBES

In 1878, Forbes marvelled at the variety of wild figs. identifying the 'waringins' and 'kawats' as the tyrants of the vegetable world.

A MONG the most attractive shrubs were the species of figs, of which there was an endless variety. The whole group of the *Artocarpeæ* is remarkable for beauty of foliage and fruit—as the hollow receptacle in which their minute flowers and true fruits are developed is often popularly called—for their striking habit and for their useful products. Some of them, as the india-rubber producing waringins and kawats species of *Urostigma* (*U. microcarpum*, and *consociatum*), are among the giants of the vegetable world, and its most relentless parasites and tyrants. Brought by some wandering bird or fruit-eating quadruped to the cleft of a high tree, the seed germinating drops down all round its host long tendril-like roots, which in a few seasons become indissoluble bonds that interlace, grow together, and close up the tree-stem that gave it its support, till its life is choked out, and only here and there, before it finally disappears, can it be seen through lat-ticed apertures, like an Inquisition martyr built into the wall. The young kawat grows, shoots upward its top and

> spreads her arms,
> Branching so broad and long, that on the ground
> The bended twigs take root; and daughters grow
> About the mother-tree, a pillared shade.

Less stately but not less beautiful are the shrub forms, the species of Hamplas (*Ficus microcarpa, amplas,* and *politoria*) whose rough leaves provide the natives with ready-made sandpaper; the *Ficus cordifolia*, the Amismata (*Ficus aspera*), and the Kihedjo—a bushy shrub, whose fruit, always in profusion along its branches, is when ripe of a rich purple hue, and unripe of the brightest vermilion or carmine colour, in bril-liant contrast to its dark foliage; while the semi-parasitic climbing *Ficus radicans* delights to cling to the tallest trees of the forest. Its fruit, which is as large as an orange, is put forth throughout the whole extent of its stem in profuse abundance, massed in clusters in every stage of growth; and as these in their passage to maturity assume all the different brilliant hues by which rich orange changes into the sombre shades of purple, the effect against the background of the tree-stem and of its own singularly chaste foliage is striking in the extreme, and is one of those objects that the eye can meet every day with renewed pleasure.

Henry O. Forbes, *A Naturalist's Wanderings in the Eastern Archipelago: A Narrative of Travel and Exploration from 1878 to 1883*, Harper and Brothers, New York, 1885, pp. 77–8.

72
Strangling Fig-trees

E. J. H. CORNER

Corner has explained the extraordinary lifestyle of the strangling figs that Forbes stigmatized as 'tyrants' of the forest.

IG-TREES whose trunks are composed of a basket-work of interlacing and anastomosing roots are called strangling figs because normally they begin life on other trees and gradually squeeze them to death. Birds, squirrels and monkeys, which eat the fruits, drop the seeds on the branches of forest-trees where they grow into epiphytic bushes that hold on by strong roots encircling the branches. From thence their roots spread down the trunk of the supporting tree to the ground, where they grow vigorously. Side-roots encircle the trunk, joining up with other side-roots where they touch, and aerial roots grow straight down into the soil from various heights. In other cases, the epiphytic bush may send at an early stage an aerial root straight to the ground and from this root, which is like a perpendicular cable, side-roots grow towards the trunk, as though they were able to see it, encircling it and ramifying over it. In either case, the supporting trunk becomes enveloped in a basket of fig-roots, through the crown of its support. As the fig-roots and their

149

supporting trunk increase in thickness they press upon each but the fig-roots, being the stronger, slowly crush the bark of the support against its wood with the effect that the supporting tree is gradually ringed and its limbs begin to die back, its crown becoming stag-headed and uneven. A long struggle ensues between parasite and host, but if the fig-plant is vigorous it surely kills its support and finally stands in its place on a massive basket of roots. This 'radical trunk' may reach a hundred feet high, according to height of the branch on which the seed germinated, and the initial cables that descend from the young epiphyte are commonly mistaken for the stems of climbers that have grown up from below. The dead trunk of the supporting tree rots away for many years in the basket of fig-roots. How long it takes to strangle a big forest-tree, we do not know but from the sprouting of the seed to the independence of the fig-tree can scarcely be less than a hundred years. Some kinds, like *F. sundaica*, *F. caulocarpa*, *F. benjamina* and, especially, *F. tinctoria*, are very destructive, yet others like *F. annulata* and *F. consociata*, appear seldom to kill their support, and, in fact, every transition to the ordinary climbing plant is displayed by our wild species. Considering how vigorous they are and how easily their seeds are distributed, it is a problem why strangling figs do not occur on most big trees in the forest. In parks and 'padangs' that are little cared for, they are generally common, occurring on every tree which is the roosting place of birds. Possibly ants carry off and eat many of the fig-seeds.

In addition to the basketing roots which encircle the support, some strangling figs develop aerial roots from their branches and even from their twigs. Such roots may hang in festoons. They remain fine and slender till they reach the ground and then one or more in a cluster thickens into a stout limb, like a trunk supporting the branch, and such is called a *pillar-root*. Trees with this habit we may term *banyan-trees* because it is the manner of growth of the famous Indian Banyan (*F. benghalensis*). By dropping new pillar-roots from their branches, as they continue to grow out, the crowns of

The 'waringin' or strangling fig, whose trunk (in the words of Wallace) 'is itself a forest of stems and aerial roots'. From Alfred Russel Wallace, *The Malay Archipelago: The Land of the Orang-Utan, and the Bird of Paradise*, 10th edn., Macmillan and Co., London, 1883.

banyans are extended far beyond the limits of ordinary trees and those of old specimens may cover vast areas. Only one Malayan species has this habit, namely the *Jejawi* or Malayan Banyan (*F. microcarpa*). The rest of our strangling figs have only basket-roots with, or without, tufts of aerial roots from the lower part of the branches or from their trunks.

Normally no strangling fig develops a main trunk from the top of its basket of roots. Instead, several twigs of the epiphytic bush grow out strongly and as they sag under their weight new twigs break from their uppersides to sag and branch in their turn, so that there is built up a many-limbed, wide-spreading and flat-topped crown with drooping lower branches from the characteristic shape of which a strangling fig can at once be distinguished in the canopy of the forest. But if they have been planted in the ground, as in generally the case with *F. religiosa* and *F. rumphii,* or if their seeds have been dropped on a rocky cliff or sea-shore, then they stand on a short trunk of their own which, at a height of ten to twenty feet, breaks up into the typical, many-limbed crown. On the granite coasts and the limestone hills, the roots of these figs travel for extraordinary distances, up to several hundred feet, in the clefts between the rocks and, ramifying over their faces, bind them together as with so many cables. It is no exaggeration to say that some of the little islands on the East Coast, which are composed merely of enormous boulders, are held together by the strangling figs that grow on them, principally the species *F. superba* and *F. caulocarpa*.

E. J. H. Corner, *Wayside Trees of Malaya*, Malayan Nature Society, Kuala Lumpur, 1940, pp. 527–9.

73
The Palm Scene

E. J. H. CORNER

Palm trees are richly represented in the forests of South-East Asia. Corner has explained how these plants, as a group, are marvellous for their antiquity, variety, elegance, and utility.

O F all land plants, the palm is the most distinguished. A columnar stem crowned with giant leaves is the perfect idea, popular or philosophic, of what a plant should be. It suffers no attrition through ramification. In all the warmer parts of the earth this form stamps itself in grand simplicity on the landscape. It manifests itself in more than two thousand species and several hundred genera, every one restricted more or less by climate, terrain, and geographical history. The present distribution of palms resembles an immense chessboard on which we see the last moves of a great game of life. Kings and queens are Malaysian and Amazonian. The major pieces have moved into America, Africa, and Asia, and the pawns have reached the islands. There are fragments of the early moves in the Cretaceous rocks, dating back 120 million years. A fan-palm has been reported from the Triassic of Colorado, and we do not know when the game began or whence it was derived. All we can say is that the palms are as old, if not older, than any other form of flowering plant and that they have endured while the rest have pressed forward into modern trees, climbers, herbs, and grasses, ramified, extended, twisted, and simplified. We find palms in the meadows, steppes and deserts, on the mountains, and all through the tropical and subtropical forests. Whether surrounded by grass-blades, towering trunks, or tree-ferns they maintain their rigid character as if this great family had been pitched, as a block of special creation, into the Mesozoic world, and around, through, and over it the subsequent streams of life had flowed. The palm is an evolutionary challenge, primitive, standardized, and viable.

We approach a tropical shore and coconut palms extend along it. We enter a tropical river and other palms are drawn up on the banks. They burst from the canopy of the broadleafed forest; they hide in its shade; they obstruct its walks; they entangle its trees; they line its rivulets. They dot the landscape of native agriculture. They distinguish the villages. They blot out the landscape under commercial agriculture. They troop across the derelict countryside and cluster at a water-hole. They are stationed along city streets and decorate the parks. We tread on their flooring, shelter beneath their roofing, rest on their matting, and eat of their substance. We should know well what palms are.

In warm climates the people have grown up accustomed to palms, using them in all these ways, playing under them from childhood and making playthings from them, perhaps reverencing them, but always caring for them. When the forest must be hewn back, the palms are spared by that primitive trait which mingles admiration with necessity. The local kinds are known through custom, story and legend, but no science or botany of a palm family has emerged. Strangers to the palm lands sketch and photograph, gather seed for their distant gardens and greenhouses, and rejoice generally in the realization of book-knowledge, but they find the palms too massive and intractable for ordinary scientific approach. It is necessary to live with the palms for many years in order to appreciate them. The rustle of the moorland grass lies overhead; the debris of fallen leaves and inflorescences is unaccommodating. So we find that few scientists have been able to cope with palms and that fewer still have made the effort to build up palm science. We find, in fact, no major group of plants so neglected in its study.

E. J. H. Corner, *The Natural History of Palms*, Weidenfeld and Nicolson, London, 1966, pp. 1–3.

74
The Durian Tree

GEORGIUS EVERHARDUS RUMPHIUS

Acclaimed as arboreal wonders of South-East Asia are the durians, elegant trees endemic to the region, whose huge, spiny fruits contain a creamy flesh nauseous to the uninitiated but held beyond esteem by the habitué among humankind and equally among the beasts of the forest—bear, tiger, pig, or elephant alike. During his years of residence in Ambon, Rumphius inevitably encountered durians. He provided a characteristically erudite description of the cultivated variety.

T HE Durian is held by many to be the most excellent fruit of the Indies, but since newcomers are averse to it for a long time because of its heavy odor, such judgment is not universal. The tree is very tall, nay among the edible fruit-bearing trees the very tallest. It crown is not dense but sparse, nevertheless it has spreading branches; the trunk is angular at the bottom and looks as if winged, with a bark of an even gray veering towards yellow which, among other things, is distinctive of this tree. The leaves have an ordinary shape, not unlike those of a cherry tree, though the edges are not notched at all, and therefore resemble the leaves of the nutmeg tree. They are half a span long, two inches wide, on top smooth and bright green, and on the underside of a faded color or like that of a rough brick; the stems or feet of these leaves have also a singular character which one does not find with other trees: for they look swollen and at the end they have a shape resembling a knee.

Its bloom consists of large flowers on thick stems hanging close together in a cluster, but not on the twigs which bear the leaves but on thin and thicker branches close to the trunk: clusters on the thin branches have five to eight flowers, but the thicker ones bear clusters of from twelve to thirty. Each bud is covered with two or three pale-green and concave little leaves which are shed as soon as the blossom is full grown. The flower itself is also remarkable, its lower part resembling a silver salt-cellar or also like the spittoon ordinarily used when eating Pinang, with below a round stomach in the shape of a heart that comes to a narrow neck and then suddenly opens up again into a wide mouth formed by five little leaves, containing five spoon-shaped leaves standing so close to the salt-cellar mentioned before that they seem to form a body with it. They enclose it at first within a large oblong bud, but those that are open curl backwards with plaited edges, because they are limp there; otherwise they are not unlike the petals of a *Narcissus*, though of a dirty white, with the lower part resembling that pale yellow salt-cellar or beaker. Inside stand five tiny and thin leaflets like slips of cloth, again of a dirty white, and divided into seven or eight short filaments bearing on top naps that are quite red and plaited, and twisted in several ways like the blossom of the Capok-tree. Right in the center one finds a long fiber with a little yellow knop standing on top of an oblong and granular knop, from whence comes the fruit. The flowers hang closed like that for a long time, and open only gradually, mostly after the noon and fall down the following night, leaving the naked fiber with its little knob. The smell of this bloom is heavy and not pleasant, and the same thing must be said of the fruits, even those which have not been opened yet. And although so many flowers hang together only three or five come to perfection, or at most ten or twelve on a cluster, to wit those on the heaviest branches, while many of the young fruits are destroyed by parrots.

The fruits are round globes, about the size of small man's head, and shaped like a curled-up hedgehog; some are round and some are oblong with a thick and hard, though not a wooden, rind which is covered with thorny and stiff points that are as angular as diamonds cut long and pointed. They do not wound unless one presses hard against them.

On the outside they are yellow-green and hang from their thick stems. Each globe can be opened lengthwise, and if one

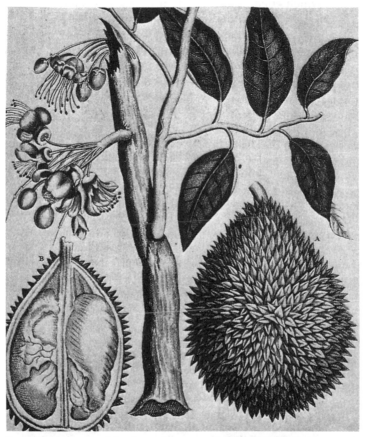

Rumphius's figure of the shoot, flowers, and fruit of the durian.

looks for the seams with a knife, one can separate it into five pieces, but since the seams may be difficult to find one can also kick it with the foot until it splits; and if they won't do this they are then considered not ripe yet. Within this thick and thorny husk are five little rooms or cells containing two, three or four kernels which look a little like dove's eggs and are of a substance like a Chestnut; these kernels are encompassed by a white and viscous meat and clothed in a thin fleece which effects that they do not stick to each other. And it is this meat (very much like as to the cream of milk, or also not unlike *Mangjar Blanco*, which are egg custards) that is most important and what is eaten of this fruit, by sucking it off these kernels. The taste is mild or somewhat luscious, and not unlike those egg custards, but the smell is quite nasty and unpleasant for the newcomers to the Indies and for those who are not used to them, because it comes close to the smell of rotting onions; which smell is also given off by the whole fruits even if they have not been opened, and it can fill an entire house with it. But as unpleasant the smell may be, the taste, on the contrary, is a dainty one. But there are many, and though they lived in the Indies for a long time, who cannot get used to the fruit because of the aforesaid nasty smell, and such people are afeared to sit in a place where the Durians are eaten when they themselves are not partaking of it. But as soon as one has tasted of it one does no longer smell that nauseous odor, and gradually becomes so used to this fruit that one comes to esteem it as the most delicious one in all the Indies.

Its wood is white on the outside but inside it tends toward a russet color; furthermore, it is made of long fibers, is straight, firm and durable, wherefore the Natives use it for the masts of their ships, and our own people have now also come to imitate them because these are handsome, tall and straight trunks. One does not climb these trees to get the ripe fruits but let them fall down on their own, because it is too perilous, and also from fear that someone might have one of these heavy fruits fall on his head.

E. M. Beekman (ed. and trans.), *The Poison Tree: Selected Writings of Rumphius on the Natural History of the Indies*, University of Massachusetts Press, Amherst, 1981, pp. 93–5.

75

The Durian

ALFRED RUSSEL WALLACE

Wallace described this 'most esteemed' fruit in ebullient terms. He also warned of the hazards. Indeed, in Sarawak I have met a man blinded in one eye by a falling durian fruit.

T HE banks of the Sarawak River are everywhere covered with fruit trees, which supply the Dyaks with a great deal of their food. The Mangosteen, Lansat, Rambutan, Jack, Jambou, and Blimbing, are all abundant; but most abundant and most esteemed is the Durian, a fruit about which very little is known in England, but which both by natives and Europeans in the Malay Archipelago is reckoned superior to all others. The old traveller Linschott, writing in 1599, says:—'It is of such an excellent taste that it surpasses in flavour all the other fruits of the world, according to those who have tasted it.' And Doctor Paludanus adds:—'This fruit is of a hot and humid nature. To those not used to it, it seems at first to smell like rotten onions, but immediately they have tasted it they prefer it to all other food. The natives give it honourable titles, exalt it, and make verses on it.' When brought into a house the smell is often so offensive that some persons can never bear to taste it. This was my own case when I first tried it in Malacca, but in Borneo I found a ripe fruit on the ground, and, eating it out of doors, I at once became a confirmed Durian eater.

The Durian grows on a large and lofty forest tree, some-what resembling an elm in its general character, but with a more smooth and scaly bark. The fruit is round or slightly oval, about the size of a large cocoanut, of a green colour, and covered all over with short stout spines the bases of which touch each other, and are consequently somewhat hexagonal, while the points are very strong and sharp. It is so completely armed, that if the stalk is broken off it is a difficult matter to lift one from the ground. The outer rind is so thick and tough, that from whatever height it may fall it is never broken. From the base to the apex five very faint lines may be traced, over which the spines arch a little; these are the sutures of the carpels, and show where the fruit may be divided with a heavy knife and a strong hand. The five cells are satiny white within, and are each filled with an oval mass of cream-coloured pulp, imbedded in which are two or three seeds about the size of chestnuts. This pulp is the eatable part, and its consistence and flavour are indescribable. A rich butter-like custard highly flavoured with almonds gives the best general idea of it, but intermingled with it come wafts of flavour that call to mind cream-cheese, onion-sauce, brown sherry, and other incongruities. Then there is a rich glutinous smoothness in the pulp which nothing else possesses, but which adds to its delicacy. It is neither acid, nor sweet, nor juicy, yet one feels the want of none of these qualities, for it is perfect as it is. It produces no nausea or other bad effect, and the more you eat of it the less you feel inclined to stop. In fact to eat Durians is a new sensation, worth a voyage to the East to experience.

When the fruit is ripe it falls of itself, and the only way to eat Durians in perfection is to get them as they fall; and the smell is then less overpowering. When unripe, it makes a very good vegetable if cooked, and it is also eaten by the Dyaks raw. In a good fruit season large quantities are preserved salted, in jars and bamboos, and kept the year round, when it acquires a most disgusting odour to Europeans, but the Dyaks appreciate it highly as a relish with their rice. There are in the forest two varieties of wild Durians with much smaller fruits, one of them orange-coloured inside; and these are probably the origin of the large and fine Durians, which are never found wild. It would not, perhaps, be correct to say that the Durian is the best of all fruits, because it cannot supply the place of the subacid juicy kinds, such as the orange, grape, mango, and mangosteen, whose refreshing and cooling qualities are so wholesome and grateful; but as producing a food of the most exquisite flavour it is unsurpassed. If I had to fix on two only, as representing the perfection of the two classes, I should certainly choose the Durian and the Orange as the king and queen of fruits.

The Durian is, however, sometimes dangerous. When the fruit begins to ripen it falls daily and almost hourly, and accidents not unfrequently happen to persons walking or working under the trees. When a Durian strikes a man in its fall, it produces a dreadful wound, the strong spines tearing open the flesh, while the blow itself is very heavy; but from this very circumstance death rarely ensues, the copious effusion of blood preventing the inflammation which might otherwise take place. A Dyak chief informed me that he had been struck down by a Durian falling on his head, which he thought would certainly have caused his death, yet he recovered in a very short time.

Alfred Russel Wallace, *The Malay Archipelago: The Land of the Orang-Utan, and the Bird of Paradise*, 10th edn., Macmillan and Co., London, 1883, pp. 74–6.

76
Bat Flowers

E. J. H. CORNER

The flowers of durians are pollinated by bats and show features held in common with other bat-pollinated trees. As Corner has explained, some are wondrously bizarre.

THE calabash tree (*Crescentia*) of America, the sausage tree (*Kigelia*) of Africa, and the midnight-horror (*Oroxylon*) of Asia are bat-pollinated bignoniaceous trees. The nocturnal baobab (*Adansonia*) of Africa, and the cotton trees (*Ceiba*) and durian trees (*Durio*) of Asia are bat-pollinated members of the *Bombax-Malva* set of families. Some nocturnal caesalpinioid flowers of America, as *Bauhinia megalandra* and *Eperua falcata*, are bat-pollinated; so may be the Asiatic members of the mimosoid *Parkia*, whereas the American with red and yellow colours are probably bird-pollinated. The papilionaceous *Mucuna* has bird-, bat-, and insect-pollinated flowers. The European purple loosestrife (*Lythrum*) is an insect-pollinated ally of the bat-pollinated tropical trees *Duabanga* and *Sonneratia* of Asia. Red-flowered wild bananas are said to be bird-pollinated, those with purple and brown flowers bat-pollinated.

Bat-flowers are also large, strong, as fitted to the bat's claws, and copiously suppled with watery nectar. They differ from the bird-flowers in opening at dusk, in their lurid yellow-green, red-brown, or purple-brown colours, in their wide mouth, allowing roomy entrance, and in the strong smell, which may be a foxy or fishy stink, a smell of sour milk, or a strange essence of cucumber. Often, too, these flowers are borne in hanging inflorescences, or they face downwards, suiting the bat's posture. They are bird-flowers adapted to bats, as the brightly coloured butterfly-flowers adapt themselves to moths. But what of the history of this association? Bats eat fruits, sup nectar, and catch insects; thus they impinge on the life of plants. The answer is not in books, which are now too specialized, but waits the biologist who can appreciate both plants and animals in tropical life.

E. J. H. Corner, *The Life of Plants*, Weidenfeld and Nicolson, London, 1964, p. 206.

77
Midnight Horror

E. J. H. CORNER

Bat-pollinated plants often extend their blooms in strange ways, the better to entice their chosen clientele. Naturally, these 'bat flowers' also open by night. This habit has prompted Corner to coin a name for one of the most curious examples in South-East Asia.

THIS grotesque tree fills us with astonishment. Botanically it is the sole representative of its kind: aesthetically, it is monstrous.

The enormous leaves look like branches, so regularly are the leaflets displayed. But each leaf develops as a unit and when it withers it breaks up gradually in regular order from the tip to the base: the leaflets fall off singly and the main stalk and its side-stalks break up at the joints: the bits accumulate round the base of the trunk like a collection of limb-bones, so that we may call it the 'Broken Bones Plant'. The leaves are crowded near the end of the stem or its branches, and saplings, which remain unbranched until after their first flowering at a height of some 15 ft., look like gigantic umbrellas. When the saplings flower, the inflorescence develops from the apical bud and therefore further upward growth of the main stem is prevented. When the inflorescence has finished flowering, the leaves below it fall off and the leafless stem is left as a pole with a few sabre-like pods dangling from its extremity ... wherefore, we may call it the 'Tree of Damocles'. Then, after 3–4 weeks in a leafless state, one or more lateral buds on the stem break out and grow into side-branches which, in due course, flower, fruit, shed their leaves and branch in their turn: and, thus, the big trees are constructed sympodially with open irregular crown and a few lanky ascending limbs. Each branch seems to flower independently of the others so that flowers, fruits and growing twigs may be found on the same tree.... After the sapling stage, the tree loses its most characteristic appearance, yet the umbrella-like groups of big leaves with the inflorescence in the centre are always distinctive.

The flowers are nocturnal. The corolla begins to open about 10 p.m., when the tumid, wrinkled lips part and the harsh odour escapes from them. By midnight, the lurid mouth gapes widely and is filled with stink. Before sunrise the corolla is detached and slips off over the long style. The flowers are pollinated by bats which are attracted by the smell and, holding to the fleshy corolla with the claws on their wings, thrust their noses into its throat: scratches, as of bats, can be seen on the fallen flowers next morning.

The pods are longer than the fruits of any other Malayan tree, being equalled only by those of some climbers. They soon bend down under their weight. When they are ripe, the gauzy seeds slip out and flit away on the breeze with the jerky motion of a butterfly: so, in the noon-tide, we may call the tree the 'Midday Marvel'.

E. J. H. Corner, *Wayside Trees of Malaya*, Malayan Nature Society, Kuala Lumpur, 1940, p. 179.

Plant Wonders

∾

78
Exuberance of Life

G. B. CERRUTI

The gigantic trees of the forest form a three-dimensional substrate supporting or sustaining a myriad other forms of plant life. In this imaginative interpretation by Captain Cerruti, the scene is redolent of competition for the one essential, sunlight!

Cerruti, an adventurous Italian, arrived in Perak via Penang in 1891 with a collection of ethnographical materials made in Nias. These he sold to the new museum at Taiping, and thereafter set off to become acquainted with the 'Mai Darat' (Orang Asli) people of the interior. After early difficulties, he established good relations with the local communities, and developed a profitable trade in jungle produce. In 1901, he was appointed to the post of Perak State Superintendent of Sakais. His book, written in 1906 after returning to Italy, is tinged with Rousseau-esque sentiments of natural man but presents a fair picture of the lives of the people he met, with a rich collection of original photographic portraits.

T HE gigantic trees shoot up straight towards the sun, each one seeming to strive to outstrip the other; but a thick and even more ambitious undergrowth of plants twine round their trunks and enclose them in a tenacious embrace, then twisting, and creeping, amongst the spreading boughs, reach and cover the highest tops where they at last unfold their several leaves and flowers under the sun's most ardent gaze.

The tree, thus encircled and suffocated by the baneful hold of the climbers, lacks light and breath; the sap flows in

165

scarce quantities throughout its organism and it languishes under the shade of the close tendrils; swarms of insects increase its agony by making their food and their nests of its bark; reptiles make love within the hollows of its trunk and at last the day comes when the lifeless giant falls with a frightful crash bearing with it the murderous parasite that is the victim of its own tenacity, which first raised it to bask in the sunshine and then caused it to be crushed under the rotten weight of its former supporter.

These are furious embraces of envy and jealousy; phrenzies of egotism in the vegetable kingdom: strange expressions of formidable hate and love, of oppression and vengeance....

The sun never penetrates under this tangled mass of vegetation except where an opening has been made by the hands of the savages or by the work of lightning and hurricane.

In the dim light of its damp atmosphere the interminable rows of tall straight trunks, some stout and some slight, assume the oddest shapes which can appeal to the observer's phantasy. Now they are colonnades, adorned with pendant festoons stretching away into the distance; now they are mysterious aisles of monster temples; now they are the unfinished design of some giant architect whose undertaking was arrested by a sudden, mystic command. However fruitful may be the imagination of the artist he would here always find fresh and superb inspiration from the enthralling sight of Nature's virginal beauties.

The stagnant waters of the ponds, round which the frogs croak and the leeches crawl, are plentifully strewn with water-lilies, reeds and other aquatic plants.

On the hoary trunks of ancient trees whole families of orchids have insinuated themselves into little clefts in the bark, and flower there in the brightest of colours: red, purple, blue and also white.

Everywhere there is a joyous exuberance of life and vigour.

G. B. Cerruti, *My Friends the Savages*, Como, Italy, 1908, pp. 60–1.

79
Abundance of Rattans

ALFRED RUSSEL WALLACE

Abundant contenders in the upward tussle are the climbing palms, or rattans. Wallace described their place in the forests of Manado, Celebes (Sulawesi).

T HE chief feature of this forest was the abundance of rattan palms, hanging from the trees, and turning and twisting about on the ground, often in inextricable confusion. One wonders at first how they can get into such queer shapes; but it is evidently caused by the decay and fall of the trees up which they have first climbed, after which they grow along the ground till they meet with another trunk up which to ascend. A tangled mass of twisted living rattan, is therefore a sign that at some former period a large tree has fallen there, though there may be not the slightest vestige of it left. The rattan seems to have unlimited powers of growth, and a single plant may mount up several trees in succession, and thus reach the enormous length they are said sometimes to attain. They much improve the appearance of a forest as seen from the coast; for they vary the otherwise monotonous tree-tops with feathery crowns of leaves rising clear above them, and each terminated by an erect leafy spike like a lightning-conductor.

Alfred Russel Wallace, *The Malay Archipelago: The Land of the Orang-Utan, and the Bird of Paradise*, 10th edn., Macmillan and Co., London, 1883, p. 269.

80
Rattans Explained

E. J. H. CORNER

Corner has described the exceptional variety and abundance of rattans in South-East Asia.

T HE climbing palm is neither root-climber nor twiner, but the more generalized scrambler that hoists itself leaf by leaf, while the stem hangs as the cable to the root. The big leaf, which it inherits as a pachycaulous plant, does the mechanical work; the stem, relieved of the pressure, responds by becoming a flexible structure with long inter-nodes. The unopen leaf lengthens at the tip. The sword of the palm crown becomes a whip, barbed with hooks. It sways and blows, catching twig, bark, limb, and leaf in the surround. As the leaf opens and projects itself by basal growth, the attached hooks are pushed on and those further down the leaf-axis take over; if they cannot be disengaged the crown is thrust aside on its swaying stem. Once a grip is established, it is seldom released; if other leaves have been unsuccessful, one can hold the crown. But, as more leaves are projected, another will attach itself to the ramifications of the forest; it is the peculiarity of this sort of climber to thrive on the branching exterior of other plants. It often happens, nevertheless, that many leaves do not attach themselves, especially in the early stages of the palm's life when it is growing up from the floor of the forest, or when it is grow-ing by stream, lake, or shore at the edge of the forest, and then hanging whips become a menace to man and beast. To disengage the hooks, it is necessary to back and, in backing, other whips may be encountered; the unwary can become incredibly and most painfully entangled. One needs to be a pachyderm for immunity, and I often think that the elephant and rhinoceros have been the answer. Unattached whips, so fine and tenacious, are an ever present hazard in the forests of

Calamus ornatus (rattan) scrambling up a tree. From W. Veevers–Carter, *Riches of the Rain Forest*, Oxford University Press, Singapore, 1994.

south-east Asia and, though apparently just a side-effect of the palm's growth, they surely assist in protecting the edible bud.

Compared with other palms, this manner of growth seems to be fairly rapid. It is caused very largely by internodal elongation as well as by elongation of the leaf-tip. The larger species of *Calamus* may have internodes three to four feet long. The leaves of climbing palms have, probably, no greater photosynthetic ability than those of other palms, but the effort is put into lengthening, rather than massive consolidation. A well-known and commercially exploited climber *Calamus caesius* will produce under forest conditions a stem about thirty feet long in five or six years from seed, and this in the course of ten more years will grow to a hundred feet. Thinner stems may lengthen more rapidly and, though their effective leaf-surface will be much less as the leaves are smaller, yet the greater number of stems that can be produced from a tuft may make up any deficiency; in dense forest with few shafts of light, the leptocaul may win. The longest stem that has been measured for any kind of climbing plant was that of *Calamus manan*, recorded by the Forest Department of Malaya as 556 feet; another, considerably longer, was chewed up and trampled to bits by elephants after it had been pulled down and before it could be carried out of the forest. Thus, like two distant extremities, *Calamus* of the rain forest rivals *Macrocystis* of the sea.

Now, lengths of this kind far exceed the stature of any tree. Either the palm must have scrambled over several trees, or its stem hung in loops and lay in coils on the ground. We do not know the length to which an uninhibited climbing stem may grow, or why it should be limited. The hanging crowns and cables of these palms, however, are heavy. They snap twigs and break branches; they hook blindly on to living and dead. The supports give way, sooner or later; the crown subsides until caught again and the stem loops between the branches and coils on the ground. These are side-effects of slipping which generally cause the great lengths of stem, but they have their consequences. When the spiny sheaths of the dead leaves have rotted away, the old loops and festoons make the runways for the four-handed. And when these runways end in large bunches of edible fruits, there is the contribution of these barbed and horrid growths to the repast in the canopy.

The climbing palms of the Orient are known as rattans or, in Malay, *rotan*. It is thought that the word comes from *raut* (to pare) and to be connected with the cleaning and splitting of rattan stems for the many uses which they have: this is one of their better known aspects.

E. J. H. Corner, *The Natural History of Palms*, Weidenfeld and Nicolson, London, 1966, pp. 203–4.

81
Bamboos

ALFRED RUSSEL WALLACE

Bamboos are huge, woody grasses. They abound in great diversity in South-East Asia, growing on terrain of all kinds.

Wallace was forcibly impressed by the enormous value of bamboos as a natural resource, and enumerated the variety of ways that he saw them put to use in the Dayak villages of Sarawak.

T HEIR strength lightness smoothness straightness roundness and hollowness, the facility and regularity with which they can be split, their many different sizes, the varying length of their joints, the ease with which they can be cut and with which holes can be made through them, their hardness outside, their freedom from any pronounced taste or smell, their great abundance, and the rapidity of their growth and increase, are all qualities which render them useful for a hundred different purposes, to serve which other materials would require much more labour and preparation. The

171

Bamboo is one of the most wonderful and most beautiful productions of the tropics, and one of nature's most valuable gifts to uncivilized man.

The Dyak houses are all raised on posts, and are often two or three hundred feet long and forty or fifty wide. The floor is always formed of strips split from large Bamboos, so that each may be nearly flat and about three inches wide, and these are firmly tied down with rattan to the joists beneath. When well made, this is a delightful floor to walk upon barefooted, the rounded surfaces of the bamboo being very smooth and agreeable to the feet, while at the same time affording a firm hold. But, what is more important, they form with a mat over them an excellent bed, the elasticity of the Bamboo and its rounded surface being far superior to a more rigid and a flatter floor. Here we at once find a use for Bamboo which cannot be supplied so well by another material without a vast amount of labour, palms and other substitutes requiring much cutting and smoothing, and not being equally good when finished. When, however, a flat, close floor is required, excellent boards are made by splitting open large Bamboos on one side only, and flattening them out so as to form slabs eighteen inches wide and six feet long, with which some Dyaks floor their houses. These with constant rubbing of the feet and the smoke of years become dark and polished, like walnut or old oak, so that their real material can hardly be recognised. What labour is here saved to a savage whose only tools are an axe and a knife, and who, if he wants boards, must hew them out of the solid trunk of a tree, and must give days and weeks of labour to obtain a surface as smooth and beautiful as the Bamboo thus treated affords him. Again, if a temporary house is wanted, either by the native in his plantation or by the traveller in the forest, nothing is so convenient as the Bamboo, with which a house can be constructed with a quarter of the labour and time than if other materials are used.

As I have already mentioned, the Hill Dyaks in the interior of Sarawak make paths for long distances from village to village and to their cultivated grounds, in the course of which they have to cross many gullies and ravines, and even rivers; or sometimes, to avoid a long circuit, to carry the path along the face of a precipice. In all these cases the bridges they construct are of Bamboo, and so admirably adapted is the material for this purpose, that it seems doubtful whether they ever would have attempted such works if they had not possessed it. The Dyak bridge is simple but well designed. It consists merely of stout Bamboos crossing each other at the roadway like the letter X, and rising a few feet above it. At the crossing they are firmly bound together, and to a large Bamboo which lays upon them and forms the only pathway, with a slender and often very shaky one to serve as a handrail. When a river is to be crossed an overhanging tree is chosen, from which the bridge is partly suspended and partly supported by diagonal struts from the banks, so as to avoid placing posts in the stream itself, which would be liable to be carried away by floods. In carrying a path along the face of a precipice, trees and roots are made use of for suspension; struts arise from suitable notches or crevices in the rocks, and if these are not sufficient, immense Bamboos fifty or sixty feet long are fixed on the banks or on the branch of a tree below. These bridges are traversed daily by men and women carrying heavy loads, so that any insecurity is soon discovered, and, as the materials are close at hand, immediately repaired. When a path goes over very steep ground, and becomes slippery in very wet or very dry weather, the Bamboo is used in another way. Pieces are cut about a yard long, and opposite notches being made at each end, holes are formed through which pegs are driven, and firm and convenient steps are thus formed with the greatest ease and celerity. It is true that much of this will decay in one or two seasons, but it can be so quickly replaced as to make it more economical than using a harder and more durable wood.

One of the most striking uses to which Bamboo is applied by the Dyaks, is to assist them in climbing lofty trees, by driving in pegs. . . . This method is constantly used in order to obtain wax, which is one of the most valuable products of the country. The honey-bee of Borneo very generally hangs its combs under the branches of the Tappan, a tree which towers above all others in the forest, and whose smooth cylindrical trunk often rises a hundred feet without a branch. The Dyaks climb these lofty trees at night, building up their Bamboo ladder as they go, and bringing down gigantic honeycombs. These furnish them with a delicious feast of honey and young bees, besides the wax, which they sell to traders, and with the proceeds buy the much-coveted brass wire, earrings, and gold-edged handkerchiefs with which they love to decorate themselves. In ascending Durian and other fruit trees which branch at from thirty to fifty feet from the ground, I have seen them use the Bamboo pegs only, without the upright Bamboo which renders them so much more secure.

The outer rind of the Bamboo, split and shaved thin, is the strongest material for baskets; hen-coops, bird-cages, and conical fish-traps are very quickly made from a single joint, by splitting off the skin in narrow strips left attached to one end, while rings of the same material or of rattan are twisted in at regular distances. Water is brought to the houses by little aqueducts formed of large Bamboos split in half and supported on crossed sticks of various heights so as to give it a regular fall. Thin long-jointed Bamboos from the Dyak's only water-vessels, and a dozen of them stand in the corner of every house. They are clean, light, and easily carried, and are in many ways superior to earthen vessels for the same purpose. They also make excellent cooking utensils; vegetables and rice can be boiled in them to perfection, and they are often used when travelling. Salted fruit or fish, sugar, vinegar, and honey are preserved in them instead of in jars or bottles. In a small Bamboo case, prettily carved and ornamented, the Dyak carries his sirih and lime for betel chewing, and his little long-bladed knife has a Bamboo sheath. His favourite pipe is a huge hubble-bubble, which he will construct in a few minutes by inserting a small piece of

Bamboo for a bowl obliquely into a large cylinder about six inches from the bottom containing water, through which the smoke passes to a long slender Bamboo tube. There are many other small matters for which Bamboo is daily used, but enough has now been mentioned to show its value. In other parts of the Archipelago I have myself seen it applied to many new uses, and it is probable that my limited means of observation did not make me acquainted with one-half the ways in which it is serviceable to the Dyaks of Sarawak.

Alfred Russel Wallace, *The Malay Archipelago: The Land of the Orang-Utan, and the Bird of Paradise*, 10th edn., Macmillan and Co, London, 1883, pp. 77–81.

82
The Greater Moth Orchid, *Phalaenopsis*

F. W. BURBIDGE

Among the vegetable wonders of these forests are the multitude of epiphytes—those plants whose habit is to lodge on the trunk or limbs of others. In this way the epiphytes gain benefits, especially a high position in the canopy more exposed to the life-giving sunlight, but they take nothing from their hosts except the physical support. They cause no injury other than the shade they may cast on the foliage of their companion, or the mechanical strain of the extra load. The epiphytic way of life is followed among plants of many kinds, notably mosses, ferns, rhododendrons, and especially the orchids, in great profusion. The Greater Moth Orchid is one of the grandest examples.

Frederick William Burbidge, from whose writings this passage is abstracted, was a distinguished botanical author and, from 1879 until his death (at fifty-eight years of age), Curator of the Botanic Garden of Trinity College, Dublin, Ireland. He was originally apprenticed as a gardener as a boy, trained as a student with the Royal Horticultural Society, and found his first job at the Royal Botanic Gardens, Kew, before joining the editorial staff of *The Garden*, a horticultural publication, in the early 1870s. In 1877–8, under commission from the British horticultural firm of James Veitch & Sons to collect new and beautiful plants for introduction to cultivation, he visited South-East Asia, spending most of his time in what is now the Malaysian State of Sabah.

E PIPHYTAL orchids are essentially heat-lovers—like palms they are children of the sun. One may often travel a long way in the islands where these plants are most abundant without catching a glimpse of them; and this is especially true *of Phalænopsis grandiflora*, which is of all orchids perhaps the least obtrusive in its native habitats. This trait is, however, the unobtrusiveness of high birth, they do not care to touch the ground, but rather prefer a sphere of their own high up in the trees overhead. The plants have a charming freedom of aspect, as thus seen naturally high up in mid-air, screened from the sun by a leafy canopy, deluged with rains for half the year or more at least, and fanned by the cool sea-breezes or monsoons, which doubtless exercise some potent influence on their health—an influence which we can but rarely apply to them artificially, and the greatly modified conditions under which we must perforce cultivate them may not render this one so desirable as it sometimes appears to be abroad....

High up overhead the most lovely orchids hold their court in the sunshine: here they are really 'at home' to their winged visitors. Now and then, however, you come across a newly-fallen tree—a very monarch of the woods—which has succumbed to old age and rude weather at last, and has sunk to the earth from which it sprang a seedling generations ago; its branches laden with everything inanimate, which had made a home in its branches. Some of these ruined trunks are perfect gardens of beauty, wreathed with graceful climbing plants, and gay with flowers and foliage. The fall of a large tree, and its smaller dependents, lets in the sun, and so the epiphytes do not suffer much for a time; and one may thus observe them in all their beauty.

Burbidge's illustration of the Greater Moth Orchid (*Phalaenopsis*) 'at home'.

Here, right in the collar of the tree, is a plant of the gram-matophyllum orchid, big enough to fill a Pickford's van, and just now opening its golden-brown spotted flowers on stout spikes two yards long. There, on that topmost branch, is a mass of the moth orchid, or phalænopsis, bearing a hundred snowy flowers at least; and in such healthy vigour is it, that lovers of orchids at home—supposing it could be flashed direct to 'Steven's' in its present state—would outbid each other for such a glorious prize, until the hammer would fall at a price near on a hundred guineas, as it has done before for exceptional specimens of these lovely flowers.

There, gleaming in the sunlight, like a scarlet jewel, beneath those great leathery aroid leaves, is a cluster of tubular æschynanthus flowers; and here is another wee orchid, a tiny pink-blossomed cirrhopetalum, whose flowers and leaves scarcely rise above the bright carpet of velvety moss among which it grows.

F. W. Burbidge, *The Gardens of the Sun, or a Naturalist's Journal on the Mountains and in the Forests and Swamps of Borneo and the Sulu Archipelago,* John Murray, London, 1880, pp. 52 and 54–5.

83
Orchids in Java

HENRY O. FORBES

The complexities of pollination among the orchids epiphytic on trees in Java have been described in detail by Forbes.

I gathered the rather rare *Cymbidium stapelioides*, growing at a height of 2600 feet above the sea, flowering on a fallen tree. I brought it home, 1000 feet lower, and fixed it to a tree-stem, to which it at once took kindly. None of the flowers which were expanded when I found it were fertilised; but one of the bulbs had a stem with a solitary capsule. For three weeks the plant remained in the condition in which I found it, its large and handsome, though somewhat dull-coloured, flowers retaining their perfect freshness during all this period. I then look compassion on its barren state, and fertilised from their neighbours four of its florets. These alone of the sixteen flowers bore fruit. A couple of months later a fine new spike appeared, which I left to its own resources. For between four and five weeks it exhibited a very fine tross of twelve flowers; but not one seed-capsule was produced. The insect life at the lower station seemed quite as abundant as at the higher. This orchid possesses no nectary, and its odour, if not pleasant, is not disagreeable. The viscid disk of its pollinia is remarkable for its elasticity. After removing a pollen mass from the anther, I applied it to the stigma of another floret, and on withdrawing the pencil to which it was adhering, it sprang back with an audible snap, the viscid disk stretching quite one-eighth of an inch, without leaving pollen on the stigma, for the floret did not set a capsule. The same result followed after allowing the pollen to remain for some seconds in contact with the stigmatic surface. After the lapse of a week the viscid disk still retained its elasticity unimpaired, so much so that I was able to extend it as often as ten times for various distances up to nearly one-fifth of an inch before the connection gave way—a sharp snap always accompanying its relaxation.

One of the prettiest and commonest orchids here was a pure white *Dendrobium* (*D. crumenatum*), which suddenly appears in flower on all the trees of a district nearly on the same day. I have examined many hundreds of flowers, and I am quite sure, though I have not kept very accurate statistics of the numbers, that not one in eighty ever sets a seed capsule.

Growing terrestrially in abundance in damp shady situations is another group of this family belonging to the genus *Calanthe*. *Calanthe veratrifolia* produces quite a dense head of elegant white flowers, but the number of those that become fertilised are in enormous disproportion to those that fall off barren. I have examined plants in numerous localities, in heights amid the dense forest, as well as in more open situations; I have studied them low down, both in the sun and in the deep shade, but have invariably found that a very small proportion produces fruit. Generally the pollinia are found in the anther after the fall of the flower; but often they are absent, without any pollen being left in return on the stigma. In five different plants, out of 360 florets examined, 109 were withering with intact anthers, or had lost their pollen

179

and were unfertilised, 245 had fallen off, six only had produced capsules. These are not selected instances, but the result of the examination of five plants as they occur in my note-book. I have several times found in various species of *Calanthe*, specimens which at first I thought to be *cleistogamously* fertilised, where the ovules were enlarged in the ovary, and the flowers quite open; but close examination has shown that this is the effect of the irritation of a small species of *Hymenoptera*—a *cynips* probably.

Henry O. Forbes, *A Naturalist's Wanderings in the Eastern Archipelago: A Narrative of Travel and Exploration from 1878 to 1883*, Harper and Brothers, New York, 1885, pp. 83–5.

84
Pitcher Plants

F. W. BURBIDGE

On poor soils, especially in mountainous places, the so-called 'carnivorous' plants are able to supplement their nutrient intake by capturing small animal prey. The strange pitcher plants are notable examples in South-East Asia. Among these, the capturing device is a fluid-filled vessel (the 'pitcher') developed from an extension of the leaf-tip. Pitcher plants reach the height of diversity on the island of Borneo, and the largest and most spectacular are found on Mt Kinabalu.

The famous pitcher plants of this mountain were the chief desiderata of Burbidge and Veitch. This abstract records their delight in reaching the zone where pitchers abounded, growing alongside epiphytic rhododendrons and other glorious blooms.

ABOUT seven o'clock next morning we started on our upward journey. It was hot work at first, but we could feel it perceptibly get cooler after the first two or three thousand feet. At about four thousand feet mosses are very plentiful, the finest species gathered being *Dawsonia superba*, which fringed the path, but nowhere in great plenty. A new white-flowered species of burmannia was also gathered, and small-flowered orchids were seen. In one place a shower of small scarlet rhododendron flowers covered the ground at our feet, the plant being epiphytal in the trees overhead. It was very misty, and the moss which covered every rotten stick, and the vegetation generally, was dripping with moisture, and every sapling we grasped in climbing upwards was the means of shaking a shower-bath on us from the trees above. At about five thousand feet a dead and broken pitcher of *Nepenthes Lowi* lying in the path led to the discovery of the plant itself scrambling among the mossy branches overhead, its singular flagon-shaped ascidia hanging from the point of every leaf. It is a vigorous-habited plant, with bright green leathery leaves, the petioles of which clasp the stem in a peculiar manner. The only plants we saw were epiphytal on mossy trunks and branches, and we searched for young plants diligently, but without success. All the pitchers hitherto seen are cauline ones, and as the plant has never yet been seen in a young state, it is an open question as to whether the radical pitchers differ in shape or size, as is the case with most other species. As we ascended higher, epiphytal orchids, especially erias, dendrochilia, and cœlogynes became more plentiful, and we came upon a large-flowered rhododendron, bearing rich orange flowers two inches in diameter, and twenty flowers in a cluster! It grew on a dangerous declivity, and not one of our lazy men would venture to get it for us. Such a prize, however, was too lovely to forego, and after a wet scramble among the surrounding bushes, I secured it in good condition. Two or three other species were seen in flower, but none equal to it in its golden beauty. Casuarina trees became common, and higher up these were joined by two or three species of gleichenias, and a distinct form of dipteris. Phyllocladus also appeared, and a glaucus-leaved dianella (*D. javanica*). Here also were two of the most distinct of all rhododendrons, *R. ericifolium* and *R. stenophyllum*. On open spaces among rocks and sedges, the giant *Nepenthes Rajah*

N. Edwardsiana. From Spenser St. John, *Life in the Forests of the Far East; or Travels in Northern Borneo*, 2nd edn., Smith, Elder and Co., London, 1863.

began to appear, the plants being of all sizes, and in the most luxuriant health and beauty. The soil in which they grew was a stiff yellow loam, surfaced with sandstone-grit, and around the larger plants a good deal of rich humus and leaf debris had collected. The long red-pitchered *N. Edwardsiana* was seen in two places. This plant, like *N. Lowii*, is epiphytal in its perfect state, and is of a slender rambling habit. Highest of all in the great nepenthes zone came *N. villosa*, a beautiful plant, having rounded pitchers of the softest pink colour, with a crimson frilled orifice, similar to that of *N. Edwardsiana*. All thoughts of fatigue and discomfort vanished as we gazed on these living wonders of the Bornean Andes! Here, on this cloud-girt mountain side, were vegetable treasures which Imperial Kew had longed for in vain. Discovered by Mr Low in 1851, dried specimens had been transmitted by him to Europe, and Dr (now Sir Joseph) Hooker had described and illustrated them in the Transactions of the Linnæan Society, but all attempts to introduce them alive into European gardens had failed. To see these plants in all their health and vigour was a sensation I shall never forget—one of those which we experience but rarely in a whole lifetime!

F. W. Burbidge, *The Gardens of the Sun, or a Naturalist's Journal on the Mountains and in the Forests and Swamps of Borneo and the Sulu Archipelago*, John Murray, London, 1880, pp. 98–100.

85
Gingers

HENRY O. FORBES

Gingers abound in the tropical rain forests of South-East Asia. Forbes was intrigued by the peculiarities of fertilization among a terrestrial member of this important group of herbaceous plants.

I N the low forest a common species of the Ginger family (*Curcuma zerumbet*) abounded; but in gathering it, I observed that it was provided with one of the many contrivances for securing cross-fertilisation which are so interesting to the botanist, and give such intense pleasure to his contemplation of even the commonest flowers. The flower-stem terminates in a head of rich pink leaf-like organs called spathes, which supply a brilliant alluring mass of colour to the rather inconspicuous, odourless, though largish white flowers; the pistil, or organ for receiving the fructifying pollen from the stamens, passes through a hole in the conjoint anther, and its head is protected by a hood in the perianth from all insects and intruders which are not large enough to convey its pollen to another flower. When, however, there enters a bee or other insect large enough to fill the mouth of the flower, it comes in contact with the processes *a*, projecting from the lower margin of the compound anther, which act precisely as a lever, for when these are pushed backward by the bee pressing in, in quest of the nectar at the bottom of the flower, the anther is rotated, carrying with it the stigma or top of the pistil on to the back of the insect in the most beautiful manner. A bee that presses the long appendages of the anther, may rotate down the anther so as to carry away pollen on its back, but it will not fertilise the flower unless it is large enough to rotate the composite anther sufficiently far to bring the little tubercles, *b*, also on to its back, the pressure of which alone rotates the pistil tip on to the bee's back. It is evident that the pistil can never come into contact with the pollen of its own floret, nor can any floret be fertilised unless the insect has entered fully into a former flower, and smeared its back with a patch of pollen of some length, as long at least as the interval between the anther appendages and the pistil.

As the fertilising insect even begins to back out the lever apparatus is instantly released, and the summit of the pistil completely returns into the security of its hood.

When once fertilised the stamens thicken in their central part and, contracting in a corkscrew fashion, draw the perianth with the stamens and pistil to the bottom of the spathe out of harm's way and to make room for the next floret. Mr Darwin has drawn attention to the likeness of the *Scitamineæ* in the relation of their essential organs to those of the *Orchidaceæ*, and few examples perhaps could exhibit this similarity more than the one under notice; its pollen moreover being less friable than that in most species of its family, and singularly viscid.

Henry O. Forbes, *A Naturalist's Wanderings in the Eastern Archipelago: A Narrative of Travel and Exploration from 1878 to 1883*, Harper and Brothers, New York, 1885, pp. 247–9.

86
Rafflesia

THOMAS STAMFORD RAFFLES

The world's most extremely modified parasitic plants occur in the forests of South-East Asia. Most stupendous of these is the huge Rafflesia, first reported from Sumatra in a letter addressed to the Duchess of Somerset by Sir Thomas Stamford Raffles, one of the heroic figures of South-East Asia.

Raffles was born at sea in 1781, a few days out from Jamaica, homeward bound aboard the *West Indiaman* captained by his father, but his own career took him eastward. At the age of fourteen, he joined the East India Company as a clerk in the head office at Leadenhall Street, London. In 1805, he was appointed assistant to the Chief Secretary and in 1807, Chief Secretary of the Company's new Presidency of Penang. In 1810, he became the agent of the Governor-General, the Earl of Minto, with his headquarters at Malacca from where, in 1811, he launched a successful invasion of Java. Raffles governed Java until 1816 when, under the settlement between the British and the Dutch at the conclusion of the Napoleonic wars, he transferred to Bencoolen (Bengkulu), Sumatra. Early in 1819, with the authority of the EIC's headquarters in Calcutta, he stopped on the island of Singapura for a momentous week (29 January–7 February) during which he concluded the treaty establishing British rights, leaving William Farquhar to become the first Resident. In 1824, Raffles finally left South-East Asia, but his health was permanently injured and he died prematurely in 1826.

The plant described in this abstract was later named after Raffles.

T HE most important discovery throughout our journey was made at this place. This was a gigantic flower, of which I can hardly attempt to give anything like a just description. It is perhaps the largest and most magnificent flower in the world, and is so distinct from every other flower, that I know not to what I can compare it—its dimensions will astonish you—it measured across from the extremity of the petals rather more than a yard, the nectarium was nine inches wide, and as deep; estimated to contain a gallon and a half of water, and the weight of the whole flower fifteen pounds.

The Sumatran name of this extraordinary production is Petimum Sikinlili, or Devil's-Siri (beetle) box. It is a native of the forests, particularly those of Passumah Ulu Manna.

This gigantic flower is parasite on the lower stems and roots of the Cissus Angustifolia of Box. It appears at first in the form of a small round knob, which gradually increases in size. The flower-bud is invested by numerous membranaceous sheaths, which surround it in successive layers and expand as the bud enlarges, until at length they form a cup round its base. These sheaths or bracts are large, round, concave, of a firm membranaceous consistence, and of a brown colour. The bud before expansion is depressive, round, with five obtuse angles, nearly a foot in diameter, and of a deep dusky red. The flower, when fully expanded, is, in point of size, the wonder of the vegetable kingdom; the breadth

Rafflesia Arnoldi, reproduced in Lady Raffles's *Memoir*.

across, from the top of the one petal to the top of the other, is three feet. The cup may be estimated capable of containing twelve pints, and the weight of the whole is from twelve to fifteen pounds. The inside of the cup is of an intense purple, and more or less densely yellow, with soft flexible spines of the same colour: towards the mouth, it is marked with numerous depressed spots of the purest white, contrasting strongly with the purple of the surrounding substance, which is considerably elevated on the lower side. The petals are of a brick-red, with numerous pustular spots of a lighter colour. The whole substance of the flower is not less than half an inch thick, and of a firm fleshy consistence. It soon after expansion begins to give out a smell of decaying animal matter. The fruit never bursts, but the whole plant gradually rots away, and the seeds mix with the putrid mass.

If I am successful in obtaining a draftsman, your Grace shall have a perfect representation of it. I have made a very rough sketch of it myself, but it is not in that state that I could venture to present it. It seems to be a flower unknown to most of the natives, as well as to naturalists; its colours red, yellow, and purple, and most brilliant. The chemical composition being fungous, it would not keep; and not having sufficient spirits, we could not preserve it entire. A part of it, with two buds almost as big as a child's head, will be sent home.

Lady [Sophia] Raffles, *Memoir of the Life and Public Services of Sir Thomas Stamford Raffles, by his Widow*, 2nd edn., James Duncan, London, 1835, Vol. 1, pp. 343–5.

87
Fungi

E. J. H. CORNER

Fungi have a special place in the ecology of the tropical rain forests of South-East Asia, as John Corner has explained.

F UNGI do not figure in the usual brief of wildlife or habitat conservation. No voice has been raised on their behalf. They, however, do the dirty work by clearing up, very largely, the mess of dead vegetation. The combination of putrescible plant remains with a host of fungal scavengers, especially the higher fungi, stokes the power plant of the forest. Over the years fungi can render a trunk into clouds of spores which settle as manna for animalcules at the beginning of food-chains and into friable rubble which is tilth for the soil and material for root-absorption. The more substantial the vegetation, the greater is the variety of fungi needed for its degradation. The high and varied forest of Peninsular Malaysia contains an inestimably rich assemblage of higher fungi essential for its continuance. From end to end of the Peninsula hyphae permeate the humus, dead wood and bark, fruit-husks, seed-coats, living and dead roots, and extend in these dead parts into the canopy. Their presence is, however, not obvious until they fruit, which they do seasonally, as over all the world.

Despite the general uniformity of the perhumid climate, the lowland fungi of Peninsular Malaysia fruit seasonally in March to May and August to October or November. These seasons apparently correlate with the return of wet weather after relatively dry periods of several weeks. Prolonged vegetative growth during the rainy weather in most cases does not lead to fruiting. That growth must be checked by the dry spell and, then, on the return of the rain, the hyphae change by some means unknown, from diffuse foraging to compact growth as fruit-bodies. Suddenly, at these times, there appear on the forest-floor countless toadstools, puffballs, clubs, cups and brackets, in explanation of what has been occurring. The expanded fruit-bodies seldom last more than a few days or a week and species and genera fruit in succession. Unless one is on the spot for the few critical days, many fungi will be overlooked.

First come small fruit-bodies of such as *Marasmius* and *Mycena*, growing on fallen leaves and twigs—first to be soaked with rain. Then begin the terricolous agarics such as *Amanita, Boletus, Russula,* and *Lactarius,* to be followed by other genera and by the more slowly growing, tough and woody, fruit-bodies of polypores and stereoid fungi. . . .

There are some exceptions. Certain species of ephemeral habitats or those with short-lived mycelium respond to slight local variations in the weather, such as freak storms in a dry period. In addition, the perennial brackets of woody polypores and stereoid fungi are present at all times of year but they, too, respond seasonally by adding, twice a year, a new layer of tubes or of hymenium. Thus, although the forest is never devoid of some fruit-bodies, for most of the time there are few signs of its fungus wealth.

E. J. H. Corner, 'Higher Fungi', in Earl of Cranbrook (ed.), *Key Environments: Malaysia*, Pergamon Press, Oxford, 1988, pp. 88–90.

88
Ant Plants

HENRY O. FORBES

The interaction of vegetable and animal is nowhere more remarkable than in the South-East Asian ant plants. These show a huge variety of strange adaptations to an existence apparently of mutual benefit to both partners. Forbes found examples in Java, and investigated the role of ants in the development of the peculiarities of the plant.

T HE 14th of June is to me memorable as being the day on which for the first time I saw in its native habitat, and gathered there, that most singular of the vegetable productions of the Indian Archipelago, the *Myrmecodia tuberosa* and *Hydnophytum formicarum*. Their most striking characteristic will be indelibly marked in my remembrance by the sensations other than mental, by which their acquaintance was made.

In tearing down a galaxy of epiphytic orchids from an erythrina tree, I was totally overrun, during the short momentary contact of my hand with the bunch, with myriads of a minute species of ant (*Pheidole javana*), whose every bite was a sting of fire. Beating a precipitous retreat from the spot, I stripped with the haste of desperation, but, like pepper-dust over me, they were writhing and twisting their envenomed jaws in my skin, each little abdomen spitefully quivering with every thrust it made. Going back, when once I had rid myself of my tormentors, to secure the specimens I had gathered, I discovered in the centre of the bunch a singular plant I had never seen before, which I perceived to be the central attraction of the ants. It was called *Kitang-kurak* by my boy, who said it was the home of the ants. I was overjoyed with the revelation that a slice struck off by my knife, made of an intricate honeycombed structure swarming with minute ants—a living formicarium.

In the space of a short search I found, generally high on the trees, abundance of specimens of both genera, which, not without several futile attempts and many imprecations and groanings on the part of my boys, were brought to the ground; and, at the ends of a pole over their shoulders, up which the infuriated dwellers would ascend to spread over their bare bodies to their frequent discomfiture, they were at last safely deposited in a spot in Mr Lash's garden, where I could examine them with comfort without disturbing their inhabitants.

[Following is a description of] the general appearance of the epiphyte: a spine-covered bulb surmounted by a

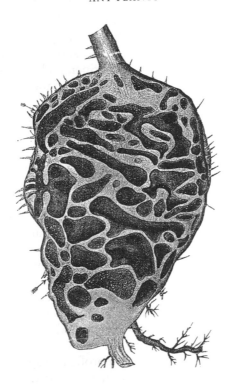

Forbes's illustration of a transverse section of the stem of the ant plant, *Myrmecodia tuberosa.*

cylindrical axis bearing leaves and minute flowers, while the longitudinal section on the opposite page shows the complicated system of galleries—some of them papillated—inhabited by the ants.

Observing the ants often employed in carrying out whitish particles, I at first conjectured that the irritation of their digging out a dwelling must have induced the swelling of the bulb; and, curious to see the *modus operandi* of its commencement, I decided to raise a few of them from seed. This turned my attention to their flowers and fruit. The flowers are produced in deep spine-protected pits on the axis surmounting the bulb, and are remarkable for the extreme rapidity with which the cycle of their functional changes are performed. The pellucid white flower appears, and is followed by an orange, watery fruit, whose seeds ripen and often germinate in the little pits where they grow, all within the space of thirty-six hours.

Some years later Dr Burck, of the Buitenzorg Gardens, most kindly showed me specimens and microscopic slides illustrating some interesting observations he had made on these flowers: that the corolla segments rarely open (though a slight touch can effect it): that the pollen grains exsert their pollen tubes while still in the anthers; and that both the external and the internal surfaces of the lobes of the pistil are covered with papillæ, indicating that these surfaces are functionally active.

I have never observed these flowers approached by the ants that infest the interior, nor by any other insect, which to gain admission to the flower, even if open, must be very small indeed. The anthers and the pistil do not seem to reach maturity together, yet it would seem that self-fertilisation alone can take place; perhaps the tubes of the pollen grains which fall to the bottom of the corolla manage to reach the lower lobes of the pistil and produce fecundation.

The seeds I planted germinated with great freedom, and I cultivated quite a number of young *Myrmecodia,* whose growth I watched with the greatest interest. Many of them I kept quite isolated from the interference not only of the *Pheidole javana,* which seems to be the only species of ant which lives in these plants in their native state, but of all other species, and I was surprised to find that from their very earliest appearance *this curious galleried structure arose without the presence of the ants,* and that the plants continued to grow and thrive vigorously in their absence as long as I cultivated them. Some bulbs had a single canal reaching to their centre from a round orifice opening generally close to the little tap-root; others presented one or two loculi in the interior, without any communication at first with the exterior, partially full of a spongy substance looking like its own degenerated tissue. These chambers invariably developed a spongy pith—which in a section it was not difficult to trace out in advance in the still fleshy substance—towards and to open at last at one or more spots on the exterior of the bulb. Secondary galleries, arising in the same manner as the primary, soon formed communicating channels, extending with age, throughout the whole of the growing bulb. At a later period, in Amboina, where the *Myrmecodia* and the *Hydnophytum* were very abundant, I found many specimens containing a large central and quite isolated chamber full of water—not rain-water—round which radiated the galleries tenanted by ants and their larvæ of the same species as in Java.

Henry O. Forbes, *A Naturalist's Wanderings in the Eastern Archipelago: A Narrative of Travel and Exploration from 1878 to 1883*, Harper and Brothers, New York, 1885, pp. 79–82.

89
Korthalsia

E. J. H. CORNER

The exact nature of the relationship between insect and plant is still more obscure in the case of the fish-tail rattan, *Korthalsia*, described by John Corner as creating an ant 'shelter' within the sheathing leaf-base.

WHERE the leaf-stalk joins the sheath in all its species there is a well-developed ligule which may reach several inches long and be so conspicuously convex as to form a sort of legging on the stem; for this reason it is called the ocrea. The species are distinguished by the form, size, and spininess of the ocrea. The old and dry leaf-sheaths persist for a long time; stems over one hundred feet long may be clothed with the pallid dead sheaths. The ocreas also persist and, as thin hard convex shells firmly pressed to the stem, they make excellent shelters for ants if they can get in. They enter by biting a hole or two in the soft, living ocrea of the young leaf and make a nest inside. As more leaves are developed, they enter more houses until, with strip development, they occupy the whole stem.

We pause in the excitement of a first expedition through the sweating glades beneath the dipterocarps, and a faint rustle fades into the trees. It comes again and vanishes as widely. We think of snakes, wasps, bees, and look around, but can discern no obvious source of the mystery. Yet now it is repeated right, left, and on all sides as a series of tiny rattles through the bushes into the canopy. An uncanny feeling shivers over our clammy bodies that we are watched by a host of invisible onlookers. But is this snake underfoot any more than the trailing stem of an old rattan? We bend down in relief to examine it and, just as the sound commences, a small ant at a hole in an ocrea beats its mandibles on the dry cover. Instantly a rattle comes from the box, to be taken up by the next and the next along the stem into the trees. We are standing in an old clump of *Korthalsia* and all its stems are rattling. The sentry has alerted the soldiers and the alarm is transmitted from post to post as a sort of 'action stations' to repel boarders up to the crown in the tree-tops. We lift the stem and out rush the black ants with ferocious bites.

E. J. H. Corner, *The Natural History of Palms*, Weidenfeld and Nicolson, London, 1966, pp. 210–11.

Invertebrate Marvels

❧

90
Insects of Burma

F. KINGDON WARD

In December 1930, on their one expedition together, Kingdon
Ward and my father were amazed at the variety of insect life to be
found in the Burmese jungle.

W E had started a collection of insects, mainly beetles, and
this occupation gave us plenty of interest. Whenever
we came to a large log of wood or a stone, we gathered
round it armed with killing bottles, and proceeded to roll it
over if we could. The sudden light startled the underworld
into life. Small beetles scurried this way and that. There were
vicious-looking centipedes and bloated wood-lice running
madly about. Little black scorpions turned up their tails and
adopted an aggressive attitude. These last were more common inside the wood logs than under them—especially
where white termite ants had been at work. Those who are
familiar only with English or even with European forests
would be surprised at the work performed by the hordes of
insects and other creatures which work in the dark in the
Burmese jungle. Even at this off-season, prodigious numbers
of small sappers and miners were at work. A thick tree trunk
is reduced to dust in a few months by a termite army. Nor
were all the insects we discovered subterranean. Butterflies
and grasshoppers, dragonflies and beetles were numerous on

195

warm afternoons in every open place. It was surprising how many of the smaller grasshoppers were one-legged, as though they had each lost a limb during some titanic upheaval, or perhaps only in domestic strife with the more bulky females. Huge locusts with a bright green fuselage, utterly sluggish when the morning mist lies on the ground, became active in the heat of the day, when the shade temperature rose to 70°. These locusts are awkward in the air, flying clumsily and rather slowly when disturbed; but their colour keeps them concealed; often the first intimation one had of their presence was a whirr of wings. They would travel in a straight trajectory, as though loosed from a gun, until they hit against an obstacle. Usually they fell down, but sometimes they clung to the frail support of a leaf or stem. They never seemed to have the power to change their direction while in flight and always kept on their course until stopped suddenly by impact.

Most of the cold-weather butterflies we saw were small drab, shade-loving insects, their wings dazzle-painted with bars and spots. They are weak, and fly slowly, with a zigzag, dipping motion.

F. Kingdon Ward, *Plant Hunter's Paradise*, Jonathan Cape, London, 1937, pp. 42–3.

91
Butterflies of Sulu

F. W. BURBIDGE

Butterflies and moths reach peaks of abundance and variety at the tropical latitudes of South-East Asia. The botanist, Burbidge, enjoyed their special richness in the Sulu Islands, Philippines, and wisely did not disparage them for their taste in liquid foods.

O F all the smaller forms of animal life in temperate countries the butterflies are the most absolutely beautiful. In the tropics they are especially so, being there found of the largest size and most lovely hues. In the rice fields and by the open pathways, lively little golden-winged kinds flutter in the sunshine. Some are quite wholly golden, others amber, with black fringes to their wings; many varieties enliven the river margins, and others sail aloft around the tops of the great forest trees. The nearly dry bed of a forest stream is an attractive spot to many of the finest tropical butterflies, especially if it be chequered with shade and sunshine. In such a place they may be seen by the hundred, flitting, fluttering, skimming or wobbling to and fro, enlivening the cool greenery with their colour, beauty, and variety of motion. Here you see them at home and happy. Their colours defy description, so variable do they appear as seen in the sunlight; sulphur and black, amber and blue, velvety bands, purple shot with bronze, wings of blue, inclining to green, and of green inclining to blue, and of velvety blackness banded with pea or apple-green, are only a few of their combinations. Their beauty of presence is so satisfying, that we almost forget their life history, the egg so dainty in form, and often so beautiful in sculpture, the caterpillar, attractive in its way, and chiefly remarkable for its leaf-eating powers; then the long sleep in a silken hammock, and finally a sunny awakening into life and beauty as a daintily painted butterfly. There must be something in the climate or vegetation of the Sulu islands especially favourable to insect life, and nowhere else did I see butterflies so plentiful as here, not only in the forest and by the river, but around the houses of Meimbong itself.

The site of the market being littered with fragments of fruit and other *debris*, was especially attractive to them; on being disturbed they fluttered away in crowds, only to return almost immediately to feast on the wasted sweets, and to open and close their gorgeous wings in the sunshine.

F. W. Burbidge, *The Gardens of the Sun, or Naturalist's Journal on the Mountains and in the Forests and Swamps of Borneo and the Sulu Archipelago*, John Murray, London, 1880, pp. 201–2.

92
Rajah Brooke's Birdwing

HENRY O. FORBES

Among the most gorgeous of papilionid butterflies of South-East Asia is Rajah Brooke's birdwing. This butterfly was first collected in Sarawak by Wallace who named it *brookeana* in honour of the Rajah. Males gather at salt-springs or seepages where they present a brilliant sight. Females are vastly outnumbered in wild populations, and rarely seen. Here is Forbes's note, from his camp by hot springs in Sumatra.

T HE magnificent *Ornithoptera brookeana*, whose favourite resort was the stones that cropped out above the hot water, and which were of a temperature but little below 130 °F. This butterfly has a bar of the richest lake dividing the head from the thorax; its blue-black wings are banded on the upper side with the most sparkling metallic emerald, and the under sides slashed with metallic green and blue, which glittered and flashed in the sunshine, in whose brightest hours alone they made their appearance.

Henry O. Forbes, *A Naturalist's Wanderings in the Eastern Archipelago: A Narrative of Travel and Exploration from 1878 to 1883*, Harper and Brothers, New York, 1885, p. 227.

93
Curious Butterflies

ALFRED RUSSEL WALLACE

The large birdwing butterflies fascinated Wallace, who was particularly intrigued at the extraordinary mimicry shown by females of the Great Mormon, *Papilio memnon*.

T HE first is the handsome Papilio memnon, a splendid
butterfly of a deep black colour, dotted over with lines
and groups of scales of a clear ashy blue. Its wings are five
inches in expanse, and the hind wings are rounded, with
scalloped edges. This applies to the males; but the females are
very different, and vary so much that they were once supposed to form several distinct species. They may be divided
into two groups—those which resemble the male in shape,
and those which differ entirely from him in the outline of
the wings. The first vary much in colour, being often nearly
white with dusky yellow and red markings, but such differences often occur in butterflies. The second group are much
more extraordinary, and would never be supposed to be the
same insect, since the hind wings are lengthened out into
large spoon-shaped tails, no rudiment of which is ever to be
perceived in the males or in the ordinary form of females.
These tailed females are never of the dark and blue-glossed
tints which prevail in the male and often occur in the females
of the same form, but are invariably ornamented with stripes
and patches of white or buff, occupying the larger part of the
surface of the hind wings. This peculiarity of colouring led
me to discover that this extraordinary female closely resembles (when flying) another butterfly of the same genus but of
a different group (Papilio coon); and that we have here a case
of mimicry similar to those so well illustrated and explained
by Mr Bates. That the resemblance is not accidental is
sufficiently proved by the fact, that in the North of India,
where Papilio coon is replaced by an allied form (Papilio
Doubledayi) having red spots in place of yellow, a closely-
allied species or variety of Papilio memnon (P. androgeus),
has the tailed female also red spotted. The use and reason of
this resemblance appears to be, that the butterflies imitated
belong to a section of the genus Papilio which from some
cause or other are not attacked by birds, and by so closely
resembling these in form and colour the female of Memnon
and its ally, also escape persecution. Two other species of this
same section (Papilio antiphus and Papilio polyphontes) are

Wallace's illustration of two different females of the birdwing, *Papilio memnon*.

so closely imitated by two female forms of Papilio theseus (which comes in the same section with Memnon), that they completely deceived the Dutch entomologist De Haan, and he accordingly classed them as the same species.

But the most curious fact connected with these distinct forms is, that they are both the offspring of either form. A single brood of larvæ were bred in Java by a Dutch entomologist, and produced males as well as tailed and tailless females, and there is every reason to believe that this is always the case, and that forms intermediate in character never occur.

Alfred Russel Wallace, *The Malay Archipelago: The Land of the Orang-Utan, and the Bird of Paradise*, 10th edn., Macmillan and Co., London, 1883, pp. 128–30.

94
Butterfly Swarms

L. WRAY JR.

Huge gatherings of butterflies have been recorded in South-East Asia. Some have appeared to be directed migration—but from where, and whither, remain unsolved mysteries. This short observation is abstracted from the journal of a trip to the interior hills of southern Perak, Malaysia, by Leonard Wray Jr.

Wray was the son of a pioneer British planter of the same name in what is now Peninsular Malaysia. He became Curator of the museum at Taiping, Perak, and undertook several general collecting expeditions in exploration of the interior of that State. He is also credited with early experimental plantings of Para rubber in Perak and instituted trial tapping in 1897. 'Wray's camp', on Gunung Tahan, Peninsular Malaysia, is named after him and he is commemorated by the name *wrayi* given to five birds new to science at the time, described from his collections. This abstract is taken from the account of his first trip to the highlands of the Main Range, in 1888.

ON the 25th we were able to leave Tapa. We then had 22 Sakais, and the heavy baggage had to be put into two boats and poled up the river to Kuala Woh, which place we reached after a walk of two and-a-half hours, the track crossing the Batang Padang River twice. The whole way, wherever there was an opening in the jungle, we met with swarms of yellow butterflies. There must have been millions of them spread over the country. In places they were settled so thickly that the ground could not be seen. Some of these patches were two and three feet in diameter, and after driving away the butterflies the ground was quite yellow from pieces of their wings and dead ones. I have never seen such a sight before, almost any sweep of a butterfly net would catch a dozen or more. In the afternoon it came on to blow, just before a shower of rain, and all the butterflies at once took up positions on the undersides of the leaves of trees and

201

plants and on the lee sides of the stems and roots. They were all of one species of Terias (*Terias hecabe*), and the Malays said that they had appeared about a week before we saw them. The whole of the next day's march they were quite as numerous, though we rose to an altitude of 1,130 feet above sea level, and they were also fairly common as high as the camp on Gunong Batu Puteh, which we reached on the day after.

L. Wray, 'Journal of a Collecting Expedition to the Mountain of Batang Padang, Perak', *Journal of the Straits Branch of the Royal Asiatic Society*, Vol. 21, 1890, pp. 124–5.

95
Catching Moths

ALFRED RUSSEL WALLACE

By night, butterflies are supplanted by their even more diverse and numerous relatives, the moths. Wallace was an enthusiastic collector and made his record catch of moths while lodging at Rajah James Brooke's hilltop bungalow on Bukit Peninjauh, some 30 kilometres up the Sarawak River from Kuching. Careful detective work led to the rediscovery of this site a few years ago by Sarawak Museum staff.

O N one side of the cottage there was a verandah, looking down the whole side of the mountain and to its summit on the right, all densely clothed with forest. The boarded sides of the cottage were whitewashed, and the roof of the verandah was low, and also boarded and whitewashed. As soon as it got dark I placed my lamp on a table against the wall, and with pins, insect-forceps, net, and collecting-boxes by my side, sat down with a book. Sometimes during the whole evening only one solitary moth would visit me, while on other nights they would pour in, in a continual stream, keeping me hard at work catching and pinning till past midnight. They came literally by thousands. These good nights were very few. During the four weeks that I spent altogether on the hill I only had four really good nights, and these were always rainy, and the best of them soaking wet. But wet nights were not always good, for a rainy moonlight night produced next to nothing. All the chief tribes of moths were represented, and the beauty and variety of the species was very great. On good nights I was able to capture from a hundred to two hundred and fifty moths, and these comprised on each occasion from half to two-thirds that number of distinct species. Some of them would settle on the wall, some on the table, while many would fly up to the roof and give me a chase all over the verandah before I could secure them....

... on twenty-six nights I collected 1,386 moths, but ... more than 800 of them were collected on four very wet and dark nights. My success here led me to hope that, by similar arrangements, I might in every island be able to obtain abundance of these insects; but, strange to say, during the six succeeding years I was never once able to make any collections at all approaching those at Sarawak. The reason of this I can pretty well understand to be owing to the absence of some one or other essential condition that were here all combined. Sometimes the dry season was the hindrance; more frequently residence in a town or village not close to virgin forest, and surrounded by other houses whose lights were a counter-attraction; still more frequently residence in a dark palm-thatched house, with a lofty roof, in whose recesses every moth was lost the instant it entered. This last was the greatest drawback, and the real reason why I never again was able to make a collection of moths; for I never afterwards lived in a solitary jungle-house with a low boarded and whitewashed verandah, so constructed as to prevent insects at once escaping into the upper part of the house, quite out of reach.

Alfred Russel Wallace, *The Malay Archipelago: The Land of the Orang-Utan, and the Bird of Paradise*, 10th edn., Macmillan and Co., London, 1883, pp. 85–7.

96
Ornithoscatoides

HENRY O. FORBES

While chasing butterflies in Java, Forbes found himself rivalled by a more elaborate mimic—a spider that used its resemblance to a bird's dropping to entice its prey. His specimen became the type of a new genus, appropriately named *Ornithoscatoides*!

I had been allured into a vain chase after one of those large, stately flitting butterflies (*Hestia*) through a thicket of prickly *Pandanus horridus*, to the detriment of my apparel and the loss of my temper, when on the bush that obstructed my farther pursuit I observed one of the *Hesperiidæ* at rest on a leaf on a bird's dropping. I had often observed small Blues at rest on similar spots on the ground, and have often wondered what the members of such a refined and beautifully painted family as the *Lycænidæ* could find to enjoy at food seemingly so incongruous for a butterfly. I approached with gentle steps but ready net to see if possible how the present species was engaged. It permitted me to get quite close and even to seize it between my fingers; to my surprise, however, part of the body remained behind, and in adhering as I thought to the excreta, it recalled to my mind an observation of Mr Wallace's on certain Coleoptera falling a prey to their inexperience by boring in the bark of trees in whose exuding gum they became unwittingly entombed. I looked closely at, and finally touched with the tip of my finger, the excreta to find if it were glutinous. To my delighted astonishment I found that my eyes had been most perfectly deceived, and that the excreta was a most artfully coloured spider lying on its back, with its feet crossed over and closely adpressed to its body.

The appearance of the excreta rather recently left on a leaf by a bird or a lizard is well known. Its central and denser portion is of a pure white chalk-like colour, streaked here and there with black, and surrounded by a thin border of the

dried-up more fluid part, which, as the leaf is rarely horizontal, often runs for a little way towards the margin. The
spider, which belongs to a family, the *Thomisidæ*, possessing
rather tuberculated, thick, and prominent abdomened bodies,
is of a general white colour; the underside, which is the one
exposed, is pure chalk white, while the lower portions of its
first and second pair of legs and a spot on the head and on the
abdomen are jet black.

This species does not weave a web of the ordinary kind,
but constructs on the surface of some prominent dark green
leaf only an irregularly shaped film of the finest texture,
drawn out towards the sloping margin of the leaf into a narrow streak, with a slightly thickened termination. The spider
then takes its place on its back on the irregular patch I have
described, holding itself in position by means of several
strong spines on the upper sides of the thighs of its anterior
pairs of legs thrust under the film, and crosses its legs over its
thorax. Thus resting with its white abdomen and black legs
as the central and dark portions of the excreta, surrounded by
its thin web-film representing the marginal watery portion
become dry, even to some of it trickling off and arrested in a
thickened extremity such as an evaporated drop would leave,
it waits with confidence for its prey—a living bait so artfully
contrived as to deceive a pair of human eyes even intently
examining it.

Henry O. Forbes, *A Naturalist's Wanderings in the Eastern Archipelago: A Narrative of Travel and Exploration from 1878 to 1883*, Harper and Brothers, New York, 1885, pp. 63–5.

97
Fireflies

JOHN CAMERON

While butterflies gild the day, the glittering firefly brightens the sultry night in many a mangrove, as described by Cameron at Singapore in the 1860s. Modern Singapore has preserved a small relic of this special habitat at Sungei Buloh nature reserve, a true jewel of natural heritage.

T HESE swamps, as I have remarked when describing the Singapore river, are filled and discharged by the rise and fall of the tide. At high water they look pretty enough, for the mangroves are covered over to above their roots, and display only their thick green bushy tops. At low-water, on the other hand, the muddy bottom is exposed and glistens half wet in the sun, with the dull, dirty roots of the mangroves standing naked out of the mud like the ribs of an inverted umbrella. Passing these swamps on a sultry night, especially at low water, and when there is no moon, the sight is a very peculiar one, certainly never to be met with in temperate climates. The bushes literally swarm with fireflies, which flash out their intermittent light almost contemporaneously; the effect being that for an instant the exact outline of all the bushes stands prominently forward, as if lit up with electric sparks, and next moment all is jetty dark—darker from the momentary illumination that preceded. These flashes succeed one another every three or four seconds for about ten minutes, when an interval of similar duration takes place; as if to allow the insects to regain their electric or phosphoric vigour. The Malays here and in many parts of the Archipelago have jewels made for night wear, set, not with pearls or stones, but with little round cages about the size of a pea, in each of which a firefly is imprisoned; the little insect, excited by the narrowness of its cage, gives out even more brilliant and more frequent flashes than when at large. The jewel could have no more pretty setting; it is also a very cheap and a very harmless one, as the firefly is set free before the night is over. I have read somewhere that these insects are impaled on little golden needles, as in the agonies of death they emit a more brilliant lustre. This must be a mistake, however, for I have found that the strength of the flashes they give out is in proportion to their vitality, and if this is in any way impaired, as by the loss of a leg or a wing, the bright flash becomes dull and often extinct. It is difficult to believe that the light of these insects is phosphorescent; it certainly has much more the appearance of electricity, for it is a sharp bright spark and not a dull lustre, and if not under the control of the animal is at least affected by its passions. If they are irritated, as by confinement, or if a branch of a bush on which they are clustered be roughly shaken, they will flash out much more rapidly and brilliantly than when enjoying themselves undisturbed.

John Cameron, *Our Tropical Possessions in Malayan India* ..., Smith, Elder and Co., London, 1865, pp. 80–1.

98
Weaver Ants

HENRY N. RIDLEY

Even the more obnoxious insects of South-East Asia can be astounding in their habits. The extraordinary mode of nest-building by the aggressive, viciously stinging red ant, known for obvious reasons as the 'weaver ant', *Oecophylla smaragdina*, or to Malaysians and Indonesians as *kerengga* (modern spelling), was recounted by Henry Ridley, Director of the Botanic Gardens, Singapore, from 1888 to 1911.

Ridley is celebrated as the pioneer of effective methods of propagating and of tapping Para rubber trees, which had first been introduced in 1877 to Singapore and to Kuala Kangsar, Perak, and subsequently became the mainstay of a prosperous plantation industry throughout tropical South-East Asia.

E VERY person in the Straits must be acquainted with the ferocious red ant commonly known as the Caringa, but although it is so abundant, and obnoxious, it seems that its ferocity and the sharpness of its bite are almost all the facts generally known about it. It is, however, a very interesting animal, not only on account of its peculiar intelligence and courage, but also on account of its remarkable nest-building. I cannot find that the methods of making leaf nests as practiced by the Caringa has ever been described, and as it is very curious I will here submit some account of it. The nests are built in the leaves of any tree suitable to the ants, provided that the leaves are not too stiff to bend, or too small to fasten together conveniently. Usually a tree is selected which is attacked by one of the scale insects upon the honey-like exudations of which these ants live to a large extent. If possible the nest is built over leaves or stems infested by the scale insects, so as to include them in the nest, and in any case other scale insects are carried into the nest for the food supply when requisite. When the food supply is finished, the ants leave the nest and go to another tree.

When a nest is to be built a number of ants seize one edge of a leaf in their jaws and by sticking the claws of the hind legs into an adjoining leaf steadily draw the two edges together. Usually one ant commences the work; then others come up and assist, till finally a large number can be seen holding on tightly. The structure of the legs is evidently adapted for this work, as they are remarkably long and furnished with very sharp hooked claws. If the edges of the two leaves are still too far apart, and one ant cannot reach both edges a chain is made. One ant grasps one edge with its jaws, another seizes him gently but firmly by the notch above the abdomen in its jaws. A third repeats the operation on the second and holds the second leaf by its hind claws. In this manner the leaves are gradually pulled together till the edges almost or entirely meet. The ants can remain in this strained position for a very long time, but usually in a few minutes others come up and commence to sew the leaves together with silk. This is done in the following way. One or two ants come from the interior of the nest, each bearing a larva in its mouth, the tail of the larva pointing outwards. They then commence by applying the tail end of the grub to the edge of one leaf irritating it by quivering the antennae over and upon it. The grub emits a thread of silk which is fixed apparently by the antennae of the ant to the leaf-edge. The sewer then runs across to the other leaf drawing the thread from the grub and fixing it there, and thus it goes backwards and for-wards from leaf-edge to leaf-edge till a strong web of silk blinds the two leaves together. No silk is used in lining the nest, but any holes or spaces between the leaves, are closed with a curtain of silk. When a grub's silk-producing power is exhausted, it is taken back to the interior of the nest and another one fetched. The rapidity with which the work is done is wonderful. I partially opened a nest on a Velvet apple tree (*Diospyros discolor*) tearing open a space at one end about four inches each way, by raising one of the leaves which had previously been sewn to two others. The ants seemed much excited, but soon recommenced to repair the damage. First one, then another, and eventually ten or a dozen seized the edge of the leaf in the way above described and began to pull it back into the old position. The operation took about ten minutes. The leaf seemed to move by short slight jerks, but slowly and steadily. Just as they had got it close to the other leaf, a gust of wind blew it open again and the ants had to recommence. In less than a quarter of an hour the leaves were again held in apposition and the sewing had begun.

H. N. Ridley, 'On the Habits of the Caringa', *Journal of the Straits Branch of the Royal Asiatic Society*, Vol. 22, 1890, pp. 345–6.

99

Leeches

GEORGE MAXWELL

The greatest frisson for the newcomer to South-East Asian forests, is the first encounter with the notorious land leeches. Their habits were described graphically by Maxwell, who knew them well from much experience in the forests.

T HE ants are not as bad as the leeches. Walk you never so lightly, the weight of your footsteps gives the news of your approach, and upon the leaves and grass-stalks and the decaying vegetation that lies everywhere underfoot, the brown forest leeches stand up in eager anticipation. They are of all sizes, from the baby that is scarcely thicker than a thread to the full grown one of an inch and a half long. They stand on their tails, swaying their bodies and bowing their heads on every side to discover the direction from which the sound comes. They have a quaintly fantastic, mincing appearance, from which the Malays borrow a simile to express the affected walk of the damsels of their country.

But when a leech sees the object of its search there is no further delay—no more bowing and curtseying; it races towards its goal. The head is thrust out as far as it will reach, and the mouth seizes hold of whatever it may touch, a leaf or blade or the bare soil. The body is bent into a great loop that brings the tail up to the head. Then the long body straightens again, and the head is thrust forward once more. Each step is the full length of the body, and the leech covers the ground in graceful sinuosities that remind one of galloping greyhounds.

And when the leech gets on to you it wastes no time. Should there be no opening at the top of your boot, and should the folds of your putties afford no entrance, it climbs until it reaches the place where your knickerbockers button at the knee. This is the place where it generally finds access.

But it is immaterial to the leech where it gets at you: get at you it will. If every other opening is unavailable, it will, if not picked off sooner, climb until it reaches your neck. The sense of smell seems to be strongly developed in these pests, for when your blood begins to flow after a leech has dropped off you, gorged and pear-shaped, all the leeches that get upon you subsequently make their way to the one place. Sometimes you may pick off a handful of leeches that hang in a cluster, all clotted with gore and slime, round the side of your knee, and find that you have only three or four other leeches on the whole of the rest of your body.

It adds to the difficulties of attempting to pick a way over a carpet of fallen twigs and crackling leaves, when you see that a leech is racing to catch your boot. In another two or three strides it will reach you. To move your foot before you can seize hold of it may mean that you may snap a dry branch underfoot, and alarm the animal you are stalking; to let the leech get on to you, means that unless you stop to pick it off it will leave a punctured wound upon you that will cause you some days of considerable irritation; and to stop to pick it off may mean that another leech, or perhaps two, will take advantage of the delay to climb upon you unawares. Among your winged worries are mosquitoes, horse-flies, and an occasional skirmisher from a wasp's nest.

I well remember the leeches in this patch of forest, for one of the bites ulcerated, and some months elapsed before it was cured.

George Maxwell, *In Malay Forests*, William Blackwood and Sons, Edinburgh and London, 1907, pp. 99–101.

Quadrupeds and Others

∿

100
Orang-utan

SPENSER ST JOHN

In the mid-seventeenth century Europeans were astounded to learn that a large, red-haired, forest-dwelling anthropoid ape inhabited parts of the great islands of Sumatra and Borneo. In the first travellers' tales, myth and fantasy combined to attribute many near human characteristics to this 'man of the forest' (*orang hutan* in the Malay language) and illustrators gave rein to their imagination. By the later half of the eighteenth century, seafarers had brought home specimens (live and dead) and the anatomy of orang-utans became better known. With the emergence of theories of evolution in the 1800s, interest in them intensified. Museums clamoured for specimens, and the roving naturalist-collectors responded. Accounts of the slaughter by Wallace, Beccari, Hose, and others whose writings feature in this anthology are not edifying.

A brief but objective first-hand account of the habits of this uniquely South-East Asian ape was provided by Spenser St John who spent fourteen years in Borneo, first as British Commissioner stationed in Kuching and subsequently, from 1856 to 1862, as British Consul-General in Brunei. His book, *Life in the Forests of the Far East*, was an immediate best seller and was followed rapidly by a revised and augmented second edition. This abstract is from the latter. Note that St John uses both the name 'orang utan' and the Sarawak vernacular 'mias' (more correctly spelt 'maias', cf. 'mawas' in Indonesia).

212

T HE districts most frequented by the orang utan within the territories of Sarawak, are the Sadong and Lingga, and in those it is generally found where the old jungle stretches uninterruptedly for miles over low swampy lands, dotted here and there with hills and gentle risings, on which noble fruit-trees, rivalling the giants of the forest in magnitude, offer a tempting repast to them. Wherever there have been extensive clearings on which the thickly growing young jungle covers the land, or where the soil yields only the mangrove or the nipa or nibong palms, orang utans are seldom or never found. And this may be readily accounted for by the habits of these animals, which always move from tree to tree and seldom descend to the earth, except in search of water. In the old forest they advance leisurely along the strong branches, and having with one hand secured a firm hold by means of the twigs, stretch out the other to the boughs of the neighbouring tree, and then swing themselves onward, moving, if frightened, at a very rapid rate, or if the boughs be in a favourable position, they grasp those that meet together in one hand, and, thus supported by the mingling twigs, continue their course. As they advance along the large outstretching branches, they appear to be almost walking upright, as the great length of their arms enables them almost to touch their feet without stooping. In their tame state I have often watched them move across a lawn, and then they appear to walk with their fore feet, and drag along their hinder ones like a man who, having lost the use of his legs, employs a pair of crutches. They lean their weight on their knuckles. In the young jungle, or the palm swamps, they could not move from tree to tree, and therefore avoid them. The habits of the orang utan are not gregarious, as they are generally found alone, or attended with a young one, though sometimes two or three of the latter keep together. The infants cling so closely to their mothers that it is almost impossible to tell they are there; and the female does not appear to be in the slightest degree incommoded by their presence.

213

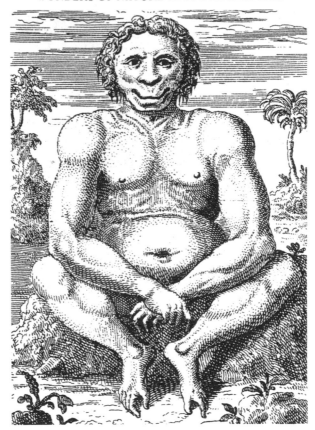

Beeckman's picture and description of the 'Oran-ootan' evidently owed more to imagination and hearsay than direct observation. From Captain Daniel Beeckman, *A Voyage to and from the Island of Borneo in the East-Indies*, T. Warner and J. Batley, London, 1718.

The orang utan always builds itself a nest to rest in at night; it is a very simple one; having selected a horizontal forked branch of sufficient strength to bear its weight, across the angle it lays sufficient boughs to render itself comfortable: it never attempts to shelter itself against sun or rain. When wounded it always resorts to the same expedient, and quickly makes a nest in which to support itself when faint from loss of blood. As these lodgings are so readily constructed, the mias rarely returns to them, or uses them a second time; so that they are to be seen in every direction in the forests frequented by these creatures. They are, however, rarely to be met with on hilly ground, as at nightfall the orang utan quits the fruit-trees to retire to the swamps.

Spenser St John, *Life in the Forests of the Far East; or Travels in Northern Borneo*, 2nd edn., Smith, Elder and Co., London, 1863, pp. 234–6.

101
Game in Cochin-China

JOHN WHITE

In the early years, there was quarry in plenty for the hunter. His reward might be in magic, merchandise, or museum trophy, as John White told.

IT is difficult to conceive of the abundance of game in Don-nai: deer and antelopes are daily in the bazars, and hares occasionally; and this country of rivers is the paradise of aquatic fowls, of various descriptions, while the copses and rice-plantations are filled with birds of graniverous habits. The sportsman may in half an hour fill his game-bag to overflowing. The woods and mountains abound with wild beasts, such as elephants, tigers, rhinoceroses, &c.

These animals are all hunted by the natives; the elephant for his teeth; the tiger for his skin; and the rhinoceros for his horn. Ivory and rhinoceroses' horns are a regal monopoly. Some of these articles were offered us privately, which, to prevent trouble, we refused. The horn of the rhinoceros is formed much like a limpet-shell, but more pointed: at its base it is generally about six inches long, by four inches wide, and protrudes about six or eight inches. There is a shallow concavity occupying the whole base, resembling the limpet also in that respect. To judge of the goodness of a rhinoceros' horn, this concave part is held to the ear, and the greater the noise, resembling that of the waves on the sea-beach, the better the horn. This criterion certainly appears fallacious, if not ridiculous; but the Chinese, who are accustomed to purchase these articles, are always determined by this test. The Onamese speak with great energy of the irresistible strength and amazing velocity of the rhinoceros. They say he moves so rapidly, that it is difficult for the eye to keep pace with him; that no object in his way is any impediment to his rapid career; that he beats down rocks, walls, and large trees, with great ease; and that his track can be easily traced by the ruins in his rear. Speaking of this animal one day to the viceroy, he observed, 'You now see him here, before you, in Saigon'; and, snapping his fingers, 'now he is in Canjeo'. However hyperbolical these accounts appear to be, we may yet infer from them, that the rhinoceros is an animal of astonishing strength and speed. The common tiger of Cochin China is not greatly dreaded, but the royal tiger is a most terrific animal. The governor presented one of the latter to the commander of each ship: they were confined in very strong cages of iron-wood. That which I had was a beautiful female, about two years old, nearly three feet high, and five feet long: her skin is now in the museum of the East India Marine Society, at Salem; for, in consequence of losing, by bad weather, the stock of puppies and kids provided for her on the homeward passage, we were obliged to shoot her.

John White, *A Voyage to Cochin China*, Longman, Hurst, Rees, Orme, Brown, and Green, London, 1824, pp. 244–5.

102
Hunting Sladang in Malaya

GEORGE MAXWELL

Big game hunting brought its enthusiasts, such as George Maxwell, into contact with the beauties of nature and wildlife. Here he recounts the stalk and suspense in pursuit of gaur, the largest of the wild cattle of South and South-East Asia, *seladang* in the Malay language.

W HEN we got to the forest edge I got on my hands and knees, and crawled until I could peer over the plain. What a sight it was! Instead of the two sladang that I had seen, a herd of eleven of these magnificent animals was quietly grazing in the open plain in front of me. Not thirty yards away, and just opposite to me, were a couple of bulls. A huge gaunt cow was a little distance behind them, and beyond her—the farthest of all—but not more than seventy yards away, was the big bull of the herd. A smaller bull and some cows with calves were feeding a little way apart, and somewhat to my right. The little bay or inlet, where the plain ran into the forest, was slightly to my left. The wind blew from them to us, bringing a faint odour of the sweet rich fragrance of cattle. Only once have I had a sight of animal life that could compare with this herd of sladang; and that was when a Malay and I were alone in the depths of the wildest forest—far from any human habitation—and at midnight saw a great solitary wild elephant taking a bath at a sulphur spring, peacefully drinking and besprinkling himself, while the moonlight poured down through the silent trees and shone upon its black glistening body and long gleaming tusks.

But I had little time to watch this herd of sladang. The big bull had his head in the air, and was staring in my direction over the ridge of the gaunt cow's back. As he seemed suspicious, I was afraid that he had seen us move, and made haste

217

to fire before he should give the alarm. How clearly I see it all—the great noble head, the grey hair upon the brow, the glossy jet black of the rest of the head, the massive size and shapely curve of the horns.

I only saw his head, for the gaunt cow covered the rest of him, and, aiming to shoot clear of the cow, I aimed too high, and—missed.

The whole herd dashed away to my right, leaving in the first alarm the little bay for the open plain. The four animals in front of me presented their broadsides, but the big bull was hidden by the cow, and I was unable to get a second shot at him. With my left barrel I fired at one of the other bulls. Then suddenly the sense of the dangers of the open plain overcame the first panic, and the whole herd turned sharply and, with the big bull leading it, galloped back again over the open plain, making for the nearest cover, which was the opposite point of the little bay. They were not more than a hundred yards away, and broadside on.

George Maxwell, *In Malay Forests*, William Blackwood and Sons, Edinburgh and London, 1907, pp. 78–9.

103
The Royal Elephant Hunt

P. A. THOMPSON

The world-famous annual royal elephant 'hunt' in Thailand was devoted to the humane objective of catching fresh stock for domestication. This tradition has continued down many years, although the herds have dwindled.

Thompson, a qualified civil engineer who served in the Thai Royal Survey Department until 1905, witnessed the hunt first-hand.

I T was in March 1905 that I was able to be present at the Hunt. Our party travelled up from Bangkok by train, and on our arrival we found a launch waiting to take us to our house-boat through the streets of floating houses. On the platform of almost every house was a little altar, decked with flowers and incense sticks, to do honour to the King as he passed. As we sat at tiffin the excitement of the crowd on the bank warned us that the elephants were in sight, so taking a sampan we rowed over to a small island in the river. From this point we could look across the level plain to the jungle, two miles away. The elephants were already half way across the plain, moving forward in a compact black mass guarded by the tame tuskers on every side. Each of the tuskers was ridden by a mahout and an elephant-catcher, wearing blue uniforms and broad-brimmed sun helmets. As the herd approached the river bank the crowd scattered from before them, taking refuge behind the flanking lines of tame elephants. Straight on the leader went, down the bank, and waded out into the river. Then followed a fine sight as the great herd hesitated for an instant on the brink, and poured over the edge in a black wave, two hundred and fifty of them, slipping and sliding down the steep bank in a cloud of dust, with trumpetings and squeals. Soon they were all swimming, keeping so closely together that they formed one black patch upon the water, while the tuskers preserved their positions on every side. As they swam they held the tips of their trunks above the surface, while the mahouts, upon the backs of the tame elephants, knelt or stood upright. After gaining the other side the herd was allowed to rest for a while, and the hot thirsty animals revelled in the shallow water, taking deep draughts and squirting streams over each other in excess of joy.

At length the final drive began. Led by two tame elephants, and closely hemmed in behind, the herd pressed forward into the outer stockade, and the bars were slipped behind them. They had still to face the narrow passage through the wall, leading to the inner enclosure, and this they did not like

Elephants in an enclosure at Ayuthia. From Henri Mouhot, *Travels in the Central Parts of Indo-China (Siam), Cambodia, and Laos, during the Years 1858, 1859, and 1860*, John Murray, London, 1864.

220

at all. As before, a tame elephant led the way, but it was not until the tuskers had come up and pushed and prodded those behind that the herd swayed towards the opening, and still those in front held back. At last one made a break and with a frightened squeal ran in, and he was followed by many others. In this way fifty or sixty elephants were got inside, but then a strange thing happened. Perhaps it was the sight of the great crowd pressing closely against the posts on every side that at length made the elephants realise that they were in a trap, but, whatever the cause, they were growing very restive, and remained huddled together in the centre of the stockade. Now and then they would crush against the posts, and one big fellow made a fierce charge in the attempt to regain his freedom. Then the posts creaked ominously, for though they look so stout they are hollow with age. When the elephants came near, the crowd outside gave way and prepared to fly, should they break out, but between the posts were stationed men who thrust with long spears at the elephants, and kept them back. Matters were now at a deadlock, for no more elephants would go through the opening, and those behind were pushing forward and boring into the throng, the little tuskers charging fiercely in with the best of them. As the crush grew worse some were trampled underneath and some were lifted off their feet, while in the very middle one great tuskless male was seen high above his fellows, walking upon the backs of those who had sunk to the ground. Then, mingled with the grunts and squeals, was heard the deep roar of anger, and on the outskirts of the scrum were some who slapped the ground with their trunks in rage. It was soon apparent that many of the smaller elephants were being crushed to death, and so the tame tuskers came round and drove the whole herd back again towards the river, but a pile of fifteen was left lying on the ground. Water was brought in long joints of bamboo, and poured over the prostrate elephants. A few recovered, and with the help of the tuskers regained their feet and joined the herd, but the greater number of them were dead.

In the evening, after the crowd had gone, the rest of the herd was safely got inside the inner stockade. The next morning the wall was thronged with sightseers, and those who could find no room there crowded into the narrow space between the wall and the stockade itself. The elephants appeared to be resigned to their fate, and some were pouring dust upon their heads and blowing it over their backs with a philosophic air of disregard for their surroundings. The catchers, mounted on the tame tuskers, were riding in amongst them. They had ropes of rhinoceros hide, and at one end was a noose which they guided by means of a long bamboo. Having singled out an elephant they seized the moment when one foot was off the ground to slip the noose deftly over his hind leg, and having drawn it tight they threw down the loose end of the rope. Then men ran in between the posts, and catching the rope lashed it to a post. If the wild elephant struggled the tame tuskers forced him back, and as he approached the posts the rope was drawn in, until he was tied up against them. Only five or six elephants were caught, and the young tuskers were generally the ones to be chosen.

P. A. Thompson, *Lotus Land*, T. Werner Laurie, London, 1906, pp. 223–7.

104
Bearded Pig Migrations

E. BANKS

South-East Asia is notorious for the variety of strange pigs endemic to the region, especially on the islands that straddle the Equator and stretch from west to east. One species, the bearded pig, is found in Sumatra, across southern Peninsular Malaysia, and throughout the great island of Borneo, where it is the only wild pig. These pigs have been the quarry of mankind since the earliest Stone Age. Periodically, as Banks has related, they form huge migratory herds which it is every hunter's dream to encounter.

THE bearded pig is subject to lemming-like mass migrations, quite distinct from the annual local movements damaging rice fields, since food is not the main purpose of these changes. In seventeen years' collecting I have seen one and heard of another migration. For five to six weeks, at points sixty to a hundred miles apart, moves a steady stream of wild pigs, a few solitary, some family parties of seven or eight, many packs from fifteen to thirty or forty, occasionally convoys estimated at two hundred, sufficiently large to deter the natives from attack. Every ten minutes or quarter of an hour pigs pass by, a few large, old individuals, many of medium size, none in very fat condition. Rice crops on route are utterly destroyed but they do not deviate in search of others off line of march and food is not objective. Silent, not quarrelsome, almost furtive, intent on something, looking round but little, they push on undeterred by waiting natives, who club and spear them at river crossings until weary of pork. Whence came the pigs, and where they go none know, over a narrow front travelled this horde of pork, not to be turned from its path until exhaustion.

In October 1935 over 800 Dayaks arrived from down river for a mass assault on the pigs which were migrating across the Batang Rejang below the Pelagus rapids. The District Officer reported that well over 1500 had been killed. In November information was received that the great pig migration had ceased; later in the month it recommenced, numbers of Dayaks applied for permission to proceed up river. The migration of pigs across the Batang Rejang continued in December, lasting for three months, unprecedented even in the memory of the oldest men.

E. Banks, *Bornean Mammals*, The Kuching Press, Kuching, 1949, p. 72.

105
A Horde of Pork

JULIAN CALDECOTT AND SERENA CALDECOTT

To see the massed passage of bearded pigs on their migrations has been enough to send men near to madness!

The progress of the great bearded pig movement in 1983 through the Fourth Division of north-eastern Sarawak was pieced together in retrospect by Julian Caldecott and his wife, Serena. In the early 1980s he was working as a professional wildlife biologist with the National Parks and Wildlife Office of the Sarawak Forest Department.

T HE interior Fourth Division is vast, and there were probably several bearded pig populations migrating independently within it. We are concerned only with the upper Baram population, a migration cycle encompassing some 10 000 square kilometres and centred on the headwaters of the Baram river. A key part of this area is a mountain ridge, peaking at about 2110 metres, along which runs the international frontier between (Malaysian) Sarawak and (Indonesian) Kalimantan Timur. This ridge, according to our surveys and the reports of local people, shelters an exceptionally rich oak forest about 50 kilometres long, and the trees of this forest seem to fruit, at least lightly, early in most years. The bulk of the Baram population of pigs started in 1983 near this ridge.

Blundering down steep, forested slopes, or trotting nose-to-tail through the hill-rice fields to splash into the shallows and swim across stream, came group after group, most 30–60 strong, some numbering 100 or more. Three communities on the Baram hazard to guess how many groups crossed in the vicinity of their longhouse each day in this two- to four-month period, yielding roughly these numbers of individual bearded pigs: 50 000, 36 000, 9000. These 95 000 pigs crossed about 6 kilometres of river-length, but the same thing was happening across at least 40 kilometres of the Baram and another

224

10 kilometres of the Silat, so the total travelling population could have been as high as 800 000. It is likely, however, that the pigs channelled themselves across portions of the river with relatively easy banks, and we suspect that the population numbers at least a million.

This 'horde of pork' paid its toll. The people of the Baram are heavily armed, and both practised and enthusiastic hunters. In a sample of 581 families living on the upper Baram, for example, each possessed on average slightly more than half a shotgun (one between two), two spears or spear-blowpipes and three hunting dogs. During 1983 as the pigs crossed the Baram and Silat, each of 577 families on these rivers killed an average of nearly 33 bearded pigs (according to data from interviews, treated conservatively). Allowing for the execution of stragglers outside the main migration and the relatively few communities not covered by our survey, it seems that at least 20 000 bearded pigs were slaughtered as the migrating wave-front rolled over the Baram and Silat in 1983, or roughly 8 per cent of the total travelling population.

After running the gauntlet of the Baram and Silat, the pigs travelled on in their urgent search for food, picking their way through the complex mosaic of the interior. Some probably went west, to be killed by the people of the Tinjar river, but most seem to have veered to the north, either following the Baram valley towards Long San, or orbiting Gunung Murud Kechil in the wild lands between the rivers. Joining forces south of the Akah river, the pigs, swept northeastwards to divide again around the Kelabit settlement of Long Lellang in late 1983 and early 1984. One mass passed to the south, heading due east across the southern end of the Tamabu Range to reach Pa Dali in March 1984, and then to climb up into the oak forest on the Kalimantan border (which was fruiting very prolifically in April). The other wave travelled north from Long Lellang, up the western flank of the Tamabu Range to the Penan community of Pa Tik, and thence partially north-east into the Murut country of the Fifth Division, and partially east towards Kalimantan.

So, between early 1983 and early 1984, a large portion of the bearded pig population of upper Baram completed a roughly oval journey, starting and ending on the Kalimantan border east of the Baram, apparently to take advantage of the fruiting oak forests there.

J. & S. Caldecott, 'A Horde of Pork', *New Scientist*, 15 August 1985, pp. 34–5.

106
The Babirusa of Celebes

ALFRED RUSSEL WALLACE

A pig of truly extraordinary appearance, and of largely unknown habits in its natural state, is the babirusa or 'pig-deer' of Celebes (Sulawesi), described here by Wallace.

T HE Babirusa or Pig-deer, [is] so named by the Malays from its long and slender legs, and curved tusks resembling horns. This extraordinary creature resembles a pig in general appearance, but it does not dig with its snout, as it feeds on fallen fruits. The tusks of the lower jaw are very long and sharp, but the upper ones instead of growing downwards in the usual way are completely reversed, growing upwards out of bony sockets through the skin on each side of the snout, curving backwards to near the eyes, and in old animals often reaching eight or ten inches in length. It is difficult to understand what can be the use of these extraordinary horn-like teeth. Some of the old writers supposed that they served as hooks, by which the creature could rest its head on a branch. But the way in which they usually diverge just over and in front of the eye has suggested the more probable idea, that they serve to guard these organs from thorns and spines, while hunting for fallen fruits among the tangled thickets of rattans and other spiny plants. Even this, however, is not satis factory, for the female, who must seek her food in the same way, does not possess them. I should be inclined to believe rather, that these tusks were once useful, and were then worn down as fast as they grew; but that changed conditions of life have rendered them unnecessary, and they now develop into a monstrous form, just as the incisors of the Beaver or Rabbit will go on growing, if the opposite teeth do not wear them away. In old animals they reach an enormous size, and are generally broken off as if by fighting.

Alfred Russel Wallace, *The Malay Archipelago: The Land of the Orang-Utan, and the Bird of Paradise*, 10th edn., Macmillan and Co., London, 1883, pp. 276–7.

107
The Flying Lemur

ALFRED RUSSEL WALLACE

South-East Asian animals of many sorts have adapted to arboreal life in the great tropical forests by evolving flight membranes of varying extent which provide the means to glide from tree to tree and often also permit subtle in-flight manoeuvres. One such is the strange mammal commonly known in English as the 'flying lemur' or 'colugo'. The enquiring Wallace attested to its aerial skill.

T HIS creature has a broad membrane extending all round its body to the extremities of the toes, and to the point of the rather long tail. This enables it to pass obliquely through the air from one tree to another. It is sluggish in its motions, at least by day, going up a tree by short runs of a few feet, and then stopping a moment as if the action was difficult. It rests during the day clinging to the trunks of trees, where its olive or brown fur, mottled with irregular whitish spots and blotches, resembles closely the colour of mottled bark, and no doubt helps to protect it. Once, in a bright twilight, I saw one of these animals run up a trunk in a rather open place, and then glide obliquely through the air to another tree, on which it alighted near its base, and immediately began to ascend. I paced the distance from the one tree to the other, and found it to be seventy yards; and the amount of descent I estimated at not more than thirty-five or forty feet, or less than one in five.

Alfred Russel Wallace, *The Malay Archipelago: The Land of the Orang-Utan, and the Bird of Paradise*, 10th edn., Macmillan and Co., London, 1883, p. 135.

108
Wallace's Flying Frog

ALFRED RUSSEL WALLACE

Wallace was also the discoverer of a gliding tree-frog. The English vernacular name, Wallace's Flying Frog, still commemorates him.

ONE of the most curious and interesting reptiles which I met with in Borneo was a large tree-frog, which was brought me by one of the Chinese workmen. He assured me that he had seen it come down, in a slanting direction, from a high tree, as if it flew. On examining it, I found the toes very long and fully webbed to their very extremity, so that when expanded they offered a surface much larger than the body. The fore legs were also bordered by a membrane, and the body was capable of considerable inflation. The back and limbs were of a very deep shining green colour, the under surface and the inner toes yellow, while the webs were black, rayed with yellow. The body was about four inches long, while the webs of each hind foot, when fully expanded, covered a surface of four square inches, and the webs of all the feet together about twelve square inches. As the extremities of the toes have dilated discs for adhesion, showing the creature to be a true tree-frog, it is difficult to imagine that this

Wallace's illustration of the flying frog named after him shows the extensive webbing of its large fore and hind feet. These structures support the frog in gliding flight, an ability which is counted as an extreme adaptation to arboreal life in the South-East Asian evergreen tropical rain forests.

immense membrane of the toes can be for the purpose of swimming only, and the account of the Chinaman, that it flew down from the tree, becomes more credible. This is, I believe, the first instance known of a 'flying frog', and it is very interesting to Darwinians as showing, that the variability of the toes which have been already modified for purposes of swimming and adhesive climbing, have been taken advantage of to enable an allied species to pass through the air like the flying lizard.

Alfred Russel Wallace, *The Malay Archipelago: The Land of the Orang-Utan, and the Bird of Paradise*, 10th edn., Macmillan and Co., London, 1883, pp. 38–9.

109
Bats in Bamboo

HENRY N. RIDLEY

There are some strange, specialized mammals associated with bamboo. The flat-headed bats of South-East Asia are able to squeeze into the safe roost space of bamboo internodes through the narrowest of fissures by virtue of exceptionally flattened skulls, first observed by Ridley in the Singapore Botanical Gardens.

A large clump of the bamboo *Dendrocalamus pendulus* Ridley which had died after flowering in the Botanical Gardens Singapore was being cut down in May and one of the coolies while cutting the culms up into lengths and splitting them noticed a strange noise within a joint. On splitting it up three or four bats flew out but there being more inside he brought it to me tied up. On taking it to the museum and carefully opening it Dr Hanitsch and I found no less than twenty-three bats of which four were adult females and nineteen were young ones. One of these was still clinging to the mother and sucking. The joint of bamboo in which these bats were enclosed was a foot in length and the diameter of the hollow inside was 2 inches. The septa at each node were perfect and unbroken, and the only possible entrance was made by a crack on one side which allowed of a narrow slip to be pushed outwards so that a triangular aperture a quarter of an inch across in its widest part appeared in the upper septum.

Through this very small space all these bats must have crept. The inside of the bamboo was wet and dark coloured and there were some dipterous larvae within.

In another clump of the same kind of bamboo, two other joints containing young bats of apparently the same kinds were opened. In one joint when opened, it having been felled and left for some days in the sun all the bats were dead and decomposed. They nearly filled the joint and were apparently about thirty in number. In the other several bats had escaped but there were a number of young ones and one half grown. Specimens of these bats were sent to the British Museum where Mr Oldfield Thomas examined them and found them to be *Tylonycteris pachypus* (*Vesperugo pachypus* Dobson). He writes, 'This bat has an exceedingly flattened skull and thus may account for its ability to get through a crack only a quarter of an inch wide. I never heard of specimens found in such a place before.'

H. N. Ridley, 'Bats in a Bamboo', *Journal of the Straits Branch of the Royal Asiatic Society*, Vol. 50, 1908, pp. 103–4.

110
Boa and Pig

ANON.

The python (often, mistakenly, called 'boa') that has swallowed a pig (or a deer, or a dog) gives us an archetypical reptile story of South-East Asia. Such gigantic snakes are still occasionally encountered.

B OA constrictor was sent for my inspection, which had that morning swallowed a pig belonging to some Chinese at Sungi Kranjie. It would appear that the snake had been seen lurking about the stye several days previous to his last meal which cost him so dear; he artfully however escaped the owner of the swine, who had ineffectually attempted his capture or destruction on these occasions; but on the morning in question, the Boa succeeded in getting entrance into the stye, and, having helped himself to a Porker, found himself in the dilemma of the Weasel in the Barn,—he could not get out again. The owner came upon him in this state of helplessness, and, having called comrades to his assistance, secured the victim, torpid from his voracious exertions, and brought him in triumph into Town.

Now you will say there is nothing novel in all this, nevertheless the disparity of size between the carcase of the pig and the jaws and body of the snake struck me so forcibly, and appeared so extraordinary, that I forthwith proceeded to ascertain the exact relative proportions, and found them as follow. The snake was twelve feet, nine inches long, transerve diameter of jaw inside three and a half inches, neck round nine inches, greatest girth of body at thickest part, when pig was out, eleven and a half inches. The pig weighed thirty seven catties and a half, or rather more than fifty pounds, was a good three fourths grown young sow, and lay apparently without a mark of violence upon its body, not a hair ruffled, legs unbroken; indeed old Isaac Walton never dealt more tenderly with his frog than the Boa had seemingly done with young Piggy. Upon closer examination it was however discovered that the ribs were broken, but as the animal remained in its place of sepulture some hours, sufficient gases had been generated to rectify the effects of the crushing and restore piggy to her pristine comeliness of shape; the contrast therefore was the more striking, but still it is quite inconceivable, how the animal was ever swallowed, how the head of the pig passed the jaws of the snake; would I think puzzle a conjuror to determine; and how the snake felt I leave to the consideration of some hopeless Dyspeptic. So distended were the walls of the abdomen by the unusual meal, that the whole pig could be seen plainly through them; they became diaphanous and thin as gold beater's skin. The vitality of the monster equalled his voracity, for, despite the numberless blows of clubs on its head, two hours after the pig had been cut out of the abdomen, I saw the tail firmly coil itself around a stake. Boa met with poetical justice, for, the same evening, he descended into the very little less ravenous maws of some Chinese, who looked upon the flesh as something exceedingly piquant and appetizing, and eagerly they strove amongst themselves who should possess the largest share of it.

Anon., 'Miscellaneous Notices', *Journal of the Indian Archipelago*, Vol. 2, No. 2, 1848, pp. iii–iv.

111
The Irrawaddy Dolphin

JOHN ANDERSON

In past times the Irrawaddy swarmed with its eponymous dolphin, a species confined to the South-East Asian region. It is unusual among dolphins in its specialization for life in the freshwater environment of the larger river systems.

The first careful description was provided by John Anderson, Superindendent of the Indian Museum at Calcutta. As medical officer on two British expeditions to 'Western Yunnan' (now Burma) in the 1870s, Anderson encountered the Irrawaddy dolphins and, combining his medical and zoological skills, conducted detailed anatomical and behavioural research on the species.

O N my second voyage, although a constant outlook was kept, dolphins were not met with until the steamer had reached Yenanyoung, about one hundred miles above Prome. After the first dolphins had been encountered, they were seen almost daily in the deep reaches of the river as far as our destination, Bhamo, which is about 550 miles in a straight line from the sea, and about 800 miles by the windings of the river. The Tapeng, which flows down from the high Chinese valleys to the east of Bhamo, joins the Irawady about a mile above the town, and at the mouth of the Tapeng many dolphins of all ages are generally to be seen disporting themselves in the long deep reach of the Irawady that occurs there. But during the rains, when the Tapeng and the other affluents of the great Burmese river, such as the Khyendwen and Shuaylee, are in flood, they are ascended by these dolphins. They are also numerous in the deep channels of the lower and middle defiles, and indeed may be generally observed in the majority of the deep reaches. The Shans of Upper Burma assert that the dolphins are not to be found beyond a point thirty miles above Bhamo, where the course of the river is interrupted by rocks, and which they style *Labine*, or Dolphin Point, from the circumstance that, according to them, it is the residence of certain *Nats*, who there impose so heavy a toll on dolphins as to deter them from proceeding upwards....

The Irawady dolphin has much the characters of its marine fellows, being generally seen in small schools which frequently accompany the river steamers, careering in front and alongside of them, as is the custom of dolphins of the sea. Occasionally, however, a solitary individual may be observed, but this is the exception, as two or three are usually associated together, hence this may be considered as a gregarious form. In the defile below Bhamo, where the river runs for ten miles over a deep bed 40 to 60 fathoms in depth and from 200 to 500 yards in width, and defined by high, wooded hills on either side, numerous troops of dolphins may be observed passing up and down, rising every minute or two to the surface to emit the short blowing sound, which ends in the more feeble one of inspiration, and all night through this sound may be heard. They never leave the deep water, and when they rise to breathe (which they do in periods varying from 70 to 150 seconds, although occasionally exceeded) the blow-hole is first seen, then at the end of inspiration the head disappears and the back comes into view, and is gradually exposed as far as the dorsal fin, but the tail flippers are rarely visible. The act of breathing is rapid, so much so indeed that it requires a very expert marksman to take aim and fire before the animal disappears. I have observed some of them disporting themselves in a way that has never yet been recorded of Cetacea, as far as I am aware. They swam with a rolling motion near the surface, with their heads half out of the water, and every now and then nearly fully exposed, when they ejected great volumes of water out of their mouths, generally straight before them, but sometimes nearly vertically. The sight of this curious habit at once recalled to me an incident in my voyage up the river when I had been quite baffled to explain an exactly similar appearance seen at a distance, so that this remarkable habit would appear to be not uncommonly manifested. On one occasion I noticed an individual standing upright in the water, so much so that one-half of its pectoral fins was exposed, producing the appearance against the background as if the animal was supported on its flippers. It suddenly disappeared, and again, a little in advance of its former position, it bobbed up in the same attitude, and this it frequently repeated. The Shan boatmen who were with me seemed to connect these curious movements with the season—spring—in which the dolphins breed.

The food of the Irawady dolphin is apparently exclusively fish. The fishermen believe that the dolphin purposely draws fish to their nets, and each fishing village has its particular guardian dolphin which receives a name common to all the fellows of his school; and it is this superstition which makes it so difficult to obtain specimens of this Cetacean. Colonel Sladen has told me that suits are not unfrequently brought into the Native Courts to recover a share in the capture of fish, in which a plaintiff's dolphin has been held to have filled the nets of a rival fisherman.

John Anderson, *Anatomical and Zoological Researches ... and a Monograph on the Two Cetacean Genera* Platanista *and* Orcella, London, 1878, Vol. 2, pp. 300–1.

112
Turtles of Talang-talang

JAMES BROOKE

On the sandy beaches of South-East Asia, laying turtles hauled out in huge numbers. In 1842, James Brooke visited the Talang-talang islands of Sarawak, his new fiefdom.

I had here an opportunity of seeing a turtle deposit its eggs, which it did in the following manner:—when on the sand it wandered from place to place, and tried several by digging a little, apparently rejecting them as unfit: at length, having made its choice, it buried its nose, and began scooping the sand with its hinder feet in a most deliberate and easy manner, throwing the sand to a considerable distance. It often stopped in its work, and recommenced, and so dug till the body was pretty well buried, and the hole a depth of three or more feet. It then took its station over the hole, and began to lay its eggs, which it did at intervals, for a length of time, to the number of two hundred and thirty; and all the while was perfectly indifferent to the proximity of numerous spectators. Having deposited its eggs, it filled the hole with its hinder fins, and beat down the sand both on the spot and all around, and then retired, not directly (for the track would have been a guide to the nest), but in numerous tortuous courses, round and round, and finally took its departure for the sea at a point distant from its eggs. The Malays on watch have small sticks with flags on them, and as each turtle deposits its eggs, they mark the spot with one of these, and the following morning take the eggs, and store them ready for sale. With all their vigilance, however, numbers escape their observation, and some nests they purposely spare. When the young come forth, the sand (which is small) is said to be literally covered with them, and as they make directly for the sea, the sharks and other fish devour great numbers. These two islands are picturesque and beautiful, with fine wood, and they would make a charming estate for the growth of nutmegs and coffee, for the soil is good. At present they abound with limes and chillies, and have a few wild plantains, all of which thrive well.

Captain R. Mundy, RN, *Narrative of Events in Borneo and Celebes*, James Murray, London, 1848, Vol. 1, pp. 306–7.

113
The Vu Quang Ox

VU VAN DUNG ET AL.

Considering the density and ubiquity of people and the consequent depletion of original populations of large land animals of South-East Asia, it is astonishing that a totally new species of wild ox should remain undiscovered to the outside world until vouched for by remnants of its carcass in 1992!

The authors were members of a research team assembled to collect material and to investigate the distribution and behaviour of this strange montane forest ox in Vietnam. Known in the vernacular as *Sao la* or 'spindle horn', it has been named *Pseudoryx nghetinhensis* and has since been found to extend to adjoining parts of Laos.

I N May 1992 the discovery of three pairs of horns in the only remaining area of pristine forest in northern Vietnam led to the description of a new species of ox. A total of 20 specimens have now been found, most of them consisting of only the horns and part of the skull. The Ministry of Forestry in Vietnam is enlarging and upgrading protected areas in the suspected 4000-sq-km range of the Vu Quang ox and surveys are under way in two proposed reserves in neighbouring Laos where the ox is also reported to occur. Meanwhile a local campaign is necessary to inform villagers of the valuable nature of this species and to ban further hunting.

Vu Van Dung, Pham Mong Giao, Nguyen Ngoc Chinh, Do Tuac, and John MacKinnon, 'Discovery and Conservation of the Vu Quang Ox in Vietnam', *Oryx*, Vol. 28, No. 1, 1994, p. 16.

A portrait of the newly discovered Saola, Spindle horn or Vu Quang Ox. Reproduced with permission from *Oryx*, Vol. 28, No. 1, 1994.

Birds

∾

114
The Great Contrast

ALFRED RUSSEL WALLACE

It was the birds, more than any other group of animals, that drew Wallace's attention to the faunal divide that now bears his name, and that is marked by the deep waters of the Macassar Straits. At its southern extremity, 'Wallace's Line' passes between Bali and Lombok.

T HE great contrast between the two divisions of the Archipelago is nowhere so abruptly exhibited as on passing from the island of Bali to that of Lombock, where the two regions are in closest proximity. In Bali we have barbets, fruit-thrushes, and woodpeckers; on passing over to Lombock these are seen no more, but we have abundance of cockatoos, honeysuckers, and brush-turkeys, which are equally unknown in Bali, or any island further west. The strait is here fifteen miles wide, so that we may pass in two hours from one great division of the earth to another, differing as essentially in their animal life as Europe does from America. If we travel from Java or Borneo to Celebes or the Moluccas, the difference is still more striking. In the first, the forests abound in monkeys of many kinds, wild cats, deer, civets, and otters, and numerous varieties of squirrels are constantly met with. In the latter none of these occur; but the prehensile-tailed Cuscus is almost the only terrestrial mammal seen, except wild pigs, which are found in all the islands, and deer (which have probably been recently introduced) in Celebes and the Moluccas. The birds which are most abundant in the Western Islands are woodpeckers, barbets, trogons, fruit-thrushes, and leaf-thrushes: they are seen daily, and form the great ornithological features of the country. In the Eastern Islands these are absolutely unknown, honeysuckers and small lories being the most common birds; so that the naturalist feels himself in a new world, and can hardly realize that he has passed from the one region to the other in a few days, without ever being out of sight of land.

Alfred Russel Wallace, *The Malay Archipelago: The Land of the Orang-Utan, and the Bird of Paradise*, 10th edn., Macmillan and Co., London, 1883, pp. 14–15.

115
Hornbill Casque

HENRY O. FORBES

Hornbills are the most majestic of the forest birds of South-East Asia. Forbes investigated the anatomy of the astonishing casque that surmounts the bills of these birds.

I shot several specimens of *Bucerotidæ*, the white-crested *Hydrocisa albirostris*, and the great hornbill (*Buceros galeatus*), whose heavy scarlet hammer-fronted casque, which it uses to beat with far-resounding thuds the branches of the trees, draws upon it a severe persecution, as in Palembang each head commands a large price, for out of its dense white ivory-like consolidated horn, are manufactured studs and sleeve-links of great beauty. The casque in most species of this family is a cancellated structure permeated by blood-vessels so teased out as to give it great lightness, that it is difficult to under-stand why in this species it should be so solid and heavy; yet, notwithstanding, no bird could flit about more lightly in the tree-tops, or gather its food more agilely. In a longitudinal section of the head and casque of this bird, the thick horny hammering portion has behind it a layer of dense bone to which osseous bars radiate towards the occipital condyle, where the head joins with the neck, and pass above and around the brain cavity, to protect it in a most beautiful way from shock. The brain cavity is thus lodged below the line of shock, and is besides separated from the casque by padding in the shape of a cartilaginous joint. To Professor Flower I am indebted for directing my attention to the beautiful section in the Museum of the Royal College of Surgeons, whose structure had indeed led him to infer, before he knew the fact, that the bird must use its head as a hammering instrument.

Henry O. Forbes, *A Naturalist's Wanderings in the Eastern Archipelago: A Narrative of Travel and Exploration form 1878 to 1883*, Harper and Brothers, New York, 1885, p. 154.

116
Hornbill and Young

ALFRED RUSSEL WALLACE

The bizarre nesting behaviour of hornbills struck Wallace as 'stranger than fiction'.

I had the good fortune to obtain a male, female, and young bird of one of the large hornbills. I had sent my hunters to shoot, and while I was at breakfast they returned, bringing me a fine large male, of the Buceros bicornis, which one of them assured me he had shot while feeding the female, which was shut up in a hole in tree. I had often read of this curious habit, and immediately returned to the place, accompanied by several of the natives. After crossing a stream and a bog, we found a large tree leaning over some water, and on its lower side, at a height of about twenty feet, appeared a small hole, and what looked like a quantity of mud, which I was assured had been used in stopping up the large hole. After a while we heard the harsh cry of a bird inside, and could see the white extremity of its beak put out. I offered a rupee to any one who would go up and get out the bird, with the egg or young one; but they all declared it was too difficult, and they were afraid to try. I therefore very reluctantly came away. In about an hour afterwards, much to my surprise, a tremendous loud hoarse screaming was heard, and the bird was brought me, together with a young one which had been found in the hole. This was a most curious object, as large as a pigeon, but without a particle of plumage on any part of it. It was exceedingly plump and soft, and with a semi-transparent skin, so that it looked more like a bag of jelly, with head and feet stuck on, than like a real bird.

The extraordinary habit of the male, in plastering up the female with her egg, and feeding her during the whole time of incubation, and till the young one is fledged, is common to several of the large hornbills, and is one of those strange facts in natural history which are 'stranger than fiction'.

Alfred Russel Wallace, *The Malay Archipelago: The Land of the Orang-Utan, and the Bird of Paradise*, 10th edn., Macmillan and Co., London, 1883, p. 137.

117
Megapodidae

ALFRED RUSSEL WALLACE

The nesting habits of the megapodes or maleos are unique. Their eggs are incubated, not by the parent bird but by external warmth. Wallace found that those on Lombok made use of the heat of decomposing vegetation within the egg mound, while those of Celebes (Sulawesi) rely on the black beach sand.

241

THE Megapodidae are a small family of birds found only in Australia and the surrounding islands, but extending as far as the Philippines and North-west Borneo. They are allied to the gallinaceous birds, but differ from these and from all others in never sitting upon their eggs, which they bury in sand, earth, or rubbish, and leave to be hatched by the heat of the sun or of fermentation. They are all characterised by very large feet and long curved claws, and most of the species of Megapodius rake and scratch together all kinds of rubbish, dead leaves, sticks, stones, earth, rotten wood, &c., till they form a large mound, often six feet high and twelve feet across, in the middle of which they bury their eggs. The natives can tell by the condition of these mounds whether they contain eggs or not; and they rob them whenever they can, as the brick-red eggs (as large as those of a swan) are considered a great delicacy. A number of birds are said to join in making these mounds and lay their eggs together, so that sometimes forty or fifty may be found. The mounds are to be met with here and there in dense thickets, and are great puzzles to strangers, who cannot understand who can possibly have heaped together cartloads of rubbish in such out-of-the-way places; and when they inquire of the natives they are but little wiser, for it almost always appears to them the wildest romance to be told that it is all done by birds. The species found in Lombock is about the size of a small hen, and entirely of dark olive and brown tints. It is a miscellaneous feeder, devouring fallen fruits, earth-worms, snails, and centipedes, but the flesh is white and well-flavoured when properly cooked.

* * *

It is in this loose hot black sand, that those singular birds the 'Maleos' deposit their eggs. In the months of August and September, when there is little or no rain, they come down in pairs from the interior to this or to one or two other favourite spots, and scratch holes three or four feet deep, just above high-water mark, where the female deposits a single large egg, which she covers over with about a foot of sand,

and then returns to the forest. At the end of ten or twelve days she comes again to the same spot to lay another egg, and each female bird is supposed to lay six or eight eggs during the season. The male assists the female in making the hole, coming down and returning with her. The appearance of the bird when walking on the beach is very handsome. The glossy black and rosy white of the plumage, the helmeted head and elevated tail, like that of the common fowl, give a striking character, which their stately and somewhat sedate walk renders still more remarkable. There is hardly any difference between the sexes, except that the casque or bonnet at the back of the head and the tubercles at the nostrils are a little larger, and the beautiful rosy salmon colour a little deeper in the male bird, but the difference is so slight that it is not always possible to tell a male from a female without dissection. They run quickly, but when shot at or suddenly disturbed take wing with a heavy noisy flight to some neighbouring tree, where they settle on a low branch; and they probably roost at night in a similar situation. Many birds lay in the same hole, for a dozen eggs are often found together; and these are so large that it is not possible for the body of the bird to contain more than one fully-developed egg at the same time. In all the female birds which I shot, none of the eggs besides the one large one exceeded the size of peas, and there were only eight or nine of these, which is probably the extreme number a bird can lay in one season.

Every year the natives come for fifty miles round to obtain these eggs, which are esteemed a great delicacy, and when quite fresh are indeed delicious. They are richer than hens' eggs and of a finer flavour, and each one completely fills an ordinary teacup, and forms with bread or rice a very good meal. The colour of the shell is a pale brick red, or very rarely pure white. They are elongate and very slightly smaller at one end, from four to four and a half inches long by two and a quarter or two and a half wide.

After the eggs are deposited in the sand they are no further cared for by the mother. The young birds on breaking the shell, work their way up through the sand and run off at

once to the forest; and I was assured by Mr Duivenboden of
Ternate, that they can fly the very day they are hatched.

Alfred Russel Wallace, *The Malay Archipelago: The Land of the Orang-Utan,
and the Bird of Paradise*, 10th edn., Macmillan and Co., 1883, London,
pp. 156 and 265–6.

118
The King Bird of Paradise

ALFRED RUSSEL WALLACE

On the Aru Islands, Wallace finally achieved his passionate ambi-
tion: to collect a Bird of Paradise. The wonderful plumage of these
birds was already well known in Europe, where ladies fancied
exotic decorations for their hats and frocks. The traditional trade
skins were crudely dressed, and the birds appeared to lack legs.
Thus grew a legend which was perpetuated in the Latin name used
by Linnaeus, *Paradisea apoda* (i.e. without legs). All birds of the
group are now protected across their range from the Aru Islands
through Papua New Guinea.

T HE first two or three days of our stay here were very wet,
and I obtained but few insects or birds, but at length,
when I was beginning to despair, my boy Baderoon returned
one day with a specimen which repaid me for months of
delay and expectation. It was a small bird, a little less than a
thrush. The greater part of its plumage was of an intense
cinnabar red, with a gloss as of spun glass. On the head the
feathers became short and velvety, and shaded into rich
orange. Beneath, from the breast downwards, was pure
white, with the softness and gloss of silk, and across the breast
a band of deep metallic green separated this colour from the
red of the throat. Above each eye was a round spot of the
same metallic green; the bill was yellow, and the feet and legs
were of a fine cobalt blue, strikingly contrasting with all the
other parts of the body. Merely in arrangement of colours

and texture of plumage this little bird was a gem of the first water, yet these comprised only half its strange beauty. Springing from each side of the breast, and ordinarily lying concealed under the wings, were little tufts of greyish feathers about two inches long, and each terminated by a broad band of intense emerald green. These plumes can be raised at the will of the bird, and spread out into a pair of elegant fans when the wings are elevated. But this is not the only ornament.

Wallace's illustration of two birds of paradise, the King (upper) and Twelve-wired (lower).

The two middle feathers of the tail are in the form of slender wires about five inches long, and which diverge in a beautiful double curve. About half an inch of the end of this wire is webbed on the outer side only, and coloured of a fine metallic green, and being curled spirally inwards form a pair of elegant glittering buttons, hanging five inches below the body, and the same distance apart. These two ornaments, the breast fans and the spiral tipped tail wires, are altogether unique, not occurring on any other species of the eight thousand different birds that are known to exist upon the earth; and, combined with the most exquisite beauty of plumage, render this one of the most perfectly lovely of the many lovely productions of nature. My transports of admiration and delight quite amused my Aru hosts, who saw nothing more in the 'Burong raja' than we do in the robin or the goldfinch.

Thus one of my objects in coming to the far East was accomplished. I had obtained a specimen of the King Bird of Paradise (Paradisea regia), which had been described by Linnæus from skins preserved in a mutilated state by the natives. I knew how few Europeans had ever beheld the perfect little organism I now gazed upon, and how very imperfectly it was still known in Europe.

Alfred Russel Wallace, *The Malay Archipelago: The Land of the Orang-Utan, and the Bird of Paradise*, 10th edn., Macmillan and Co., London, 1883, pp. 443–4.

119
The Eastern Palaearctic Migration

IAN C. T. NISBET

Each year, by a miracle of long-distance navigation and feats of winged endurance, thousands of millions of migratory birds return to South-East Asia from northern breeding grounds and augment the populations of resident species.

The origins and routes of the migrants have been explained by Ian Nisbet, a physicist by profession but an ornithologist by inclination, who played an active part in an intensive bird-banding campaign organized during the 1960s by the Zoology Department, University of Malaya. He subsequently moved to the USA, where he continued to apply his energies to ornithology and wildlife conservation.

THERE is a major faunal boundary in Asia at about the 90th meridian, and many of the birds breeding to the east of this line (on the central Siberian plateau and in the Far East) belong to different species from their western counterparts. Almost all of these populations migrate to winter in East or Southeast Asia, although a number of them also enter India from the northeast. The ecological problems posed by these migrations are quite different from those of the western and central Palaearctic. Except for some western populations which must cross or circumnavigate the Gobi, there are no major deserts or mountain barriers to be overcome. However, the area suitable for insectivorous birds in midwinter is limited, for under the cold winds of the northeast monsoon the 10 °C isotherm moves in January down to the Tropic of Cancer. The area of land further south (excluding New Guinea and Australia which are reached by few migrants) is only some $1\frac{1}{2}$ million square miles, and has to support the birds breeding in a region five or six times larger. Moreover these winter quarters are broken up into a complex pattern of islands and peninsulas, forcing the birds to make difficult or dangerous sea-crossings. The whole region was largely under forest before its clearance by man: until very recently the habitats available for open country birds in tropical Southeast Asia must have been sparse.

According to standard reference books, there are somewhat more than 350 species of land birds which breed in the eastern Palaearctic (east of 90 °E and north of the Himalayas) and can be classified as long-distance migrants, in that a substantial part of their population spends the winter in the tropics. Eight of these are widespread North American species which have established peripheral populations in northern Siberia; these birds migrate back across the Bering Straits each year to winter in Central or South America. Correspondingly, half a dozen Asian species have peripheral populations in Alaska, which migrate back to spend the winter in the Old World tropics.

A further 34 species breeding in the eastern Palaearctic belong to the western migration system, and fly southwest in the autumn to winter in southwestern Asia or Africa. Correspondingly, a number of species of the western Palaearctic fly east to winter in Southeast Asia. Most of these anomalous cases probably represent species which have only recently extended their breeding ranges, but have not yet established corresponding new wintering grounds. Some of the east–west migrations are so extraordinary that they deserve special comment. For example, Wheatears from Alaska and from northern Scandinavia all converge on migration to winter in Africa, as do Willow Warblers from Scandinavia and eastern Siberia. In contrast, Arctic Leaf Warblers from the same areas all winter in Southeast Asia. The Amur Falcon migrates from northeast Asia to southern Africa by way of India and across the Arabian Sea—yet is almost unknown in Indochina. Conversely, Pechora Pipits from north European Russia appear to migrate to the Philippines and the eastern islands of Indonesia, keeping so far east that the species has never been recorded on the mainland of Southeast Asia.

I. C. T. Nisbet, 'The Eastern Palaearctic Migration System in Operation', in Lord Medway and D. R. Wells, *Birds of the Malay Peninsula*, Witherby, London, Vol. 5, 1976, pp. 57–8.

120
First Wild Argus

WILLIAM BEEBE

William Beebe, passionate about pheasants, visited South-East Asia in the 1920s to obtain living specimens for the collections of the New York Zoological Society, where he ultimately became Director of Tropical Research. On the bank of the Mujong River, a tributary of the Baleh, the great southern arm of the Batang Rajang, Sarawak, sunset provided his first sighting.

S TRAIGHT down stream the sun was hidden in a blaze of yellow and gold clouds before it sank, resulting in an unusually long tropic twilight. Then an afterglow tinted the eastern clouds high over the upper Mujong, violet and pale wine color. The two banks of the river became darker, duskier green, and finally all but the sky-mirrored outermost leaves changed to black. The sky was pale blue; the muddy water a nameless, beautiful brown. The banks were lifeless most of the day, the jungle folk keeping to the inner forests. Now, however, in the cool of early evening, birds' voices were heard. Small flocks of fruit pigeons dashed over the trees, large mynas perched on tall plum trees, and a family of gibbons shook the branches of a tree in the distance. In a black concavity of the pale, clayey bank a lighter spot appeared, framed by bushes. My glasses showed a wild boar, fore-feet stamping, tushes gnashing and twisted tail flicking. Had he not been against the blackest shadow he would have been invisible, as he was coated with the mud of the banks. The flies gave him no peace, and he soon turned and climbed awkwardly into the dark jungle behind. The first flying fox of the evening now appeared, flapping slowly and gracefully as a heron, and by turns soaring like a pelican; then a score of these giant, five-foot bats came into sight, high in air. As the mynas flew from their trees to some distant roost, the bats swung up to the clusters of fruit and enveloped them like starfishes on oysters, swinging around head downward and eating away with all their might. They take the place, in flight along the rivers, of herons, of which I saw none in Borneo. A brace of bluish ducks larger than teal flew across the river, and distant shrills announced the evening concert of the great five o'clock cicadas.

Then came unannounced, the sight of sights. A few paces to the right of the wild boar's wallow, my eye caught a movement against the water-washed bare face of clay. Fortunately I was looking along the tops of the barrels of my glasses, a habit of mine when locating anything by eyesight, the finding of which requires instant but inconspicuous adjustment of the lenses. I pushed them up into focus and there sprang into clear-cut delineation what my eyes had refused to separate from the shadows of the bank,—a male argus pheasant drinking from a rain pool a yard or more from the moiled current of the river. It was half crouched, and the motion of the head, alternately raised and lowered, was all that betrayed the bird. The long wings, the gracefully twisted tail-feathers were as motionless as if carved in cameo against the earthern bank. I watched it thus for a minute, two minutes, then my attention wandered for a moment to some creature near at hand, and when I looked back the bird was just disappearing. I had seen my first wild argus, brief though the glimpse had been.

W. Beebe, *Pheasant Jungles*, G. P. Putnam's Sons, New York and London, 1927, pp. 210–12.

121
Cave Swiftlets

LORD MEDWAY

Among the most intriguing of ornithological wonders are the cave swiftlets of South-East Asia that produce the edible nests of commerce. The edible component is, in fact, a hardened form of saliva secreted by hypertrophied sublingual glands. The most prized 'white' nests consist entirely of this substance. In second-grade nests, this salivary 'cement' serves to bind together extraneous materials in the construction, such as feathers or strands of vegetation.

These birds are also remarkable in uttering a distinctive rattle-like vocalization, using sound frequencies within the human hearing range. This call provides them with the capacity to orientate by echo-location. They are thus able to fly into the total darkness of caves, where they roost and build their nests. The following extract describes the changing pattern of activity and noise through the day and night in such breeding caves in Sarawak.

N IGHT is no barrier to these birds, and they fly freely within the cave or outside it at all hours of the day. Still, a long series of watches at cave mouths (principally at Niah, in Sarawak) has shown that, despite this freedom, there is a regular diurnal pattern of movement. Activity reaches a first maximum at dawn in a huge outpouring of birds from the cave mouth—at Niah by thousands a minute. To start with, very few birds return against the onslaught, but within half an hour the exodus begins to dwindle and the influx to swell until the two are roughly balanced. If the weather stays fine, in and outward traffic are soon reduced and remain low—one or two hundred a minute each way at Niah—and more or less equal throughout the heat of the day. At all times of day, birds leaving the cave fly in a loose stream one or two hundred feet above the canopy, on over the forest until they disperse and begin to feed; those returning mostly drop down from the heights and enter above the outgoers.

In the late afternoon the outflow again rises appreciably but never achieves the intensity of the morning flight; the last bird may leave the cave only a quarter of an hour before nightfall. At the same time others gather outside, and drift and circle high in the sky, often in loose flocks, calling incessantly. As the light fades they begin to drop on downspread wings and swoop through the sunset into the black gape of the cave mouth. Inside, the great chambers of Niah become thick with calling birds, milling in the hot twilight in their thousands. As night finally falls the inrush is fiercest and the crescendo of noise at the cave mouth changes character as the birds are enveloped in darkness and 'switch on' their rattling echo-location call.

Birds continue to enter the cave long after dark. Night traffic is difficult to gauge in the vast caverns at Niah, but in caves with smaller mouths it can be assessed accurately. Such a cave is Meraja at Bau, colonised by *C. maxima*, where two small arched mouths eight and nine feet high are the only access to a large cave which runs the length of the limestone mountain. Here watch was kept through all of one night in July 1957, in one of the two archways. Official sunset was 6.15 p.m. local time. At the low latitudes of Borneo seasonal variation in sunrise and sunset times are very slight; the day is always about twelve hours long, with three-quarters of an hour of twilight before dawn and after sunset. The evening of the vigil was dull at first after rain, but later cleared and the full moon shone brightly until 10 p.m.

By 5 p.m. the valley below was already full of homing birds; about twenty-five entered each minute, and five left on the evening sortie. It was dark soon after 7 p.m., by when outgoing traffic had ceased and there were only a few incomers each minute, but birds continued to enter the cave. At 8.30 p.m. the average rate had risen again to ten in each minute, at 10 p.m. four birds entered per minute, and by midnight the rate had dropped to one a minute. Still they came in sporadically, but at about 2 a.m. other birds began to come up from the galleries below and gather in the entrance hall behind the mouth. Here, by 3 a.m. the crowd of circling birds was very dense, and the total din of their echo-locating call was deafening. At 3.21 the first bird out was recorded and at 3.33 the last in. By 4.30 about four were leaving each minute, and out-traffic remained constant at this rate until dawn when it accelerated with characteristic abruptness.

Lord Medway, 'Cave Swiftlets', in B. E. Smythies, *Birds of Borneo*, Oliver and Boyd, Edinburgh and London, 1960, pp. 62–4.

Caves

❧

122
Klouwang and Its Caves

L. H. WALLON

On the west coast of the northern tip of Sumatra, an overwhelming effect is created by the combination of stupendous karst scenery in an island setting, together with the swarming cave swiftlets and the nest-collectors' strange apparatus.

In 1879, Monsieur L. H. Wallon, Civil Engineer of Mines in the Dutch administration, penned a description of the islands and caves near Keluang. His original account was later translated into English by D. F. A Hervey, from whose version this abstract is taken.

O N turning the point of the island, I could not repress an exclamation of surprise. In front of us was a magnificent cave inhabited by millions of swallows, whose piercing cries mingled with the deep murmur of the sea, produced, on their reverberation from the distant depths of the cavern, an awe-inspiring sound, which had no ordinary effect upon the mind.

One could not but feel small in the presence of these grand phenomena of Nature, and silently wonder at the work and its Creator.

The first moments of wonder and admiration passed, we entered the cavern, an immense subterranean canal some fifteen to twenty metres high and ten to twelve metres in width: bambu scaffoldings, extraordinary at once for their lightness and boldness of construction, enable the Atchinese to collect the swallows' nests.

253

Ten metres from the entrance, a fresh surprise awaited us. A submarine communication between the cavern and the sea allows a gleam of light to penetrate at the bottom of the water, and this, in its passage, illuminates the fish whose scales flash countless colours scattering everywhere multi-coloured reflections with fairy-like effect.

The subterranean canal soon turns to the right, penetrating into the heart of the island, whither it continues its course for a great distance, for the murmur of the sea reverberates endlessly; but the darkness prevented our going any farther.

Between this point, E.S.E., and the port is another avenue, the two entrances to which are above the sea; they are at an elevation, the one of twenty metres, the other of about thirty-five metres; for some time we could not find a point where it was possible to land; everywhere the sea-worn rock was vertical when it did not overhang us; at last, two-hundred metres farther on, we found a spot where the rock had fallen down and where we could land; we then contrived, sometimes by leaping from rock to rock, sometimes by making use of the unevennesses on the surface of the wall of rock, to reach the upper entrance, where a marvellous sight repaid us for our trouble. A vast cavern lay open before us. At our feet and at a depth of about thirty metres was a black unfathomable gulf, whence arose the deep murmur of the waters. About fifteen metres below, to the right, was the other entrance, resembling an immense window opening upon the sea. Before us the cavern seemed to extend indefinitely into the shade, and the green and blue tints of the rock growing gradually darker and darker formed a strange contrast to the magnificent pearl-grey of the stalactities which hung on our right; above us the rock was of a dead white, whilst the floor of the cavern, which seemed to be the ancient bed of a torrent, presented a series of striking and sharply-marked tiers of colour, resembling a painter's palette. The most brilliant decorations of our pantomimes could give but a feeble idea of the magnificent tableau we had before us.

Leaping from rock to rock, we descended to the floor of the grotto, which is formed of pebbles and water-brought soil; this floor rises with a gentle slope towards the interior; after one hundred paces all became so dark around us, that we were obliged to light torches; on every side crossed each other in flight millions of swallows, which deafened us with their piercing cries, while our torchlight lent to the gigantic bambu scaffoldings the most picturesque effect; every time they flared up the cavern was illuminated to great distances, and we suddenly perceived an inextricable web of bambus, white rocks and streamlets, which appeared to multiply as we advanced, when suddenly all vanished in darkness; the effect was most fantastic.

The soil of the cavern, in which we sank up to our knees, is light and dry, being formed of the excrement of the swallows; insects breed there in great numbers and the glare of the torches reflected on their armour produced a splendid play of light. The soil seemed made of precious stones flashing across at each other at our feet.

As we advanced, the subterranean passages multiplied and grew narrower; it was a labyrinth out of which we thought at one moment we should be unable to find our way, for our torches were beginning to be used up, and we were not very sure as to the direction we ought to take. We now heard to the left a dull sound which indicated another communication with the sea, perhaps with the cavern we first visited. Then a little further to the right we descried a feeble glimmer of light at the vault of the cavern, but it was impossible to reach this opening, owing to its great height.

The cavern probably extends under a great portion of the island, but unfortunately our torches were burnt out, and we were obliged, to our great regret, to return to the ship without having explored the whole of it.

L. H. Wallon, 'Klouwang and Its Caves, West Coast of Atchin: Travelling Notes of M. L. H. Wallon', trans., D. F. A. Hervey, *Journal of the Straits Branch of the Royal Asiatic Society*, Vol. 8, 1881, pp. 156–8.

123
Caves at Sungei Batu

D. D. DALY

No visitor can fail to be impressed by the grandeur of the huge, arching caves that form within the rugged limestone of South-East Asian karst outcrops. The open mouth is often fringed with delightful ferns, begonias, and other botanical wonders. Behind it lies a vast darkness, redolant with strange odours and unfamiliar sounds, tumultuous with bats, swiftlets, and other wildlife. The existence of large caves at Batu, near Kuala Lumpur, was first brought to public attention in 1879. Today, it is difficult to identify the caves described by D. D. Daly in the excerpt below; they may have been destroyed by quarrying.

The writer served with the Selangor police. On this trip in 1879, he accompanied Captain B. Douglas, the Resident of Selangor, Mr Syers, the Superintendent of Police, Lieutenant R. Lindsell of the 28th Regiment, some policemen, and Orang Asli guides (here called 'Sakeis'). The party left Klang at 8 a.m. by steam tender, followed the river 17 miles to Damansara, landed, and rode ponies for 13 miles by a 'good road' and four miles further by jungle trail to reach Kuala Lumpur.

FROM Kwala Lumpor to the caves, along a jungle track, all over very good soil, chocolate-coloured loam, and passing through groves of numerous fruit trees, a ride of about nine miles in a northerly direction brought us to the foot of a limestone hill, about 400 feet high, with steep perpendicular sides. The white clefts of the hill glistened in the sunlight and at once indicated limestone formation. Durian trees grow at the base of this hill and threw their lofty branches, laden with fruit at this season. Half way up the hill, and through the rich-soiled flat at the base runs a bubbling crystal streamlet over many-coloured quartz and blue and limestone pebbles, such as would gladden the heart of a trout-fisher to take a cast over.

After reaching the hill we climbed about 50 feet over rocky boulders and stood opposite a large gateway, hollowed out of the limestone hill, a great cavern, looking black and ominous as we faced it, and the scent of the bat's manure was strong. This is called the 'Gua Lambong' (or swinging or hanging cave), No. 1. Here the *Sakeis* and others commenced their notes of warning as to the deep holes in this cave, and the party entered with cautious steps. The writer tried hard to take up a modest retiring position in the rear, like Mark Twain when there were rumours of Arabs at the Pyramids of Egypt, but he found that other members were also anxious to show their humility in staying behind, some stopped to tuck up their trowsers on account of the bat's manure, another walked very suddenly on one side and stopped and closely examined the nature of the limestone formation, and the worst cast of timidity was of one who foremost at the start, suddenly wheeled round to the rear saying he wanted to light a cigar. However, having lighted torches the gallant representative of H.M.'s 28th Regiment took the lead and boldly advanced. After a few yards' walking on the soft elastic layer of the bat's manure, we had to throw away the damar torches, as the rosin from the damar that dropped on the manure set fire to it, and in their place long split bamboos were used for torches, which answered admirably.

The appearance of this cave was very grand. On a main bearing of N. N. W. we walked for about a quarter of a mile over rocks and then gently over dry deposits of bat's manure, which were from 3 to 6 feet deep. The roof and sides of the caves, which were 50 to 70 feet high and some 60 feet wide, were beautifully arched, presenting the appearance of a great Gothic dome, with curved arches and giant buttresses. Verily there was a stillness and sublimity in this work of nature that even surpassed the awe of the holy place raised by human art.

Hanging from the conchoidal arches of this vaulted dome were thousands of bats, whose flitting fluttering noises resembled the surging of the sea on an iron-bound coast. Arriving at the end of the cave we came upon an opening in the limestone crust above, which shed a soft light over the scene, a subdued tinge over the green-crusted walls at the top and a softer halo on the bright crystals of the stalactites. Carefully taking away specimens of the stalactites and stalagmites we wended our way back to the entrance, and only reached it as the torches were nearly finished.

There is a sort of alcove hollowed outside this entrance to the right hand by nature out of the rocks. A model cook-house with its stoves, fire places and all that would be necessary for the most fastidious Eastern cook.

It seemed a pity to leave such a delightfully cool atmosphere for the heated exhalations without, but another attraction awaited us and a cry of 'Durians' recalled us to the most solid comforts of this life. Quantities of durians grew on the trees at the base of this hill—a sure sign of good soil in the Malay Peninsula—and after having a good meal of this delicious fruit, after a quarter of an hour's walk in a northerly direction, we were led by Mr Syers and the *Sakei* to No. 2 Cave called 'Gua Belah' (or the divided cave). This cave was much lower in height than the last, but contained very fantastical limestone formations. The bearing was N. N. E. through these caverns, for about 100 yards, but there were branches which might be explored if sufficient time allowed. Outside these two caves were very original drawings made by the *Sakei* with charcoal on the limestone walls, reminding us of our first efforts at making sketches of the human form.

No. 3 Cave, 'Gua Lada' (Pepper cave) called from the numerous chili trees growing near the entrance, is reached after another half a mile in a northerly direction.

This and No. 2 Caves are both entered from the base of the hill, no climbing required like 'Gua Lambong' (No. 1). This is planned in one vault running S. S. E., 90 yards long, with two side corridors at right angles on either side, and the crystalline deposits are more perfect than in No. 1 Cave. Here the limestone columns have joined the stalactites, and the stalagmites are more perfect. In some places, there are great pulpits overhung with canopies, whose brilliant crystalline fringes sparkle again in the garish glare of the torches, inducing the visitor again to think of this as a great church of nature. Here, fantastically carved out of the rock, may be seen imitation umbrellas and couches and baths partly filled with bright waters that have dropped through the limestone ceiling.

It is strange that fossils could not be found anywhere. Nothing but thousands of tons of bat's dung—itself a great fortune in guano.

D. D. Daly, 'Caves at Sungei Batu in Selangor', *Journal of the Straits Branch of the Royal Asiatic Society*, Vol. 3, 1879, pp. 116–19.

124
The Dark Cave at Batu

WILLIAM BEEBE

Beebe's note of the 'Dark Cave' at Batu in the 1920s vividly described the dramatic subterranean scene and the rich variety of wildlife inhabiting the lightless environment. Nowadays, the large, upper cave and other satellite grottoes are dedicated to Hindu worship, and tens of thousands of people visit the cave complex each year.

T HEN we stopped suddenly, and looking up I saw a great cliff looming high overhead. It was clothed in green, except where it was out at elbow with patches of raw, white limestone. Before I left the car, a strong scent—unpleasant, exciting, and entirely strange—was wafted down on some current of air from the cave.

A stiff climb of a hundred yards brought me to the mouth of the dark cave—a great, gaping, black hole, the edges draped with graceful vines. I entered and, after going a hundred feet, looked back and saw an exquisite bit of the tropical land-scape: palms, distant blue mountains, and white clouds framed in the jet-black, jagged aperture.

The great height was overwhelming; the graceful dome-like summit of the cavern stretched up and up into the very vitals of the mountain. Then I plunged into darkness and lighted my electric searchlight, which seemed at first the merest bit of light ray. On and on I went, and at last, far in the distance, perceived a faint glimmer from high overhead. A rustling sound at my feet drew my light downward, and there were untold thousands of great brown cockroaches, all striving to bury themselves out of sight in the soft, sawdust-like flooring, the century-old guano of the bats. I had to go with great care, for huge jagged rocks and deformed stalag-mites obstructed the path in every direction.

I reached the rift in the lofty roof, and the glare blinded me for the moment, although it was tempered with a tracery veil of green. I had already begun to adapt myself to the ever-lasting darkness. At my feet the light fell softened, diluted with a subterranean twilight. In the centre of this part of the cave, directly under the cleft in the roof, was a curious, gigantic stalagmite, still forming from the constant dripping two hundred feet overhead—a stalagmite of great size and extreme irregularity. . . .

For a long time I sat here, finding the odor of the bats less pungent than elsewhere, and here I watched the ghostly creatures dash past. From the inky darkness of some hidden fissure they dropped almost to my face; then, with a whip of their leathery wings, they turned and vanished in the dark cavern ahead. The noise their wings made was incredibly loud; sometimes a purring, as fifty small ones whirred past together, then a sharp singing, and finally an astonishing whistling twang as a single giant bat twisted and flickered on his frightened way.

Another sound was the musical, hollow dripping of slowly falling drops on some thin resonant bit of stone, a metronome marking the passing of inky black hours and years and centuries; for in this cavern there are no days. Every noise I made, whether of voice or footfall, was taken up and magnified and passed upward from ledge to ledge, until it reached the roof and returned again to me. It was changed, however,—wholly altered; for it seemed that no sound of healthy creature could remain pure in this durable darkness, the sepulchre of unburied bats, the underworld of hateful, bleached things, of sunless, hopeless blackness. The obscurity seemed, by reason of its uninterrupted ages of persistence, to have condensed, the ebony air to have liquefied. There was no twilight of imagination, inspired by knowledge of coming day. Only quiet, eternal night.

From the black gulf ahead came, now and then, low distant mumblings, mingled with the shrill squeaks of the bats, and into this vocal void I now plunged, with the searchlight playing at my feet to avoid tripping and falling. I found that I had entered a veritable Dante's Inferno, and pictured to myself some still more dreadful round as presently to open out ahead. The sighing, gibbering, squeaking spirits or devils were there in multitudes, brushing my face or fighting among themselves as they clung to the slippery fissures high, high overhead. More than once my light led me down a small, blind side lane, into which I stumbled as far as possible. At the end of one such corridor was a roundish hole leading irregularly downward, far beyond the rays of my light. Another contracted very slowly, until the damp walls touched my head and sides and I drew nervously back, glad to escape from the sense of suffocation—as if the walls were actually closing about me, inevitably, irrevocably.

Every stone I overturned revealed numbers of tall, slender spirals—the homes of dark-loving snails; and ever the roaches in their myriads hurried away from my light. Then I came upon tragedy—fitly staged in this black hell. A commotion on the black mould directed me to where a poor bat had recently fallen, having by some accident broken his shoulder, and lay, like fallen Lucifer, gnashing his teeth and helplessly turning from side to side. More than this, two horrible gnomes fled at my approach—a long, sinuous serpent, white from its generations of life within the cave, and a huge centipede, pale, translucent green, sinister as death itself. I shuddered as I beheld this ghastly tableau,—serpent and centipede both emblematic of poisonous death, preparing to feast upon a yet living bat, devil-winged and devil-faced.

The predatory ones escaped me, though I wanted the snake. I put the bat out of his misery, his evil squeaking rage at fate remaining undiminished to the very last breath. On his nose were the great leaves of skin which aided him in dodging the obstacles in his path of darkness—organs which had failed him for a fatal moment.

Farther on I turned sharp corners and wound my path around strange angles, disturbing unending hosts of bats and finding many recently dead, together with innumerable skeletons half buried in the guano. Now and then a centipede fled from my tiny pencil of light, and once I broke open a nest of stinging ants, blind but ferocious, which attacked me and made me flee for several yards headlong, heedless of bruising, jagged obstacles.

Then my feet sank suddenly in ooze and water, and, flashing the light ahead, I saw it reflected from the ripples of an underground river flowing with no more than a murmur out of one yawning hole into the opposite wall of the cavern.

William Beebe, *Pheasant Jungles*, G. P. Putnam's Sons, New York and London, 1927, pp. 171–5.

125
Caves at Biserat

W. W. SKEAT

Many authors have made comparisons with cathedrals, and the sculptural beauty of the great limestone caverns of South-East Asia clearly arouse religious sentiment in any observer, of whatever creed! To zoologists, the specialized troglobite denizens of these vast subterranean worlds are of very considerable interest. Both aspects are treated in this account of caves in southern peninsular Thailand, visited by a Cambridge University Expedition in 1899.

This passage is taken from the diary kept at the time by W. W. Skeat, a member of the expeditionary team, but edited and published after his death and many years after the events described.

26 May.

IN the afternoon I accompanied Vaughan and Annandale to the caves in Bukit Tapang, near Biserat. The first of these caves was reached after a walk of about twenty-five minutes along the Jalor 'road', as it was called, a half-made road, a good deal broken up and allowed, part of it, to relapse into jungle. Access to the first cave not very easy, the opening being some thirty to forty feet above the ground. This cave, discovered by Vaughan, was named by him the 'Cathedral Cave', on account of its architectural (and also indeed, its almost sculptural) beauty. It bore an extraordinary likeness to the 'Cathedral Cave' at Batu near Kuala Lumpur. It was entered by a circular aperture at the top. From fifty to a hundred yards along the face of the cliff, at a level of about twenty to thirty feet below the floor of this cave, a second cave some two hundred yards long, which we named the 'Corridor Cave', ran into the very heart of the hill. About half way along this second cave was an extensive domed cavern, very dimly lighted. It was in this cavern of the Corridor

Cave that some specimens of a peculiar specialized fauna—specialized pedipalps, specialized spiders, specialized scorpions, even specialized woodlice, were discovered by our two zoologists. The breadth of this cave varied from fifteen to thirty feet, its height from thirty to sixty. Every yard, however, had its own peculiar features. The only light was in the domed portion, and there was a strong wind, almost increasing to a gale at times, that blew outwards throughout the first half, between the mouth and the dome, and inwards into the hill beyond the dome. The cave was inhabited by two species of bats and the whole of the floor of the cavern was carpeted with layer upon layer, some no doubt of a considerable depth, of bat guano.

Beside these two caves there was a deep well-like pit, also discovered by Vaughan, who descended it as far as our seventy-foot Alpine rope would allow him to do so. He reported that below that point there was a sheer drop, which allowed him to count ten before a pebble reached the bottom; he estimated this hole to be quite three hundred feet in depth.

W. W. Skeat and F. F. Laidlaw, 'The Cambridge University Expedition to Parts of the Malay Peninsula, 1899–1900: Personal Accounts by the Late W. W. Skeat and Dr. F. F. Laidlaw', *Journal of the Malayan Branch of the Royal Asiatic Society*, Vol. 26, Pt. 4, 1953, pp. 36–8.

126
Caves of Niah

NIGEL CAMERON

Of the many huge caverns that ramify within the towering karst limestone outcrops of South-East Asia, the vast complex at Bukit Subis, Niah, Sarawak, is among the best known through years of research and investigation. The floor plan of the Great Cave at Niah exceeds 10 hectares in extent, and its animal inhabitants include myriads of cave swiftlets and bats.

The scene that met the eye in the mid-1960s was vividly described by Nigel Cameron, a visitor from Britain who wrote from a geographical perspective.

I T is an arduous hour's tramp to the caves, partly on plankwalk in stretches liable to flooding from the little Subis River that winds round the foot of the Niah outcrop.

A sharp clamber from the cicada hiss and the echoing birdsong of the jungle with its parasite encrusted trees, and the first cave is reached.

Here in the dim interior are the roofless huts the birds-nesters inhabit in the season of collecting. Here under the slope of the long roof with its contorted stalactites, the algae of striking greens and the ferns of the floor which turn like a regiment to face their commander the sun, glow with the coming of afternoon and the reflected sunlight.

Mouth of the Great Cave

Through this cave and out along the face of the outcrop the West Mouth of the Great Cave suddenly yawns like the jaws of an enormous shark, toothed with stalactites, its throat diving back into deep, bat-smelling gloom. Here the jungle sounds give way to the high-pitched screaming of swiftlets and bats whose cries and whose echo-sounding clicks, as they wheel in and out of the cave continue all day and all night long.

Between six-thirty and seven o'clock in the evening perhaps about a million swiftlets flood into the cave from their day of insect-hunting over the treetops. At the same time the huge naked bats raise an ominous, heavy flutter of sound as they congregate ever nearer to the mouth while the light falls. Then, punctually at a quarter to seven, they emerge in single file along a given path under the cave-roof and fly straight and swift into the night sky.

Inside the upper lip of the cave-mouth the limestone is white, shading as the dome arches more than 200 feet above

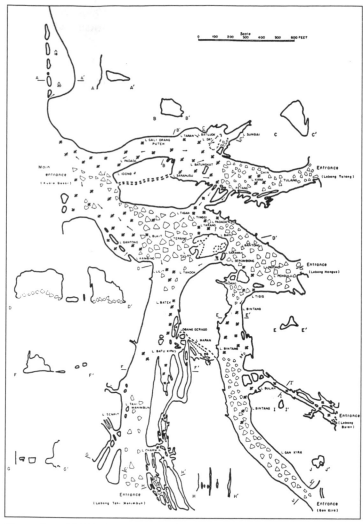

Floor plan of Niah Great Cave, Subis, Sarawak. North point is at the top of the page, and the scale bar = 600 feet (183 metres); the calculated plan area of the cave is 10+ hectares. From G. E. Wilford, *Bulletin 6: The Geology of Sarawak and Sabah Caves*, Geological Survey Borneo Region Malaysia, 1964.

the floor to greens and textured blacks. Farther in, over a floor of earth that becomes moist purple guano as you come under the nesting areas, the two throats of the cave, separated by a massive stone wall, recede into darkness loud with birds.

Mounds of guano rise precipitously, the product of millions of years of bat and swiftlet droppings. Their surface is alive with guano-flies. On one mound, called Naked Bat Hill from the colony of this species of oily-skinned and hairless bats living in the roof above it, you can catch your breath a moment and look back towards the glare of light in the cave mouth, pencilled with verticals that are the *tiang* or wooden poles used by the birdsnesters.

N. Cameron, 'Niah Caves of Borneo', *Geographical Magazine*, Vol. 40, No. 8, 1967, pp. 652–4.

The Past

∾

127
Kain Hitam

NIGEL CAMERON

Through the passage of many centuries, some great open caverns have evoked in all their human visitors a sense of mysterious beauty and repose. Nigel Cameron explored the complex system at Niah, Sarawak, and finally reached Kain Hitam, a green world that the ancient people of that place had fittingly dedicated to funerary use.

THERE are five other mouths to the cave, four of them opening to the east of the formation. An hour's stumbling progress in total dark through tunnels still, even so far from the daylight, crowded with birds on their nests, the home of the robber snakes which live on the birds, the home of scorpions scuttling between the rocks, of the blind cicadalike insect three inches long with antennae of over a foot, brings you to one or other mouth high up on the eastern cliff.

The view across the treetops in the valley is of another outcrop jungled over its summit. Forty minutes' wading through the swamp, assisted by felled logs here and there, and an exhausting climb up a cliff in the outcrop, reveals suddenly the mouth of Kain Hitam (the Black Cloth cave—so called because its owner is reputed to have sold it for a length of such material), known as the Painted Cave.

To reach it is a tremendous relief—a relief from physical exertion, from the incessant insensate screech of birds. For

268

Kain Hitam is silent. The cave is light from end to end, and bats and swiftlets live only in dark or semi-dark, finding their way by that avian echo-sounding clicking in a manner which still defies complete explanation.

Strange and Primitive Rites

The silent cave has brilliant green walls sculpted like the stygian passages from which you have not long emerged, by prehistoric currents in a prehistoric sea. The ceiling is white and almost flat. Through the breadth of the limestone rock the cave pierces, its floor diving downwards to the farther mouth—to a sort of beach on which lie a few lost and pathetic little boats of wood. The 'boats of the dead', ossuaries of perhaps a thousand years ago, rest where they were abandoned in the cathedral of strange and primitive rites.

Under this formation the river runs through a subterranean channel, and perhaps ran there in the time of early man, giving him (it is conjecture, but possible) the idea that the bones of his dead should pass the underworld river in the familiar safety of a *perahu*.

Elsewhere on a dry wall of Kain Hitam are the paintings of the same people—significantly of boats crammed with people, of strange figures captured with their arms in the air as if drowning and crying 'Help!', of a pair of fighting cocks (cock-fighting is today the popular sport of Borneo), of stylized scorpions.

Curtained off by jungle green, the light filtered green and gold and yellow through the trees at either mouth, its green algae and white ceiling glowing in the genial light, the Painted Cave must be one of the most ravishing natural beauties of all south-east Asia There is a great silence and peace there.

N. Cameron, 'Niah Caves of Borneo', *Geographical Magazine*, Vol. 40, No. 8, 1967, p. 655.

128
Glaciation of Kinabalu

LYNNE C. MYERS

Cave sites have preserved the remains of people of antiquity, their artefacts and fragments of the plants and animals that they gathered or hunted for various purposes. Such evidence has given archaeologists a reasonable picture of the human populations of South-East Asia and biological features of their environment for the past 20,000 years or so. Critical to the interpretation of these findings has been an understanding of the local climatic changes associated with transition from the final Ice Age to present conditions. A decisive factor was the recognition that the upper slopes of Mt Kinabalu, Sabah, show unmistakable signs of past glaciation. Unbelievable though it seems today, an ice cap must have crowned this peak, the highest in South-East Asia, until about 9,000 years ago.

Lynne Myers described the evidence as it unfolds before the climber. She graduated M.Sc. in Experimental Geomorphology from the University of Guelph, Ontario, Canada, in 1971 and, among other posts, was a teacher at the government middle school at Kota Kinabalu, Sabah, 1972–3.

P ROCEEDING up the mountain, the first evidence of glaciation is soon encountered. The remains of a moraine can be seen at about 10,000 feet. A moraine is a ridge of unsorted debris, deposited at the outer extremities of a glacier. Along the trail, the moraine is marked by the presence of many large, sub-angular granite boulders, scattered through a coarse, gravel matrix. The sub-angular shape of the boulders is diagnostic of glacially deposited material. (For anyone interested in seeing a much better example of a moraine, a side trip off the main trail to the Pakka Cave is well worth the effort. You must scramble across the large rocks in the stream bed until you are directly behind the cave itself. If you then face upstream and look to the right bank you will see an outcrop of much finer morainic material, just above the dry season water mark. If you climb during the rainy season the site will probably be under water!).

No evidence has yet been found of a similar morainic deposit at a lower elevation. For this reason the one at 10,000 feet is assumed to be the 'terminal moraine' of the valley glacier extending down this south face of the mountain, and thus to mark the furthest advance of that glacier down the valley. The other alternative is that there may be another moraine further down the valley which is either obscured by vegetation or has been removed by post-glacial erosion. That would mean the moraine at 10,000 feet would be a recessional moraine, marking a pause in the glacier's retreat back up the valley.

The summit area of Mt Kinabalu has been under the influence of glaciation to a marked degree, and so the glacial landforms there are numerous. The whole summit area has been 'smoothed' by the erosional action of the ice. The jagged peaks (i.e. Low's Peak) are 'nunataks', or peaks which remained above the surface of the glacier. Their jagged appearance is due to their being fractured by the alternate freezing and thawing of water in cracks during the Pleistocene Period. By comparing their appearance with the smoothness of the rest of the summit area, one can appreciate the erosional power of even such a comparatively small glacier.

The snow and ice of the glacier originally accumulated at the heads of small valleys on the mountain. The action of freezing and thawing eroded these into small amphitheatre shaped depressions called 'cirques' or 'corries'. The headward erosion of the cirques continued as the glacier grew, and when two of them, from opposite sides of the same ridge met, a gap was formed in that ridge. This small gap is known as a 'col'. There are examples of these two landforms on the summit of Mt Kinabalu.

The movement of ice grooved the underlying rocks on two scales. The smaller, sharp fragments of rock imbedded in the base of the glacier cut 'striae', usually less than an inch deep, parallel to the direction of ice flow. Larger boulders cut wider, shallow furrows up to several feet across. Post-glacial weathering has rounded and smoothed the outline of both these features so they are difficult to detect today.

L. C. Myers, 'Geomorphology', in E. R. Dingley (ed.), *Kinabalu Summit of Borneo*, Sabah Society Monograph, 1978, pp. 92–3.

129
Stegodonts from Flores

D. A. HOOIJER

Older fossil finds have come from open sites, particularly ancient fluviatile deposits. Important discoveries have shown that a primitive kind of human lived in Java (Java man or Pithecanthropus, known scientifically as *Homo erectus*) many hundreds of thousands of years ago, alongside a mixed fauna of mammals that included some that no longer exist. Few discoveries of strange fossils can have been more astounding to their finder than the collection of remains of stegodonts, large extinct elephant-like creatures, that came into the hands of the Raja of Nage Keo, Flores, in 1956.

The story was reported in a scientific journal by the late D. A. 'Dick' Hooijer, an eminent Dutch palaeontologist, who spent his long career mainly at the Rijksmuseum voor Natuurlijke Historie, Leiden, Netherlands, engaged in the study of fossil remains of large animals found in Africa, Europe and, especially, in sites in Indonesia and Malaysia.

I N December, 1956, the Raja of Nage Keo discovered fossil vertebrate remains at Ola Bula on the Soa plateau, between Ola Kile and Menge Ruda, lat. 8° 30'–8° 45' S., long. 121° 00'–121° 15' E. of Greenwich, in Central Ngada, Flores. These finds were reported by the Kepala Daerah of Flores to Dr Th. L. Verhoeven, priest at Mataloko, who visited the site in January, 1957. The fossil specimens were found lying on the grass-covered surface of a partially eroded sandstone layer, and occur over an area almost one kilometer long by a width of several hundred meters. Along the Ai Sissa, which intersects the upland plain, the fossils protrude from the river banks. Fossils were collected both by Dr Verhoeven and by

Mr C. Castillio from the surface of the plain as well as from the river banks and from the foot of a hill rising above the plain at Ola Bula. All these finds are apparently derived from the same fossiliferous sandstone, and most of them are more or less weather-worn.

Realizing at once the great importance of the finds, Dr Verhoeven contacted the Museum Zoologicum Bogoriense, and in March, 1957, the Director of the Museum, Mr A. M. R. Wegner, accompanied by Mr A. S. Dyhrberg, arrived in Flores to see the site, and to make further collections of fossils. All the specimens thus far recovered have been shipped to the Museum at Bogor, whence, by kind permission of the Indonesian authorities, Mr Wegner sent the entire collection to me for identification. It is a great pleasure to acknowledge my indebtedness to all concerned for their splendid cooperation, as a result of which these fossils, the first of their kind ever found in Flores, or in any of the Lesser Sunda Islands for that matter, are now available for study.

The collection of fossil remains from Ola Bula, which arrived at the Rijksmuseum van Natuurlijke Historie at Leiden in August, 1957, consists of several hundreds of greater and smaller bone and tooth fragments. Most of these have corroded surfaces as a result of their having been exposed to the weather, but others are better preserved, and a certain number of fragments could even be matched, such as, e.g., a pair of mandibular rami and some fragments all of the same specimen that had evidently begun to disintegrate just before its recovery from the grass plain.

To my surprise, the Ola Bula collection proved to contain the remains of stegodonts, and of stegodonts only; there is not a single identifiable tooth or bone fragment in the entire collection that belongs to animals other than *Stegodon*. The material now at hand amply justifies the following diagnosis of a new race, peculiar to the island of Flores.

D. A. Hooijer, 'A Stegodon from Flores', *Treubia*, Vol. 24, Pt. 1, 1957, pp. 119–20.

Gold of the Chersonese

ɔᴜ

130
Gold in Sumatra

HENRY O. FORBES

The ancients wrote of the Golden Chersonese, and dreamed of its treasures. Indeed, we know that there is metallic gold at places in South-East Asia. From time to time, auriferous deposits have been worked and the precious metal extracted, often by laborious manual processes and for small reward, as observed by Forbes in the 1880s.

THE recent rains had produced a flood—the greatest, it was said, for five years—which had risen from ten to twelve feet above its ordinary mark. Throughout a distance of from thirty to forty miles it had carried away pieces of the bank from three to five yards wide and from eight to ten feet deep. In these new sections large trees (stems and branches) had become exposed, buried more than six feet below the surface of the surrounding land. These sections showed the soil resting on a deep band of clay, which in turn was lying on a thick stratum of shingle, which was being again washed out, to be subjected to fresh attrition after having rested for many cycles. Below the confluence of the River Tiku, which rises among the Palæozoic rocks in the Redjang region a considerable quantity of gold is found when the river is very low, caught among the stones, larger pebbles and sand. This sand is collected—the occupation mostly of the older women—and, when freed from the larger particles, goes by the name of *bungin*; the bungin is washed in a broad cone-shaped vessel of wood—the *dulang*—by a rotatory motion, till only an extremely fine heavy black sand (*kalam*) is left. The kalam, which contains the gold is then rotated in the dulang with a little water till the heavier metal falls to the apex of the cone, whence it is carefully removed. A very successful day's washing in this fashion will bring only 1*s*. 8*d*.

Henry O. Forbes, *A Naturalist's Wandering in the Eastern Archipelago: A Narrative of Travel and Exploration from 1878 to 1883*, Harper and Brothers, New York, 1885, p. 239.

131
The Golden Coast of Kei

ALFRED RUSSEL WALLACE

For most visitors to this realm, the natural wonder of the sun's golden light has been their enduring reward. Witness A. R. Wallace, anchored 'in a very dangerous place on a rocky bottom' off the Kei Islands on the last day of 1856.

THE coast of Ke along which we had passed was very picturesque. Light coloured limestone rocks rose abruptly from the water to the height of several hundred feet, everywhere broken into jutting peaks and pinnacles, weather-worn into sharp points and honeycombed surfaces, and clothed throughout with a most varied and luxuriant vegetation. The cliffs above the sea offered to our view screw-pines and arborescent Liliaceæ of strange forms, mingled with shrubs and creepers; while the higher slopes supported a dense growth of forest trees. Here and there little bays and inlets presented beaches of dazzling whiteness. The water was transparent as crystal, and tinged the rock-strewn slope which plunged steeply into its unfathomable depths with colours varying from emerald to lapis-lazuli. The sea

275

was calm as a lake, and the glorious sun of the tropics threw a flood of golden light over all.

Alfred Russel Wallace, *The Malay Archipelago: The Land of the Orang-Utan, and the Bird of Paradise*, 10th edn., Macmillan and Co., London, 1883, p. 414.

132
A Hundred Flaming Lances

E. A. POWELL

At the rise of the sun in South-East Asia, the surging transformations of sky and sea can be jewel-like in their brilliance. As his vessel approached Borneo from the north-east, E. A. Powell saw a battleground of flaming lances resolve into a diamond-strewn Sulu Sea.

T HOUGH the velvety darkness into which we were steadily ploughing had not perceptibly decreased, it was now cut sharply across, from right to left, by what looked like a tightly stretched wire of glowing silver. Even as I looked this slender fissure of illumination widened, almost imperceptibly at first, then faster, faster, until at one burst came the dawn. The sombre hangings of the night were swept aside by an invisible hand as are drawn back the curtains at a window. As you have seen from a hill the winking lights of a city disappear at daybreak, so, one by one, the stars went out. Masses of angry clouds reared themselves in ominous, fantastic forms against a sullen sky. The hot land breeze changed to a cold wind which made me shiver. Suddenly the mounting rampart of clouds, which seemed about to burst in a tempest, was pierced by a hundred flaming lances coming from beyond the horizon's rim. Before their onslaught the threatening cloud-wall crumbled, faded, and abruptly dropped away to reveal the sun advancing in all that brazen effrontery which it assumes in those lawless latitudes along the Line. Now the sky was become a huge inverted bowl of flawless azure porcelain, the surface of the Sulu Sea sparkled as though strewn with a million diamonds, and, not a league off our bows, rose the jungle-clothed shores of Borneo.

E. A. Powell, *Where Strange Trails Go Down*, Charles Scribner's Sons, New York, 1921, p. 26.

133
Wrought in Amethysts

MRS CAMPBELL DAUNCEY

In the imagination of Mrs Dauncey, the brilliantly sunlit landscape of Panay Island, Philippines, in April 1905, evoked a veritable ransom of jewels in a setting of gold.

W E drove down to the Muelle Loney (too hot to walk at five o'clock), and when we had got on board the launch and seated ourselves in basket chairs in the bows, she steamed down the river and the estuary, and out into the channel. There was a fresh breeze blowing, and the air was delicious. As to the scenery—words fail me! The blue and green of the sea, and the mauve and rose lights reflected on Guimaras from the brilliant sunset behind us over the Panay Mountains, were like some wonderful picture wrought in amethysts and sapphires and exquisite enamels, while all along the shore line the groves of palm trees glowed in the strong light like a border of emeralds set in golden sand.

Mrs Campbell Dauncey, *An Englishwoman in the Philippines*, John Murray, London, 1906, p. 182.

134
Revelation

GEORGE MAXWELL

George Maxwell wrote of the forest sunset with something near exultation.

T HE mountain-chains melt from purple to blue, and as they recede the roughness of the forest covering becomes a velvety pile, and then an even softer texture; and finally, where grey mists melt and dissolve in the distant haze, it is not easy to know which is forest and which is sky.

Such is the view that lies beneath your eyes as you stand upon a mountain peak some four or five thousand feet above the plain. But so deep, so soft is the mantle of forest, that you may fail to realise the grandeur of the mountains. They have not the austerity that belongs to nakedness. To right and to left, where the mountain spurs run out and down to the plain, your eyes rest on slopes which, though steep perhaps, are softly undulating. Each tree melts gently into its neighbour, or partly hides it; all is green and harmonious, and the mountain offers a face which appears to be as smooth and unbroken as a pasture land. But sometimes you may see how deceptive this appearance is. It has been raining, and a great cloud comes slowly swimming landward from the sea. The direction that it takes will bring it within a mile of you. As it approaches the mountain you wonder what will happen,— whether it will rest against the mountain-side, or whether it will roll upwards through the trees. But to your amazement, when the cloud edge touches the mountain it does not stop. Then you see that the whole cloud is swimming on into the mountain. What has happened is that a mountain ravine has acted as the channel up which a current of air is rushing skywards from the plain, and into the ravine the cloud is being slowly sucked. As the cloud enters, its shape and size and colour help your eye to see both sides of the ravine, and you may vaguely estimate the depth and width of the valley that had been strangely invisible although so close. But as soon as the cloud is past and gone, the trees on both sides of the ravine seem to leap together; and, though you now know exactly where to look, waving branches and woven leaves defy your efforts to say where the entrance is. You then wonder how many similar places are hidden around you, and picture to yourself the great sea cloud hemmed in by the sides of the ravine and still swimming farther landward.

There is another time when you may have a revelation. A few minutes after sunset the westward facing mountains blaze with the refulgent glory of an afterglow. A rosy light probes the secrets that the forest hides from the noonday sun—the grandeur of wide valleys that wind an intricate way into the inmost heart of the mountains; the mystery of little deeply-shaded tributaries that fall into them on either side; the vastness of untrodden ravines and gorges; the majesty of unscaleable precipices; the terror of long straight scars that tell of landslides where trees and soil and rock have slipped in hideous disaster, leaving a wound that has cut to the very bone. For a moment all is revealed—the mantle of forest does not avail against this searching light, and you may well think that it in is the sweet exposure that the mountains blush.

G. Maxwell, *In Malay Forests*, William Blackwood and Sons, Edinburgh and London, 1907, pp. 4–5.

135
Envoi

ABDUL RAZAK BIN HASSANUDIN

FOR my close, I borrow the last stanza of a traditional Malay rhyming quatrain, composed in the 1920s by the Pehin Siraja Khatib Al-Kadhi of Brunei Darussalam.

Habis-lah pesan dagang mengarang,
Hatam-lah shaer lebih dan kurang.
Wallahu a'alam sempurna tarang,
Kalam dan dakwat sudah terlarang.

(Fulfilled is the task of a vagabond hack;
finished the work in surfeit and lack.
By the All Knowing, completeness unhidden,
the pen and the ink are henceforth forbidden!)

Pehin Siraja Khatib, Abdul Razak bin Hassanudin, *Shaer Yang Di-Pertuan,* Special Publication, Monograph series, Brunei Museum Journal, 1979.

Cambodia

Angkor: An Introduction
GEORGE COEDÈS

Angkor and the Khmers
MALCOLM MacDONALD

Indonesia

An Artist in Java
JAN POORTENAAR

Bali and Angkor
GEOFFREY GORER

Coolie
MADELON H. LULOFS

Diverse Lives
JEANETTE LINGARD

Flowering Lotus
HAROLD FORSTER

Forever a Stranger and Other Stories
HELLA S. HAASSE

Forgotten Kingdoms in Sumatra
F. M. SCHNITGER

The Head-Hunters of Borneo
CARL BOCK

The Hidden Force*
LOUIS COUPERUS

The Hunt for the Heart
VINCENT MAHIEU

In Borneo Jungles
WILLIAM O. KHRON

Island of Bali*
MIGUEL COVARRUBIAS

Java: Facts and Fancies
AUGUSTA DE WIT

Java: The Garden of the East
E. R. SCIDMORE

Java: A Travellers' Anthology
JAMES R. RUSH

The Last Paradise
HICKMAN POWELL

Let It Be
PAULA GOMES

Makassar Sailing
G. E. P. COLLINS

The Malay Archipelago
ALFRED RUSSEL WALLACE

The Outlaw and Other Stories
MOCHTAR LUBIS

The Poison Tree*
E. M. BEEKMAN (Ed.)

Rambles in Java and the Straits in 1852
'BENGAL CIVILIAN' (C. W. KINLOCH)

Rubber
MADELON H. LULOFS

A Tale from Bali*
VICKI BAUM

The Temples of Java
JACQUES DUMARÇAY

Through Central Borneo
CARL LUMHOLTZ

To the Spice Islands and Beyond
GEORGE MILLER

Travelling to Bali
ADRIAN VICKERS

Twin Flower: A Story of Bali
G. E. P. COLLINS

Unbeaten Tracks in Islands of the Far East
ANNA FORBES

Witnesses to Sumatra
ANTHONY REID

Yogyakarta
MICHAEL SMITHIES

Malaysia

Among Primitive Peoples in Borneo
IVOR H. N. EVANS

An Analysis of Malay Magic
K. M. ENDICOTT

At the Court of Pelesu
HUGH CLIFFORD

The Best of Borneo Travel
VICTOR T. KING

Borneo Jungle
TOM HARRISSON

The Chersonese with the Gliding Off
EMILY INNES

The Experiences of a Hunter
WILLIAM T. HORNADAY

The Field-Book of a Jungle-Wallah
CHARLES HOSE

50 Years of Romance and Research
CHARLES HOSE

The Gardens of the Sun
F. W. BURBIDGE

Glimpses into Life in Malayan Lands
JOHN TURNBULL THOMSON

The Golden Chersonese
ISABELLA BIRD

Illustrated Guide to the Federated Malay States (1923)
C. W. HARISSON

The Malay Magician
RICHARD WINSTEDT

Malay Poisons and Charm Cures
JOHN D. GIMLETTE

My Life in Sarawak
MARGARET BROOKE,
THE RANEE OF SARAWAK

Natural Man
CHARLES HOSE

Nine Dayak Nights
W. R. GEDDES

A Nocturne and Other Malayan Stories and Sketches
FRANK SWETTENHAM

Orang-Utan
BARBARA HARRISSON

The Pirate Wind
OWEN RUTTER

Queen of the Head-Hunters
SYLVIA, LADY BROOKE,
THE RANEE OF SARAWAK

Six Years in the Malay Jungle
CARVETH WELLS

The Soul of Malaya
HENRI FAUCONNIER

They Came to Malaya
J. M. GULLICK

Wanderings in the Great Forests of Borneo
ODOARDO BECCARI

The White Rajahs of Sarawak
ROBERT PAYN

Myanmar

Faded Splendour, Golden Past: Urban Images of Burma
ELLEN CORWIN CANGI

Philippines

Little Brown Brother
LEON WOLFF

Singapore

Manners and Customs of the Chinese
J. D. VAUGHAN

Raffles of the Eastern Isles
C. E. WURTZBURG

Singapore 1941–1942
MASANOBU TSUJI

Travellers' Singapore
JOHN BASTIN

South-East Asia

Adventures and Encounters
J. M. GULLICK

Adventurous Women
J. M. GULLICK (Ed.)

Explorers of South-East Asia
VICTOR T. KING (Ed.)

Soul of the Tiger*
J. A. McNEELY and P. S. WACHTEL

Wonders of Nature in South-East Asia
THE EARL OF CRANBROOK

Thailand

Behind the Painting and Other Stories
SIBURAPHA

Descriptions of Old Siam
MICHAEL SMITHIES

The English Governess at the Siamese Court
ANNA LEONOWENS

The Politician and Other Stories
KHAMSING SRINAWK

The Prostitute
K. SURANGKHANANG

Temples and Elephants
CARL BOCK

To Siam and Malaya in the Duke of Sutherland's Yacht *Sans Peur*
FLORENCE CADDY

Travels in Siam, Cambodia and Laos
HENRI MOUHOT

Vietnam

The General Retires and Other Stories
NGUYEN HUY THIEP

The Light of the Capital
GREG & MONIQUE LOCKHART

*Titles marked with an asterisk have restricted rights.